MARC CHAGALL ON ART AND CULTURE

BENJAMIN HARSHAV, EDITOR

Marc Chagall on Art and Culture

Including the first book on Chagall's art by

A. EFROS AND YA. TUGENDHOLD (MOSCOW 1918)

Translations from French, Russian, Yiddish, and Hebrew by

BARBARA AND BENJAMIN HARSHAV

Stanford University Press   Stanford, California

Stanford University Press
Stanford, California

Printed in the United States of America
on acid-free, archival-quality paper

Library of Congress Cataloging-in-Publication Data

Chagall, Marc, 1887–1985
  Marc Chagall on art and culture : including the first book on
Chagall's art by A. Efros and Ya. Tugendhold (Moscow, 1918) / edited by
Benjamin Harshav; translations from French, Russian, Yiddish, and
Hebrew by Barbara and Benjamin Harshav.
     p. cm.
  Includes bibliographical references and index.
  ISBN 0-8047-4830-6 (cloth : alk. paper) — ISBN 0-8047-4831-4 (pbk. :
alk. paper)
  1. Chagall, Marc, 1887 — Written works. 2. Chagall, Marc,
1887 — Aesthetics. 3. Chagall, Marc, 1887 — Criticism and
interpretation. I. Tugendhold, Y. A. (Yakov Aleksandrovich),
1872–1928. II. Efros, A. M. (Abram Markovich), 1888–1954. III. Harshav,
Benjamin, 1928– IV. Harshav, Barbara, 1940– V. Title.
N6999.C46A35 2003
709'.2 — dc21   2003007569

Original Printing 2003
Last figure below indicates year of this printing:
12   11   10   09   08   07   06   05   04

Designed by Janet Wood
Typeset by Classic Typography in 11/21 Filosofia

C O N T E N T S

The Art of Marc Chagall ➤
by A. Efros and Ya. Tugendhold. Published by
the Moscow Publishing House "Helicon," 1918.
The book was composed with the help of
the Circle for Jewish National Aesthetics "Shomir."
The publisher's logo was by El Lissitzky.

АБРАМЪ ЭФРОСЪ

Я. ТУГЕНДХОЛЬДЪ

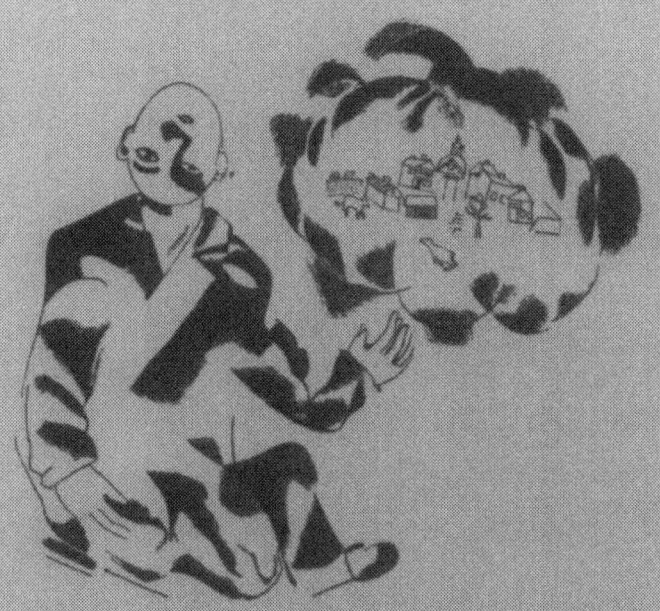

МАРКА ШАГАЛА

ИСКУССТВО

Marc Chagall (1887–1985) was a unique, individual presence in the center of modern art. The current revival of interest in his work and personality has been enhanced by the availability of works hidden in the Soviet Union since the 1920s. It also reflects the new interest in cultural aspects of art in general and in that colorful, lost world of Jewish Eastern Europe in particular. Thus, the retrospective of Chagall's early work at the Museum of Modern Art of the City of Paris in 1995 drew some 400,000 visitors, and about sixty French books and journals on Chagall were featured in the museum bookstore. Dozens of Chagall exhibitions have recently been mounted around the globe—in France, Germany, Italy, Switzerland, Finland, Russia, Japan, South America, Israel, and the United States.

A great artist, especially such a multicultural and often enigmatic artist as Chagall was, evokes our curiosity about his "intentions," his consciousness and self-understanding as an artist, his opinions on art and culture, and the vicissitudes of his private life. As Chagall himself pointed out, verbal texts were not his forte; indeed, his articulation in words is emotional or intuitive rather than analytical. Yet the texts provide a verbal ground for our readings of his life, his personality, his cultural perceptions, and his paintings. Furthermore, they are a witness account of a self-styled "Wandering Jew" and a creative artist in the twentieth century.

This book presents—for the first time in any language[1]—a comprehensive collection of Chagall's public texts: essays, articles, lectures, and speeches, written and delivered throughout his life.[2] Time and again, Chagall pondered in public on modern art, his place in it, the human situation, and Jewish culture and destiny in the twentieth century. Some of the texts were written and published or delivered in Russian or French, most of them in his native Yiddish.

It is not common knowledge that Chagall wrote poems and essays in his mother tongue, Yiddish, corresponded with dozens of Yiddish writers and Israeli leaders in Yiddish throughout his life, read Yiddish newspapers, and delivered public speeches to Yiddish audiences in New York, Paris, and Tel Aviv, especially during and after the Holocaust. Indeed, Yiddish was Chagall's basic language for the first thirty-six years of his life and again during the seven years he spent in America, though he also spoke and wrote Russian, which he acquired as a teenager, and spoke French, which he first encountered in his mid-twenties.

Chagall always wanted to be considered an Artist—international, revolutionary, Russian, or French—rather than a parochial, "Jewish" artist. Yet throughout his life, he continued to publish in Yiddish newspapers and journals, notably in the New York monthly *Di Tsukunft* and the Tel Aviv quarterly *Di Goldene Keyt*. In archives in several countries, we found manuscripts of Chagall's speeches, written out in his inimitable "childish" handwriting. It is in Yiddish that Chagall expressed his lament on the Holocaust, his concerns about the destiny of Yiddish literature and culture, and the revival of the Jewish people in Israel. It is the voice of a Jew in the twentieth century, who was accepted as an artist in the centers of modern culture and viewed the fate of his own people with love and horror. From the perspective of the Western reader, it is like an underground side of the artist's world, the solid, dark mass beneath the gleaming iceberg. It becomes even darker when we realize that Yiddish culture itself all but disappeared in the floods of history.

The present volume gathers most of Chagall's essays, lectures, and speeches on public issues, as well as two major interviews. A companion volume, *Marc Chagall and His Times: A Documentary Narrative* (Stanford University Press, 2004), tells the story of his personal life, as recorded in his autobiographical writings and hundreds of documents, private letters, and photographs. To be sure, Chagall's statements on public issues include many allusions to his private world, and the two are not easily separable. When Chagall wrote or spoke at a meeting or an exhibition opening, he touched on matters of art and culture from the position of his personal experiences and creative work; conversely, his private letters and memoirs reflect much of the cultural and political situation of his times. Thus, in many ways, the two volumes intersect and are complementary.

Chagall's lectures were never abstract theoretical statements, but rather personal, context-dependent reflections, appeals, and confessions. They were addressed to very different audiences and oriented toward specific listeners or readers—American art students or Holocaust survivors, Communists or Israeli writers, Yiddish speakers or French intellectuals. Hence the conspicuous differences in their attitudes, discourse, stereotypes, and ideas. Yet this polyphonic panorama reflects the totality of the complex personality that was Marc Chagall and should not be compartmentalized. The book is therefore arranged in chronological order, divided into seven sections, without any separation of topics or audiences, thus exposing the artist's multicultural allegiances and kaleidoscopic mind.

In addition, we translated the first book on the art of Marc Chagall, written during World War I by the Russian art critics Abram Efros and Yakov Tugendhold, and published in Revolutionary Moscow in 1918 and in a German translation in Berlin 1921. In many ways, that book defined the terms of Chagall criticism for years to come, including his achievements and his dilemmas.

All texts were carefully reconstructed from the manuscripts, translated from Russian, French, Yiddish, or Hebrew into English, and properly annotated.[3] Because the facts, details, and specific expressions are of special value to the Chagall scholar or biographer, we have tried to be as precise and close to the original as possible within the confines of idiomatic English. We rarely used earlier English translations; most were made ad hoc for specific occasions and were often either imprecise or too literal.

The introductory chapter places the material in the context of Chagall's life and times. In addition, wherever needed, we have included short introductions to specific essays. On the whole, we tried not to discuss Chagall's ideas but to let the reader interpret them in context.

Chagall never titled his lectures; most titles in this collection were either taken over from earlier publications, approved by Chagall, or supplied here. Some editorial explications or interpolations of missing or implied meanings are inserted in the text in square brackets. Other information and interpretations are supplied in numbered notes, to avoid disrupting the original document. All transcriptions of names from other languages follow a reader-friendly system.

ACKNOWLEDGMENTS

I warmly thank Anthony Calnek, Director of Publications of the Solomon R. Guggenheim Museum in New York, for his initiative to pull me into the Chagall world, as well as for the early publication of parts of this material in the catalogue *Marc Chagall and the Jewish Theater* (1992) and for the right to reproduce it here. I owe special thanks and personal gratitude to Meret Meyer-Graber who opened the family archives for me, notably the Russian texts of Chagall's early years. The Archives of the YIVO Jewish Research Institute in New York, the Art Institute of Chicago, the Israeli Knesset, the Israel Museum, and the National and University Library in Jerusalem helped me locate Chagall's manuscripts and gave me permission to publish them in English translation. Special thanks to my friend the Yiddish poet A. Sutzkever in Tel Aviv for permission to use Chagall's texts published in his journal *Di Goldene Keyt*. And thanks to the art historian Pierre Schneider in Paris for permission to reprint his interview with Chagall in the Louvre.

I am grateful to all who helped in this endeavor, especially Rivka Markus at the Knesset in Jerusalem, Nina Hayun-Mokady in Ra'anana, Marek Webb and Nikolay Borodulin at the YIVO in New York, Rafael Weiser at the National and University Library in Jerusalem, and the art historian Alexandra Shatskikh in Moscow. Daniel Feldman of the Department of Comparative Literature at Yale University prepared the index. All were knowledgeable and kind, and I thank them sincerely.

BENJAMIN HARSHAV
Yale University

INTRODUCTION **The Texts of a Multicultural Artist**

Marc Chagall was born as Móyshe Shagál ("Móshka" to his parents) in the Jewish Pale of Settlement of the Russian Empire, and buried in a Christian cemetery in St.-Paul de Vence in the French Riviera. The span between those two horizons marks the range of cultural experiences of many creative Jews in the modern age. And between those two landmarks, Chagall lived and painted in St.-Petersburg and Vitebsk, Paris and Berlin, Moscow and New York, High Falls, N.Y., and Vence, Alpes Maritimes. He visited—and was deeply impressed by—Greece and Italy, Hebrew Palestine and Yiddish Vilna, and modern Israel. Furthermore, his was not a one-way journey. He left the Jewish Pale of Settlement and came back to it, he left Russia in 1910 and came back to it in World War I, he left France for the United States in World War II and came back to it after the Holocaust. He left his childhood Bible and came back to it in modern Israel and in the National Museum of the Marc Chagall Biblical Message in Nice in the French Riviera. He accumulated "identities" and did not discard any of them.

True, not all prominent artists or scholars of Jewish origin traversed the whole road in one generation. In the case of poets or fiction writers, it was more difficult; the language in which they created had to be the language of their childhood experiences. Boris Pasternak and Ilya Erenburg, Franz Kafka and Sigmund Freud, Saul Bellow and Henry Roth were typically "second generation" in their adopted language; their parents had already moved from Yiddish-speaking small towns to the big cities and adopted a "western" language, Russian or German or English.[1] But many modern graphic artists were born in Eastern European small towns—El Lissitzky and Nathan Altman, Chaim Soutine and Jules Pascin, Ben Shahn and Mark Rothko—and "made it" in the centers of Western culture. The language of art does not have to be a "mother tongue."

In this age of multicultural studies, it is good to remember that Chagall himself was a multicultural phenomenon, a cluster of diverse and often unbridgeable cultural affinities, all nestled in one body and mind. Even his founding experience alone, his "Jewishness," was a cluster of discontinuous, even clashing cultural systems: the orthodox religious world of Lithuanian Hasidism; the merely traditional folkways and manners of his parents; the renaissance of modern Yiddish secular literature and culture; the revival of a Hebrew culture in Zionist Palestine; the Jewish nationalist atmosphere in secular Yiddish circles in New York during the 1940s, impressed by the Holocaust and the birth of the state of Israel; and the intellectual world of Jews assimilated to the dominant, Russian, French, or English cultures. Furthermore, these contradictory Jewish options were glossed over in his mind by the strong pull of the dominant

cultural spheres: Russian literature and Russian avant-garde art; the social world and aesthetic trends of French painting, thought, and poetry
after Cubism; and the technical world of French art: the production of artifacts, galleries, and museums.

An Outline of Chagall's Life

The major dates of Chagall's biography are well known, yet their cultural
dimensions are not as clear. We shall survey them here briefly, as a context for the essays of this volume.[2]

Chagall was born in the Russian provincial capital Vitebsk, in the
northeastern corner of the Jewish Pale of Settlement. It was part of Jewish
"Lithuania," or *Litah (Lite)* in Yiddish. Geographically, *Litah* was the heir
to the immense medieval Grand Duchy of Lithuania—about six times the
size of the present-day Lithuanian state—that was covered with primeval
forests and populated by Slavic peasants and Polish landed gentry. This
realm was incorporated in the medieval Polish Kingdom, but at the end
of the eighteenth century, Poland was dismantled by its neighbors and
Litah was devoured by the Russian Empire. Yet the Jews—and only the
Jews—kept the memory and preserved the boundaries of medieval
Lithuania: It was Jewish *Litah*, land of the *Litvaks*, with their particular
Yiddish dialect, food, and mentality. In the western part of *Litah* (including today's Lithuania proper, as well as some areas of Byelorussia, Latvia,
and Poland), there were several old Jewish cities, such as Brisk (Brest
Litovsk), Grodno, and Vilna (Vilnius), centers of Jewish trade and learn-
ing for half a millennium.

The eastern part of this realm, comprising most of today's Byelorussia (officially Belarus; in Yiddish, Raysn), including Vitebsk, was home to warm, emotional, simple, hard-working, and independent Jews. They lived in predominantly Jewish small towns, surrounded by a sea of Christian villages and governed by the Christian bureaucracy of the Russian Empire. An unusual population explosion among those Jews in the nineteenth century (with a growth rate twice that of the general population in Europe) spawned poverty, and fed social activities and socialist movements, as well as upward mobility, urbanization, and emigration.

These Jews were not overwhelmed by the main currents and strictures of Polish or western Lithuanian Orthodox Jewry, but adopted them in their own, relaxed way. Since the eighteenth century they were influenced by the ideals of learning promoted in western Lithuania, especially by the Gaon of Vilna (Elijah Ben Solomon Zalman, 1720–1797) and his disciples; many academies (*yeshivas*) were founded in small Byelorussian towns, where scholars studied not only Hebrew but also the more difficult Aramaic legal texts of the Talmud. Many of the important modern and secular Hebrew and Yiddish writers grew out of that education, yet revolted against it, influenced by revolutionary trends of the time. Such were the Yiddish poets H. Leyvik and A. Lyesin, whose poetry Chagall illustrated, and the great Hebrew poet Chaim-Nakhman Bialik, whom Chagall knew and revered. Chagall himself had no access to this world of learning, but he took pride in it and admired his dead grandfather David Shagal, who, unlike Chagall's coarse father who smelled of herring, was presumably a learned man and a Torah teacher.

Yet the Jews of eastern Lithuania embraced Hasidism, which was all but banned in western Lithuania. Indeed, the great eighteenth-century Jewish scholar, the Gaon of Vilna, had twice excommunicated Hasidism; his followers were called *Misnagdim* ("Opponents"). Nevertheless, in eastern Lithuania, an original Hasidic movement evolved, merging the Lithuanian ideal of learning with a Hasidic outlook and mentality; the sect was called ChaBaD—an acronym for "wisdom, insight, knowledge." It was an enthusiastic, emotional movement, fostering an optimistic, even cheerful outlook—and it was neither as strict as the western Lithuanian world of learning, nor as quarrelsome as the many competing Polish Hasidic sects. There was one sect for the whole land, led by the Lubavich dynasty, the Shneursons. The founder of the dynasty, Rebbe Shneur-Zalman (1745–1813) was born in Lyozno (Chagall's ancestral home town). Later Rebbes established their residences in the small town of Lubavich, which gave its name to the movement, and Jews—rich and poor—would travel to them for advice on religious and secular matters, as to a saint. Theirs was a spiritual, charismatic power, with an ostensibly voluntary following, that embraced most of the Jewish population of eastern Lithuania (or today's Belarus). In July 1915, Marc and Bella Chagall, secular though they were, spent their honeymoon in Zaolshe, a railroad station beyond Lyozno, in the direction to Moscow, where the Rebbe kept court in the summers. Bella's pious father was a rich supporter of the movement, and Chagall was granted an audience with the Rebbe.

Yet, contrary to common stereotypes, Chagall was not specifically influenced by Hasidism. He did not know much about its doctrine, nor could he read its classical books in the "Holy Tongue," Hebrew-Aramaic. One can only speak of general Hasidic attitudes, abstracted and folklorized, that permeated the daily life of the Jews, which may have affected Chagall's attitudes. These included an innate optimism and joyfulness; the love of music and dance; and the belief that one can serve God even in the dirtiest jobs and that feeling and spiritual intention are more important than learning and rational argument. Thus, Chagall used to paint to the music of Mozart and loved to illustrate ballet and theater. And— perhaps most relevant to Chagall's art—was the doctrine of *bitul ha-yesh*, the "cancellation of existence" or transcendence of the real, material world in spiritual elation.[3] But all that did not come from any specific learning or indoctrination; it was, as it were, "in the air," in the mentality and discourse of the people, their beliefs, and their behavior.

In his adolescence, Chagall and his peers fled this world; and when some of them looked back at it as adults, they idealized what they saw. This ethos was reinforced by modern Yiddish literature, notably the stories of Y.L. Peretz, who discovered the humane values in Hasidism and romanticized it for a secular generation. Peretz was said to have married "feeling" with "thought" (somewhat as T.S. Eliot did in a different context). Chagall, however, superimposed on this nostalgic imagery a mixture of realism and grotesque, inspired by what he called the "modernist" art of Sholem-Aleichem, the charming unreality of a fiddler on a roof, and by the Russian novelist and story teller Nikolay Gogol, whom Chagall admired and illustrated later in life.

What did influence Chagall was rather the general atmosphere of East-ern European Jewish traditions, holidays, beliefs, superstitions, morals, and manners—some derived from Jewish books and life, some influenced by the surrounding culture and folklore—that "primitive" yet total world view, that permeated the daily life of all religious Jews, Hasidic or not. He imbibed this atmosphere not from his peers (who embraced Russian cul-ture) but from his simple, ignorant parents, to whom he was grateful all his life.

Chagall's family came from a small town, Lyozno in Mohilev (or Mogilev) Province, in today's Belarus. Lyozno was a railroad station about 60 km east of Vitebsk (toward Moscow). In 1897, it had 1665 Jews, just over two-thirds of the town's population. Shneur-Zalman, the revered founder of the ChaBaD Hasidic sect and author of its founding book, *Tanya*, was born in Lyozno in the eighteenth century. Thus, Lyozno be-came a significant name in Jewish geography. Another lapsed Lubavich Hasid, Shneur-Zalman Rubashov (Shazar), secular scholar and President of Israel, greeted Chagall in Jerusalem with the words: "Our brother from Lyozno and Paris"—in this secularized context, "Lyozno" meant Jewish aristocracy and a spiritual pedigree. Chagall's friend the art critic Abram Efros mentioned Lyozno as Chagall's birthplace, and Chagall himself was uncertain; in the questionnaire for the Art Institute of Chicago in 1937 he mentioned both places: "Born: Lyozno, Vitebsk." Chagall loved to go back to his family home town, where his grandfather and a large clan (on both sides) still resided. But he was actually born in the city of Vitebsk, capital of the neighboring province, on June 25, 1887, according to the Old Style (Julian) calendar. According to the postrevolutionary New Style (Gregorian or general European) calendar, the date would be July 6, but Chagall misread it as 7/7/1887, and believed in 7 as his lucky number.

Vitebsk was the capital of a Russian Province (Gubernia). Over 52 percent of the city's population was Jewish (others included Poles, Latvians, Germans, Byelorussians, and Russians). Though small in modern terms, Vitebsk was an important railroad junction and shipping center, a major city of the Jewish Pale of Settlement, close and directly connected to Moscow and St.-Petersburg. The city grew from about 40,000 in 1880 to 65,000 in 1897, and to 106,000 in 1918. Russians ruled the city and province, yet Jews were the major force in its rapid urban, industrial, and commercial development. They produced a politically powerless yet well-to-do middle class that developed and dominated trade and manufacturing in Vitebsk Province. Urbanization attracted Jewish families, like Chagall's, from the provinces to the poor quarters of the city; and mass immigration to the West, coupled with an elite migration to the centers of Russia, opened opportunities for a fresh influx of provincial newcomers.

Móyshe Chagall was the first of eight children (followed by a boy and six girls). His mother was sixteen when he was born, and a special bond was forged between mother and son. During his childhood, he studied Hebrew biblical texts in *Heder*, the traditional religious education given at the teacher's home, and was a singer in synagogue. After bar mitzvah, his father announced that Móshka was now off his back. Like most of his

generation, the boy shed religion overnight, and gravitated toward Russian culture. It was the traditional Jewish mother who bribed a teacher to
enroll him in a Russian school, and yielding to her son's whims, brought
him to study (God forbid!) in an art school. The Russian school was a
four-year municipal high school (*uchilishche*) for children who could
already read and write. Chagall spent two years in one class, five years in
all, but never graduated. In time, he did learn to read and write Russian
more correctly than the other languages he used during his life.

The art school was a private studio of Yury (Yehuda) Pen. Pen was an
exquisite naturalistic artist of the *Peredvizhnik* school (the so-called "Itinerant" artists), who depicted Jewish types and traditions and, as Chagall
himself wrote later, "raised several generations of Jewish artists," including El(iezer) Lissitzky, Marc Chagall, and his classmate Ossip Zadkine.

Contrary to the accepted view (based on Chagall's own mystifications),
Chagall did not study with Pen for only about two months; he studied with
Pen between the ages thirteen and nineteen (perhaps on and off). It was
the formative experience of his artistic biography, though not of his personal style. Yury Pen, a devoted, hard-working professional, was Chagall's
role model, yet Chagall deserted him as he deserted his own father and
at the same time admired him all his life. Of course, Chagall demonstrated his independence: He could neither carry out nor accept Pen's
meticulous academic naturalism and precise portraiture, yet he learned
from Pen the importance of portraying the local world, its houses and
fences, and the dignity of Jewish faces and rituals—ethnography as an
object of art.

With remarkable ease, Chagall, and most young people of his generation, shifted to the Russian language. The circles of middle-class youth in
which he moved spoke Russian and recited Russian poetry, though their
parents were all Yiddish speakers. They were a mixed group of boys and
girls together—which was contrary to both Jewish religious education and
Russian gender-separate schools—in the free spirit of the time.

In 1907, Chagall went to the capital, St.-Petersburg, where Jews had
no right to live unless they had a special Right of Residence permit. He
was admitted as a "stipend student" to the Imperial School for the En-
couragement of the Fine Arts, and eventually got help from some privi-
leged St.-Petersburg Jews who valued his talent as a son of "the people."
Chagall attended several art academies, including the famous Zvantseva
art school. His influential teacher there was Lev Samoylovich (Léon)
Bakst, who soon left for Paris where he designed stage sets for Diaghilev's
Russian Ballet. Still, even then, Chagall divided his time between the
capital and his home towns of Vitebsk and Lyozno.

During 1910–1914, Chagall was in Paris, eagerly absorbing both the
contemporary avant-garde scene and the European, Christian tradition of
art. From 1911 on, he lived in the "Beehive" (La Ruche) in Paris, a building
compound housing 140 artists, mainly immigrants. He befriended several
French poets and artists, especially the avant-garde poet Blaise Cendrars,
as well as Riccardo Canudo, editor of the avant-garde art journal *Montjoie!*,
Robert Delaunay, and Guillaume Apollinaire. Apollinaire discovered
what he labeled as Chagall's "supernatural" *("surnaturel")* art thirteen
years before the foundation of Surrealism.

Apparently by that time, Chagall had learned to chat in French and fascinated his interlocutors with his "crazy" personality. Yet he could also use Russian and Yiddish. Cendrars (who spent several years in Russia) spoke and read Russian, and his wife Fela Poznanski was a Russian Jewess from a prominent industrialist family; Robert Delaunay's wife Sonia was also a Russian Jewess, and so was Raissa Maritain, whom he met after the war. There were also many Yiddish-speaking artists in La Ruche, such as "crazy" Chaim Soutine and the future Yiddish art critic Leo Kenig. Chagall was aware of the project to create "Jewish Art," promoted by Kenig and others, but he shook it off and aimed at a place in French and Russian culture.

Apollinaire introduced Chagall to the German visitor Herwarth Walden, who owned the Berlin gallery Der Sturm and published a journal with the same name, *Der Sturm*, and was a major force in promoting German Expressionism and the international avant-garde. Walden organized Chagall's first comprehensive one-man show in Berlin in the summer of 1914, including some 240 paintings and drawings. On June 15, 1914, Chagall took a train to Vitebsk to attend his sister's wedding. In August, World War I broke out, and Chagall got stuck in Russia. His great paintings of the early period were "lost" in Paris and Berlin, though many found their way to private collections and made Chagall's fame in absentia, when it was assumed he had died in the war.

In July 1915, the artist married his pre-Paris fiancée Berta (later renamed Bella) Rosenfeld. The son of a clerk in a herring-cellar married the daughter of a rich owner of three jewelry stores in Vitebsk, and he was aware of the social discrepancy. When Chagall was drafted into the army, Bella's brother found him a post in his office of war economics in Petrograd, and Chagall continued painting and exhibiting in both capitals throughout World War I. In 1916, their daughter Ida was born.

During World War I, a movement of "Jewish Art," as well as interest in Jewish religious and folk art, developed in Russia. It was not a return to religion; these were secular, populist intellectuals, atheists who discovered beauty in the tradition of their own people. Hence, religious objects and figures were idealized not for their ritual functions, but were retrospectively transformed into folklore and art. Typically, the portraits of religious Jews in Chagall's works were portraits of old people, representing the past from the point of view of a young, secular, educated generation. Chagall also painted "Rabbis" (actually, religious Jews in their traditional garb), synagogues, cemeteries—he called them "documents," because they documented the culture of the past and because those were paintings from nature, to serve as eventual material for the creations of his imagination. He was deeply affected by the expulsion "within 24 hours" of a million Jews by the Russian Army at the beginning of World War I, embraced the myth of the "Eternal" or "Wandering Jew" and his Exile existence, and later was shaken by the pogroms in the Ukraine in 1919.

The democratic Russian Revolution of February 1917 gave the Jews equal rights. The Bolshevik October Revolution appropriated that accomplishment and opened places of power for a whole generation of Jews. The Revolution also supplied a new discourse for Russian artists and intellectuals. Chagall returned to Vitebsk, and in August 1918 he was appointed Plenipotentiary for the Affairs of Art in the Province of Vitebsk by the People's Commissar of Enlightenment (education and culture) A. Lunacharsky himself. Thus "Móshka from Pokrovska Street" (near the railroad tracks), as he put it himself, became the powerful "Commissar" of Art in his native city.

On the first anniversary of the October Revolution, with the help of his pupils, Chagall decorated the whole city. He also made stage designs for the new Theater of Revolutionary Satire, TeRevSat, which served the nearby front of the Civil War; founded an Art Museum in Vitebsk; and established the famous Vitebsk People's Art College,[4] to which he invited some of the outstanding avant-garde artists of Russia as professors. Chagall never promoted Communism per se; his "Revolution" was a revolution in art. But soon he was outflanked on the artistic "Left"; the founder of "Suprematism"—a so-called "Non-Objective," or abstract school of painting—Kazimir Malevich, though invited to Vitebsk by Chagall himself, actually pushed the founder out of his school.

In the summer of 1920, Chagall moved with his wife and daughter to Moscow. He worked in Malakhovka, a "Colony" for Jewish orphans of the pogroms in Ukraine in 1919, where he taught painting and Yiddish literature. His major achievement of the Russian years were the murals painted in November–December 1920 for the new Yiddish Chamber Theater in Moscow. Yiddish, the mundane, lower-class language of his first thirty years, was now revealed to Chagall as the language of a modern, literary culture. In his youth, he had left the folkways of the Jewish religious world directly for Russian; now he came back to look at the old world from the vantage point of modern Yiddish literature.

Chagall had no real avenues to contemporary Russian theater and art. For a short time, the new avant-garde ruled in Russian art—such artists as Malevich, Kandinsky, Tatlin—and they decided to give Chagall only a third-degree bread ration. Outwitted by both the political left and the artistic left, deprived of a place in the Jewish field, unable to get quality paint, perspicacious as to the totalitarian nature of the regime (the "corset," as he dubbed it), he sought a way out. In the summer of 1922, he managed to get his paintings out of Russia, emigrated to Berlin, and finally reached Paris in September 1923.

In his second French period, Chagall became famous and affluent; he and Bella acquired a wide circle of friends among French poets and intellectuals, their house teemed with visitors, they traveled a lot in France and abroad, and in 1937 they became French citizens. Chagall mastered the art of engraving, illustrating classical books and the Bible, for which he was awarded First Prize in the Venice Biennale of 1948. Yet at the same time, Chagall maintained his ties with Jewish culture and destiny. Throughout the years, he corresponded with Yiddish writers, illustrated Yiddish books, wrote Yiddish poems, made an emotional visit to Hebrew Palestine in 1931 and to Yiddish Vilna in 1935, and promoted the establishment of a Jewish Art Museum both for the secular Hebrew culture in Tel Aviv and for the secular Yiddish culture in Poland.

When France was defeated by the German army, in June 1940, the Chagalls fled to the Unoccupied Zone (Vichy France), were stripped of their French citizenship, and at the very last moment, in May 1941, left Europe for the United States. In his American period, 1941–1948, Chagall was again close to Yiddish-speaking circles. He knew no English and read Yiddish newspapers, where he followed the emotion-laden reports on the Holocaust in Europe and the emerging state of Israel, thus reinforcing his instinctive, home-grown Jewish nationalism. Throughout the years in France, Bella and Marc spoke Russian among themselves, and probably Yiddish, too. Although Bella had a more advanced Russian education than Marc, when she wrote her memoirs in 1939–1944, she wrote them in Yiddish.

During World War II, the victories of the Red Army, nostalgia for their Russian homeland, and a belief in the ideology of utopian Socialism led many American Jews to sympathize with the Soviet Union. In the late 1930s, during the Spanish Civil War, Chagall had participated several times in the Yiddish Communist press in Paris, and he continued in New York in the 1940s. He never became a Communist, but he was attracted to their Yiddish cultural activities in America and often spoke at their events; he lent his name to the Board of the Committee of Jewish Writers, Artists, and Scientists (whose honorary President was Albert Einstein). The Committee included some prominent liberal and left-wing intellectuals in the mode of the French Popular Front of the 1930s, yet it was later pronounced as a Communist "front organization." When Bella died suddenly in 1944, her memoirs were posthumously published in another "front organization," the "Book League of the Jewish People's Fraternal Order, IWO." Back in France, in 1949, Chagall became Honorary President

of a similar "front organization," MRAP (Movement against Racism, Anti-
semitism, and for Peace), which included Jacob Kaplan, the Chief Rabbi
of France, as well as several black intellectuals. But he quietly withdrew in
1952, when he learned of Stalin's execution of the leading Soviet Yiddish
writers, his friends. As a result, he was not allowed to come back to
America until 1958 (and to Russia until 1973).

Thus, unlike many immigrant intellectuals who stayed in America, his
inability to speak the language, and his daughter Ida's persistent pressure
to return to France, convinced Chagall to leave the United States. But the
main reason for his return to Europe after the war was that in France he
was not reduced to a "Jewish" milieu, but was part of the dominant culture, he spoke the language, was welcomed by the French cultural establishment, and enjoyed major exhibitions of his work. With his young
common-law wife Virginia Haggard (with whom he communicated in
French) and their son David, Chagall moved to France in 1948, bought a
house in Orgeval near Paris and, later, in Vence near Nice. To his great
sorrow, after seven years of intimate life together, Virginia left him in
1952, and Marc married the Russian-speaking Vava (Valentina Brodsky)
with whom he lived until his death in 1985. He visited Israel several
times and finally was allowed to visit his "homeland" Russia (though not
Vitebsk!) in 1973.

Chagall spoke a charming, idiosyncratic French, albeit with a Yiddish
accent, but his French spelling was quite impossible (as we can see in
his handwritten letters to Virginia Haggard). His Russian—the only language he had studied in a school—was generally correct, but it often had

a Babelian Yiddish subtext. Important letters in those languages and in English were often written in longhand or typed by Bella, Virginia, Ida, or Vava. Chagall learned Hebrew in *Heder*, to read selected passages of the Torah but not to write or speak. He could copy biblical words or passages but never wrote anything in Hebrew. In his written lectures and letters, the many Hebrew words contained in Yiddish are often misspelled. His written Yiddish—the spoken language of Chagall's childhood and youth—uses a peculiar spelling system, reflecting his local dialect. Nevertheless, Yiddish was intimate and easy; he wrote dozens of lectures and hundreds of letters in Yiddish, and answered even trivial corespondence. His real language was the language of colors.

The last thirty-seven years in France were a period of world fame, affluence, and tremendous productivity. Chagall expanded the genres of his work to stained glass windows in churches and synagogues, tapestries, ceramics, and sculptures, which he produced with the aid of first-rate French masters.

The Modern Jewish Revolution

The cultural and geographic trajectory of Chagall's life briefly outlined above makes Chagall a typical child of the Modern Jewish Revolution—a total transformation of the Jews, their languages, education, professions, values, their very existence in geography and in world history, that occurred in the century after the pogroms of 1881–1882 in Russia.[5] Millions of Jews moved from their "primitive" or "medieval" state of existence in small towns, mostly religious, poor, and ignorant (their Hebrew religious knowledge seemed irrelevant to the European cultural world), to big cities, and to the West, or (especially after the Revolution) to the Russian capitals and the eastern part of the Soviet empire. A similar process began in the smaller Jewish communities of Western Europe a century earlier; however, only after 1882, when millions joined the transformation, did a new Jewish cultural system with mass participation emerge.

If there ever was a "reevaluation of all values" it was in this nation on the move, at this particular historical junction. The Jews embraced an ideal of European secular culture—its genres, modes of discourse, ideologies, and institutions. And they joined it in two major directions: extrinsic and intrinsic.[6] The extrinsic trend brought masses of Jews to the languages, literature, science, theater, and so on in the centers of general culture, while the instrinsic trend created a European-type culture in the internal Jewish languages, Yiddish and Hebrew.

The intrinsic revolution aimed at creating an autonomous, secular, extraterritorial Jewish national culture. It produced a gamut of Jewish ideologies and political parties; a network of secular Jewish social and cultural institutions (schools, libraries, publishing houses, research institutes, theaters, newspapers, sport and health organizations, etc.); and a rich, secular literature in both Yiddish and Hebrew, including a massive effort at translating world literature and knowledge into the Jewish languages. As European history showed, the ideal model of a nation based on language and culture without power over a territory could not survive. Thus Yiddish culture, dominant and still vital in Chagall's time, has been shrunk to a minimum today; what has survived is the library of a colorful and significant literature. On the other hand, the minor, Hebrew culture has returned to its historical homeland, settled a territory, created the state of Israel, and flourished in it.

The extrinsic trend, on the other hand, driven by a rapid assimilation of the Jews to the dominant languages and societies, produced significant contributions by Jews (to be precise: persons of Jewish origin, the "non-Jewish Jews," as they were dubbed by Isaac Deutscher) to general culture and science. It is almost impossible to imagine modern culture without the names of Marx, Einstein, Freud, Kafka, Husserl, Durkheim, Jakobson, Lévi-Strauss, Chomsky, Derrida, Salk, Oppenheimer, and so on; or without several intellectual movements, launched by coteries of assimilated Jews, such as most of the Russian Formalists, the early psychoanalysts, the Frankfurt School, the moguls of Hollywood, the creators of the nuclear bomb, and many prominent theoretical linguists and economists.

The relations of those people to their Jewish past varied widely. The founder of Phenomenology, E. Husserl, converted to Christianity when it was a requirement for a professorship in Prague, and was hardly concerned about his Jewishness until the Nazis reminded him. Einstein discovered his Jewishness when he was expelled from Germany, but then supported various Jewish causes and bequeathed his archives to the Hebrew University in Jerusalem; Freud and Kafka struggled with the problem in their private correspondence for many years, as did Chagall, yet kept it out of the bulk of their creative work.

Chagall was even closer to the Jewish domain than many of them; his basic language was Yiddish, and he stood at the crossroads of both directions, the intrinsic and extrinsic. A creative writer has to immerse himself in one language: Kafka and Celan opted for German; Peretz and Chagall's friend Opatoshu, for Yiddish. The language of painting, however, is universal; a painter could stride both social spheres. Indeed, Chagall often crossed from the extrinsic culture to the intrinsic, and back again. On the whole, he succeeded in becoming a French artist (without suppressing the Jewish topics of his paintings) and befriended many French intellectuals, yet simultaneously, throughout his life, he also kept strong emotional relations both with Yiddish literature and with the emerging Hebrew society and state of Israel.

As a child of the Modern Jewish Revolution, Chagall developed a multilingual and multicultural perspective that gave him a sense of both relativism and irony. As a Jew from the Pale, he came to European history from outside that history, and for him all periods were parallel to each other, like so many rooms in the Louvre. To use André Malraux's term, all of art history was for him a *musée imaginaire*. His was not a revolution against the art of a past that he or his parents had grown up with, saw in museums, or studied in school; and he lacked the shock of a historical upheaval. True, biographically Chagall moved from exposure to Naturalist painting to a kind of Russian Fauvism to the French post-Cubist scene. But all those coexisted for him simultaneously, and this was a voyage not in history but in geography: Vitebsk—St.-Petersburg—Paris. When Chagall discovered the second generation of Cubists in Paris, he saw it as "Art" itself.

Only from the position of the avant-garde of his time did he turn back to discover for himself the main tradition of European art. Thus, his famous "Homage to Apollinaire" (1911–1912) is dedicated to his avant-garde idols: "Apollinaire, Cendrars, Canudo, Walden," but is also influenced by the fifteenth-century Italian painter Masaccio; and his autobiography of 1922–1924 is already devoted "To Rembrandt, Cézanne, My wife, My mother," with no mention of the avant-garde. Indeed, Chagall absorbed European art in a reverse direction: first Delaunay, then Cézanne, then Delacroix, and only after World War II did he discover Monet, and later, Titian (whom he praised in the Erasmus Prize lecture in 1960).

What had kept Chagall in Paris in 1910 was not Picasso but the Louvre. Hence, his thinking about art was essentially eclectic, relativizing all trends and styles, in a "postmodernist" fashion. He was certainly not a reactionary, reverting to Renaissance or other historical art, but a painter situated in the heart of Modernism, yet responding in his own way: using various modernist devices, yet subordinating them to his idiosyncratic deformations of representation. Since for him, art history was turned upside down, he could be perceived as a precursor of both Expressionism and Surrealism. And in time, to substitute for the lack of a historical dimension, he embraced the Bible—which for him was both childhood and prehistory, both Jewish and Christian-European.

The amazed and enthusiastic reception of Chagall in Paris and Berlin was largely due to his drastic leap from a "medieval" *shtetl* to modern Paris. It was the first generation of the Modern Jewish Revolution, and it exposed a sharp clash of imaginary worlds and semiotic systems. Individualism and introspection were key characteristics of this Revolution; a person had to break out of the imposing, dense, religious and social Jewish normative community by forcefully asserting his own individuality. And this individualism, shaping his personality, was carried over to the new, adopted culture. Chagall never succumbed to or joined any political party, never affiliated with any artistic ideology or style. He was impressed by many trends, artistic and political, which he encountered in his life, yet he kept his distance.

The traditional Jewish imaginary world was ahistorical, its texts were nonnarrative. The discourse of Yiddish had folklorized that semiotic discourse: it was talkative, digressive, associative; anything could be parallel to anything else. Chagall visualized this style, different times and places coexisted on one canvas; his paintings were anything but narrative.

Questions of Identity

What, then, was Chagall's identity?

"*Marc Chagall ist Russe*"—"Marc Chagall is a Russian"—announced the first sentence of the issue of *Der Sturm* in 1923, devoted to Chagall's work. Herwarth Walden, owner of the Expressionist gallery Der Sturm, had visited Paris in 1913. Walden brought the twenty-seven-year-old original artist to Berlin and made him internationally famous. Herwarth Walden (1878–1941) himself was a Jew (his real name was Georg Lewin), yet there was hardly a trace of it in his cultural activities in pre-Nazi Germany; nor did it matter, for all but in origin he was a German.[7]

Indeed, Chagall's paintings exhibited in Berlin in 1914 contained no overtly Jewish themes or figures.[8] Nevertheless, Chagall did insert some traces of his Jewish origins. Thus, the painting "To Russia, Donkeys, and Others," created in Paris in 1912 and addressed to the avant-garde exhibition "Donkey's Tail" in Moscow (which was very Russian in its substance), also contains three little Jewish "Stars of David" floating in the black sky on the left side, along with several more, decomposed into triangles:[9] a little Jewish corner in big Mother Russia.

"Marc Chagall, French (1887–)" announces a 1937 postcard of the Art Institute of Chicago on the reverse side of a painting depicting a religious Jew in the traditional Eastern European black attire and prayer shawl. The Jew is labeled "Rabbi" (possibly by Chagall himself), yet the prototype was a beggar in Vitebsk! He was called "Rabbi," ascribing to him some importance—apparently to dissociate this exotic image from the iconography of European-style Jews. Couldn't a French artist portray an Orthodox Jew? And, as Chagall argued, didn't the Dutch Rembrandt paint such Jews?

The issue is not as funny, or as simple, as it may appear. Insofar as such labels designate the country or culture within which the artist worked, they are perfectly correct. Those who pinned this label on Chagall (including himself)[10] may have wanted to escape anti-Semitic stereotypes; a Russian or French citizen, or a scientist working within those cultures, might be offended when stigmatized as defined by his ethnic or religious origin. From the perspective of the French cultural scene, Chagall was like van Gogh, Picasso, or Modigliani, who became the artists they were when they came from their respective countries to France, as Chagall pointed out correctly.

Yet from the perspective of modern Jewish culture—in both its Yiddish Diaspora and its Hebrew Israeli varieties—Chagall was a Jewish artist, and when speaking to those societies, he never obfuscated that fact. The American leftist Yiddish poet Z. Vaynper protested the French identity in Chagall's Chicago exhibition mentioned above, saying: "Now Marc Chagall declared himself to be a French artist!... According to Marc Chagall, he is not a Jewish artist at all, but a Jew-artist in French art." Chagall vehemently responded: "Sometimes, in sleepless nights, I think that perhaps I created a few pictures that might give me the right to call myself 'A Jewish artist.'" And expressions of Jewish identity are scattered throughout his texts and letters.

The way out of such contradictions lies in abandoning the habitual essentialist "identity" for a flexible perspectivism. We cannot ask what Chagall *is* in any exclusive way, because from his texts we learn that he is all of it: French and Russian and Jewish—all at the same time. And he is both pro-Communist and pro-Zionist, as well as opposed to those ideologies; simultaneously a "Revolutionary Artist" and a critic of avant-garde formalism. And I do not mean a fuzzy medley or cosmopolitanism, for Chagall was not at all fuzzy or compromising about it. He did not blur the boundaries, but developed his own polyphony and expressed his convictions decisively, depending on the context of his discourse and relationship. Oxymoron, ambiguity, and paradox are key characteristics of modernism in literature and art—and Chagall carried them to the identity level.

Chagall had not one single identity, either in his cultural and ethnic consciousness or in his artistic style, but a cluster of identities that were mutually exclusive yet complementary in his own mental world. He maintained a network of personal and professional relationships in several languages and ideological directions, and activated his different feelings about identity in different speech situations. In short, Chagall's identity is not the essence of some abstract "self," but is dependent on specific communicative situations, their audience, language, ideology, and expectations. Yet his individualism and awareness of his kaleidoscopic consciousness often led him to insert a counter-note into whatever ideology he embraced at the moment: to demand Zionism in a speech to the Communists, or to criticize the "automatic writing" of the Surrealists and simultaneously state that he was a "surrealist" before them.

To use the earlier distinction between the two modes of Jewish secularization, we may say that the mature Chagall mostly lived in the extrinsic world, but was deeply concerned about the intrinsic culture. In his correspondence, the Israeli government was "our" government and Yiddish literature "our" literature—expressions he never used for Russia or France. Yet he sometimes claimed that his homeland was Russia and his country was France. Vis-à-vis the Jews, he was an insider living in and talking from the outside; vis-à-vis the world at large, he was an "outsider" living in and talking from the inside.

ONE **In Revolutionary Russia**
1918–1922

The Bolshevik Revolution of October 1917 placed ideology and culture at
the center of public activities and government concerns. Many intellectuals felt they had experienced an upheaval of apocalyptic dimensions, the
bloody birth pangs of a cleansed, new world, without the social distortions
of Tsarist Russia. A wave of experimentations in all the arts seemed to
match the social revolution; furthermore, the artists earned their bread
by working for the new government. The powerful People's Commissar
of Enlightenment (equivalent to a Minister of Education and Culture),
Anatoly Lunacharsky, who knew Chagall from Paris, invited him to build
a new art college in Vitebsk. In August 1918, Chagall submitted a proposal
for such a school, and on September 12, 1918, he went to the capital
St.-Petersburg, then called Petrograd, to get final approval for his project.

Thus, at the age of thirty-one, Marc Chagall was appointed Plenipotentiary for the Affairs of Art in the Province of Vitebsk. He founded the
Vitebsk People's Art College, to which he invited some of the outstanding

avant-garde artists of Russia, including Ivan Pugny, Mstislav Dobuzhinsky, El Lissitzky, and Kazimir Malevich. To explain and defend the avant-garde direction of his college, Chagall wrote his first published articles.

He also established an art museum, initiated artistic activities in several towns of Vitebsk Province, and designed the stage sets for all ten productions of the new Theater of Revolutionary Satire, TeRevSat, which served the Red Army on the nearby front of the Civil War. Chagall was totally submerged in these activities; his stubborn positions and whimsical individualism caused clashes in all directions and his creative work suffered. Indeed, this was the first—and last—public position he ever held.

We publish here two programmatic articles, which use manifesto-type discourse and revolutionary phraseology to fight both "academic" art and the Marxist party bosses.[1] For Chagall, Revolutionary Art meant a revolution in the history of art that parallels the political revolution, rather than art on proletarian themes or painted for proletarians.

Art on the Anniversary of October[2]
November 7, 1918[3]

The workers and peasants are celebrating the anniversary of their Revolution. We need not dwell on the fact that this anniversary is the first, and is a rare event in history. This is clear both to its friends and its enemies. But what speech can I—an artist—make on this anniversary? Wouldn't many feel it strange? No doubt. But that is wrong. And here is why.

Art lived and will continue to live by its own laws. But in its depths, it undergoes the same stages experienced by all humanity, advancing toward the most revolutionary achievements. And if it is true that only now, when humanity has taken the road of the ultimate Revolution, can we speak of Humanity with a capital H, even more so, can Art be written with a capital A only if it is revolutionary in its essence. Only such Art in all its media can protect its historical right to survive. Only such Art and such revolutionary creators demand our attention, receive it, excite us.

Those to whom our art seems strange and incomprehensible, those who think the importance of art is overrated in the days of mass celebration, let them be embarrassed.

No one will dare deny the political achievements of the Revolution their right to live. Open the way for them!

We are also celebrating the anniversary of Revolutionary Art, the anniversary of the collapse of the Academies of the "Professors" and the restoration of the power of Leftist Art in Russia. Perhaps it has not been understood by all activists in the arts or in all of its branches. If they have a sense of survival—they'll understand it sooner or later. But some will object to us and say: So why are you a minority? No one, at least in our city, literally no one understands you, we are all baffled by your works—while our political Revolution is supported by a majority.

But those who start to argue that this should not happen—at least in the period of human development we are now experiencing—are wrong. Yes, the creators of Revolutionary Art always were and are now a minority. They were a minority from the moment the splendid Greek culture fell. From that moment on—we—are a minority. But we shall not remain a minority! Not in vain does the earth tremble! The majority will join us when two revolutions, the political and the spiritual, systematically uproot the heritage of the past with all its prejudices. But whether the majority will be with us now or later—this does not stop us. Stubborn and imperious, obedient to the inner voice of our artistic conscience, we offer and impose our ideas, our forms—the forms and ideas of the new Revolutionary Art; we have the courage to think that the future is with us. No matter how embarrassed many are by the radical edge of Leftist Art, we have to say to our friends and our foes: Down with prejudices! Plunge head first into the sea of the people's Revolutionary Art, give yourself to it instinctively and trustingly!

And believe it: the working people, transformed, will approach that high rise of culture and Art, which some nations have experienced in the past and of which we can only dream.

The Revolution in Art
March–April 1919[4]

When we turn to our throbbing era—the very moment of general Revolution—we immediately feel freer, outside of our confining frameworks, and we frankly pose the question: how long will we remain within the bounds of "historical conditions" (which I put in quotation marks)? Isn't it better to take a risk once, and with our own determination, to oppose each arbitrary "yes" of history with a "no"? All conformity to the traditional fate of history is alien to the spirit of our age. And our future will not know a return to the past; it will not know it, for such a return would be contrary to the permanent revolution, to the revolution of the spiritual and political struggle we are going through.

From now on, we must finally understand how we find ourselves in the whirlpool of the Revolution. All areas and all elements of spiritual and material order are entirely submerged. And we need enormous strength and a truly contemporary spirit to live in our age, foreshadowing the future. What does revolution in art mean? This revolution wasn't born yesterday. In the whole history of art you encounter isolated names of revolutionary innovators, painters, composers, and poets. More than once they have rejected the stagnant culture and have created new eras. But our age has given art an extraordinary stability; it has clearly set our tasks and has freed us from the yoke of the academies and the professors.

Our age has put up a wall against the naive reasoning of European and Russian aesthetes on the isolation and inviolability of art. It puts an end to the refined discourse on the so-called "beauty" in art, which exists only for itself. It puts an end to all the literary debates and all the deadly boring discussions of "Art for art's sake." From now on, we no longer want to know what we have in our hands or what weapon we are going to use to strike you. And we consciously lose and scatter traditional definitions and the meaning of the simplest things: it hardly matters to us if such and such a thing has its own name or has no name at all. How long will the tedious debates of intellectuals on art and "Art for art's sake" go on as in the past?

The art of general Revolution is hiding behind the inaccessible "Art for art's sake." It is hiding behind the art of the closed studios and the artistic production of isolated individuals. It would be appropriate for us to dwell here on the meaning and value of what is generally called Proletarian Art.

I maintain that the situation of art in our days will go beyond the present. And while we are in the process of constructing the social and political life of today by progressively going toward the future—our Art in general, and plastic art in particular—are already within the realm of the future.

When we speak of Proletarian Art, we are usually thinking of its important and undisputed ideas and tasks; who would agree to remove its "content"? But here we encounter the "subject matter." Do you think that if the "subject matter" represents the life of a worker or of a peasant, rather than insects, and in an uninspired way, it is Proletarian Art?

No, I will never be convinced that Antoine Watteau, the painter of elegant parties and the refined reformer of the plastic art of his century, is inferior to Gustav Courbet solely because the latter represented workers and peasants on his canvases. But the art of today, like the art of tomorrow, doesn't want any "content," and only reluctantly does it accept compromises and concessions in this realm. So we must be wary about defining Proletarian Art. Above all, let us be very careful not to define it by its ideological content, in the usual sense of that word. It is precisely this aspect that we must banish definitively. Let us not shout all over: "Look, look: we are those same workers and peasants, we are struggling, we are fighting." Let us not underline it in our works. Whom do we want to impress? The voice of the masses will always recognize the truth.

No matter how bold and free we are on issues of art, we must not deprive ourselves of an important property, which is a certain sense of modesty. It is the right and the duty of each of us.

Proletarian Art will be Art which, with a wise simplicity, will be able to break internally and externally from what we can only call "Literature." In vain do you criticize life and consider it from any point of view: as long as you have not succeeded in uprooting the last traces of your former life, there will be nothing proletarian either in your art or in your life. As soon as this break is made—and it is not decided by decree—art ceases to play the role of illustration and serving somebody. And it doesn't matter what the poet, the musician, the painter represents: the sound of factory sirens or an orange peel—it is enough to understand that if one cannot ask himself how he represented it, its value is nil.

Our comrades in Petrograd are right when they assert along with us: Proletarian Art is not an art for proletarians or an art about proletarians. Let us remember once and for all: it is the Art of proletarian painters. In the person of the proletarian painter, creative gifts are combined with proletarian consciousness. He knows precisely that he himself, like his talent, belongs to the collective. Unlike the bourgeois painter who is forced to pander to the taste of the mob, the proletarian painter is constantly struggling against routine and leading the masses after him.

I repeat: we will remain indifferent to works that tell or represent the heroic struggle and the life of the workers and peasants; we do not feel the breath of the essential laws of the new Art in those works.

This is why we proletarian painters respect above all the value of the plastic language. In our refusal to admit any "subject matter" and "content," we are unshakable. Pitilessly throw out all art that contains $2 \times 2 = 4$, the closest and most accessible to the masses. This art is not worthy of our age. Oppose it, by advancing our will in action and our inextinguishable internal voice. It will be the voice of the rebels of the whole world, constantly demolishing and building a new life and culture, and it will also be the most disciplined voice, internally and externally. But always be able to obtain the maximum of output and expression. As for the subject matter in the usual sense, never mind where it comes from and what inspired it— it isn't worthy of us. Who will cast the stone at us? Only one who isn't capable of sensing the future in which we are already involved. Once and for all, let us stop asking: "Why? For what reason?" If the food given you is harmful to your health, you shout boldly: "Take this away—it is unhealthy." But here, you are offered food of the new Revolutionary Art which is necessary to preserve the beings living on earth. And it is wrong to call the art of our days by the derisive title: "The Art of the Poor."

Let us not be intimidated by the fact that we are in a minority and that no one understands us, so to speak. If the minority appreciates us with a sincere enthusiasm, we can allow the majority to turn away from us hastily and out of misunderstanding. We will then shout to them: "Fine, you will come back to us!" Ever since the decline of Greek culture, we have always been in a minority. To be the minority in art is the measure of its authenticity. But we won't be so for long. Not for nothing does the earth tremble. And the coming days will remove all uncertainties and mutual incomprehension.

Wait for the day of transfiguration!

You will be with us!

And with us the New World will awaken!

This world will force you to understand us—and you will!

My Work in the Moscow Yiddish Chamber Theater
1921–1928[5]

A revolutionary time brought with it swift, revolutionary changes. In Chagall's Art College, Kazimir Malevich promoted the abstract, minimalist, and geometrical art of Suprematism, organized as the new movement of UNOVIS (Affirmers of the New Art). Chagall published Malevich's first programatic brochure, but eventually lost all the students of his master class to the new, more radical religion of art. Chagall was all against academism and routine in painting, against realism and psychologism, and for a revolution in art, but he could not envision art without cultural representations of a "world" (however "deformed") and the individual expression of subconscious perceptions. In the summer of 1920, Chagall abandoned his college, and took his wife and daughter to Moscow.

Toward the end of 1920, the experimental Yiddish Chamber Theater, founded by Aleksey (Aleksandr) Granovsky in Petrograd, moved to the new capital of Russia, Moscow. Here they took over the apartment of a rich Jew who fled from the Revolution, built a stage in the former kitchen, and turned the living room into a theater hall with ninety seats. The artistic adviser of this theater, Abram Efros, persuaded Granovsky to invite Chagall to paint the scenery for their first performance in Moscow: three sketches by Sholem-Aleichem.

Chagall plunged into the work, and over the course of forty days, in November–December 1920, he completed his masterpiece. Instead of a painting inside a theater, he included the whole theater in his paintings: The stage was constructed by Chagall, actors' faces were painted, and all the walls were covered with murals, nicknamed "Chagall's Box."[6] Granovsky's innovative theater underwent a transformation under the impact of Chagall's painting. For a short time, it became one of the most famous theaters in Russia and in Western Europe.

Chagall recorded that experience in two articles: first, when the theater was allowed to go on a tour of the West in 1928 (based on an earlier memoir of 1921) and second, in 1944, when Shloyme Mikhoels, the Director of the soviet Yiddish theater, visited New York.

"Here are the walls," said Efros, "do what you want with them." It was an apartment, run-down, its tenants had fled. "See, here we will have benches for the audience, and over there, the stage."

To tell you the truth, "over there," I didn't see anything but a vestige of a kitchen, and "here"?

I shouted, "Down with the old theater that smells of garlic and sweat![7] Long live..." And I dashed to the walls. On the ground lay sheets;[8] workers and actors were crawling over them, through the renovated halls and corridors, among slivers, chisels, paints, sketches.

Torn tatters of the Civil War—ration cards, various queue-numbers—lay around. I too wallowed on the ground. At moments, I enjoyed lying like this. At home they lay the dead on the ground. Often, people lie at their heads and cry. I too love, finally, to lie on the ground, to whisper into it my sorrow, my prayer...

I recalled my great-grandfather, who painted the synagogue in Mohilev,[9] and I wept: why didn't he take me a hundred years ago at least as an apprentice? Isn't it a pity for him to lie in the Mohilev earth and be an advocate for me [in the World to Come]? Let him tell with what miracles he daubed with his brush in the shtetl Lyozne. Blow into me, my bearded grandfather, a few drops of Jewish truth![10]

To have a bite, I sent the janitor Ephraim for milk and bread. The milk is no milk, the bread is no bread. The milk has water and starch; the bread has oats and tobacco-colored straw. Maybe it is real milk, or maybe—fresh from a revolutionary cow. Maybe Ephraim poured water into the jar, the bastard, he mixed something in and served it to me. Maybe somebody's white blood.... I ate, drank, came to life. Ephraim, the representative of the workers and peasants, inspired me. If not for him, what would have happened? His nose, his poverty, his stupidity, his lice crawled from him to me—and back. He stood like this, smiling feverishly. He didn't know what to observe first, me or the paintings. Both of us looked ridiculous. Ephraim, where are you? Who will ever remember me? Maybe you are no more than a janitor, but sometimes by chance you stood at the box office and checked the tickets. Often I thought: they should have taken him on stage; didn't they take janitor Katz's wife? Her figure looked like a square yard of wet wood covered with snow. Carry the wood to the fifth floor and put it in your room. The water streams.... She screamed, protested during rehearsals like a pregnant mare. I don't wish on my enemies a glance at her breasts. Scary!

Right behind the door—Granovsky's office. Before the theater is done, there is little work. The room is crowded. He lies in bed, under the bed wood shavings, he planes his body. Those days he was sick.

"How is your health, Aleksey Mikhaylovich?"

So he lies and smiles or scowls or curses. Often acrid words, of the male or female gender,[11] fell on me or on the first comer. I don't know if Granovsky smiles now, but just like Ephraim's milk, his futile smiles console me. True, sometimes, I felt like tickling him, but I never dared to ask, "Do you love me?"

I left Russia without it.

For a long time, I had dreamed of work in the theater. Back in 1911, Tugendhold wrote somewhere that my objects are alive, I could, he said, paint psychological sets. I thought about it. Indeed, in 1914, Tugendhold recommended to Tairov, the director of the Moscow Chamber Theater, that he invite me to paint Shakespeare's Merry Wives of Windsor. We met and parted in peace. The goblet was overflowing.[12] Sitting in Vitebsk—commissaring away, planting art all over the province, multiplying students-enemies—I was overjoyed to get Granovsky's and Efros's invitation in 1918[13] to work in the newly opened Yiddish theater. Shall I introduce Efros to you? All of him legs. Neither noisy nor quiet, he is alive. Moving from right to left, up and down, always beaming with his eyeglasses and his beard, he is here and he is there, Efros is everywhere. We are bosom buddies and we see each other once every five years. I heard about Granovsky for the first time in Petrograd during the war. From time to time, as a pupil of Reinhardt, he produced spectacles with mass scenes. After Reinhardt's visit to Russia with Oedipus Rex, those mass scenes created a certain impression. At the same time, Granovsky produced spectacles using Jews of all kinds of professions whom he assembled from everywhere. They were the ones who later created the studio of the Yiddish theater.

Once I saw those plays, performed in Stanislavsky's realistic style. As I came to Moscow, I was agitated. I felt that, at least in the beginning, the love affair between me and Granovsky would not settle down so fast. I am a person who doubts everything under the sun, whereas Granovsky is sure of himself, and a bit ironic. But the main thing is that, so far, he is absolutely no Chagall.

They suggested I do the wall paintings for the first production and the opening of the theater. Wow, I thought, here is an opportunity to turn the old Yiddish theater upside down—the Realism, Naturalism, Psychologism, and the pasted-on beards. I set to work. I hoped that at least a few of the actors of the Yiddish Chamber Theater and of HaBimah,[14] where I was invited to do The Dybbuk, would absorb the new art and would abandon the old ways. I made a sketch. On one wall, I intended to give a general direction introducing the audience to the new Yiddish People's Theater. The other walls and the ceiling represented klezmers, a wedding jester, women dancers, a Torah scribe,[15] and a couple of lovers hovering over the scene, not far from various foods, bagels and fruit, set tables, all painted on friezes.[16] Facing them—the stage with the actors. The work was hard; my contact with the work was settling down. Granovsky apparently lived slowly through a process of transformation from Reinhardt and Stanislavsky to something else. In my presence, Granovsky seemed to hover in other worlds. Sometimes, it seemed to me that I was disturbing him. Was it true? I don't know why he did not confide in me. And I myself didn't dare to open serious discussions with him. The wall was breached by the actor Mikhoels, who was starving just like me. He would often come to me with bulging eyes and forehead, hair standing on end, a pug nose and thick lips entirely majestic.

He follows my thought, he warns me, and with the sharp edges of his hands and body he tries to grasp. It is hard to forget him. He watched my work, he begged to let him take the sketches home, he wanted to get into them, to get used to them, to understand. Some time later, Mikhoels joyfully announced to me, "You know, I studied your sketches, I understood. I changed my role entirely. Everybody looks at me and cannot understand what happened."

I smiled. He smiled. Other actors quietly and carefully snuck up to me, to my canvases, began observing, finding out what kind of thing this is. Couldn't they also change? There was little material for costumes and decorations. The last day before the opening of the theater, they collected heaps of truly old, worn-out clothes for me. In the pockets, I found cigarette butts, dry bread crumbs. I painted the costumes fast. I couldn't even get out into the hall that evening for the first performance. I was all smeared with paint. A few minutes before the curtain rose, I ran onto the stage to patch up the color of several costumes, for I couldn't stand the "Realism." And suddenly a clash: Granovsky hangs up a plain, real towel! I sigh and scream: "A plain towel?!"

"Who is the director here, me or you" he answers.

Oh, my poor heart, oh sweet father!

I was invited to do the stage for The Dybbuk in HaBimah. I didn't know what to do. Those two theaters were at war with each other. But I couldn't go to HaBimah, where the actors didn't act but prayed, and, poor souls, still idolized Stanislavsky's theater.

If between me and Granovsky—as he himself put it—the love affair didn't work out, Vakhtangov (who had then directed only The Cricket on the Hearth) was a stranger to me. It'll be very hard, I thought, to find a common language between the two of us. To an open declaration of love, I respond with love; but from hesitations and doubts, I walk away.

For example, in 1922, they invited me lovingly to Stanislavsky's second art theater to stage together with the director Diky[17] Synge's "Playboy of the Western World."

I plunged into it body and soul, but the whole troupe declared a strike, "Incomprehensible."

Then they invited somebody else and the play was a flop. Isn't it true?

At the first rehearsal of The Dybbuk, in HaBimah, watching the troupe with Vakhtangov, I thought, "He is a Russian, a Georgian; we see each other for the first time. Embarrassed, we observe one another. Perhaps he sees in my eyes the chaos and confusion of the Orient. A hasty people, its art is incomprehensible, strange.... Why do I get upset, blush, and pierce him with my eyes?"

I will pour into him a drop of poison; later he will recall it with me or behind my back. Others will come after me, who will repeat my words and sighs in a more accessible, smoother and clearer way.

At the end, I ask Vakhtangov how he intends to conceive of The Dybbuk. He answers slowly that the only correct line is Stanislavsky's.

"I don't know," said I, "of such a direction for the reborn Yiddish theater." Our ways part.

And to Zemakh,[18] "Even without me, you will stage my way. There is no other way." I went out into the street.

Back home in the children's colony in Malakhovka, I remembered my last meeting with An-sky,[19] at a soirée in 1915 it "Kalashnikov's Stock Market."[20] He shook his gray head, kissed me, and said, "I have a play, The Dybbuk, and you're the only one who can carry it out. I thought of you."

Ba'al-Makhshoves, who stood nearby, blazed agreement with his eyeglasses and nodded his head.

"So what shall I do?... What shall I do?"

Anyway, I was told that a year later Vakhtangov sat for many hours at my projects, when he prepared The Dybbuk. And they invited someone else, as Zemakh told me, to make projects à la Chagall. And at Granovsky's, I hear, they over-Chagalled twentyfold. Thank God for that.

Malakhovka 1921–Paris 1928

P. S. I just heard that the Muscovites are abroad. Regards to them!

On Jewish Art—Leaves from My Notebook
1922[21]

After less than two years as Plenipotentiary of Art in Vitebsk, Chagall had to leave his Art College. Either he was pushed out, or he was simply fed up with administration, wrangling with the Communist authorities and with artists who claimed to be more revolutionary than he was, notably the founder of the abstract school of "Suprematism" Kazimir Malevich and his follower El Lissitzky. In the summer of 1920, Chagall moved to Moscow with his wife and four-year-old daughter and found work in the framework of the new Jewish secular culture that developed freely under the aegis of Soviet equality. Chagall painted his famous murals for the Yiddish Chamber Theater and taught art and Yiddish literature at a Jewish orphanage in Malakhovka near Moscow. Thus, he was invited to express

his views on Jewish art in the new Yiddish literary-cultural journal, *Shtrom*

(which can be variously translated as "stream," current," or "torrent," that

is, in the strong current of the Revolution).

A few words, comrades, on the topic you asked me to write about at length—My opinion on Jewish art.

Just recently in Jewish artists' circles a hot debate went on about the so-called Jewish art.

In the noise and fever, a group of Jewish artists emerged. Among them was Marc Chagall.

Still in Vitebsk, when this "misfortune" happened—just returned from Paris—I smiled to myself. I was busy then with something else.

On the one hand, the "new world"–Jews[22]—that world so hated by Litvakov[23]—my shtetl alleys, hunchbacked, herringy residents, green Jews, uncles, aunts, with their questions: "Thank God, you grew up, got big!" And I kept painting them.

On the other hand, I was younger then by a hundred years, and I loved them, simply loved them. I was more absorbed by this, this gripped me more than the thought that I was anointed as a Jewish artist.

Once, in Paris, back in my LaRuche[24] room, where I worked, I heard through the Spanish screen the quarrel of two Jewish emigré voices: "So what do you think, after all, Antokolsky wasn't a Jewish artist, or Israels, or Liebermann!"

The lamp was dim and lit my painting standing upside down (that's how I work—now are you happy?!) and finally, when the Paris sky began to dawn, I laughed at the idle thoughts of my neighbors about the lot of Jewish art:[25] "OK, you talk—and I will work."

Representatives of all countries and nations! To you my appeal (I cannot, I remembered Spengler). Confess: Now, when Lenin sits in the Kremlin, there is no sliver of wood [for heating], smoke rises, the wife is angry—do you now have "national art?"

You, clever German Walden[26] and you various others who preach international art, fine Frenchmen Metzinger and Gleizes[27] (if they're still alive), you will answer me: "Chagall, you're right!" Jews, if they feel like it

(I do), may cry that the painters of the shtetl wooden synagogues (why am I not with you in one grave) and the whittlers of the wooden synagogue rattles—"Hush!" (I saw it in An-sky's[28] collection, got seared) are gone. But what is really the difference between my crippled Mohilev great-grandfather Segal[29] who painted the Mohilev synagogue and me, who painted the Yiddish theater (a good theater) in Moscow? Believe me, no fewer lice visited both of us as we wallowed on the floor and in workshops, in synagogues and in theater. Furthermore, I am sure that, if I stop shaving, you would see his precise portrait...

By the way, my father [looked like him]. Believe me, I put quite a bit of effort, no less love (and what love!) have we both expended.

The difference is only that he [Segal] took orders for signs and I studied in Paris, about which he also heard something. And yet. Both and he and others (there are such) are not yet Jewish art as a whole. Why not speak the truth. Where would it come from? God forbid it should have to come from some fiat! From Efros[30] writing an article, or because Levitan[31] will give me an "academic ration!"...

There was Japanese art, Egyptian, Persian, Greek. Beginning with the Renaissance, national arts began to decline. Boundaries are blurred. Artists come—individuals, citizens of this or that state, born here or there (blessed be my Vitebsk), and one would need a good registration or even a passport specialist (for the Jewish desk) to be able to "nationalize" all the artists.

Yet it seems to me: If I were not a Jew (with the content I put into that word), I wouldn't have been an artist, or I would be a different artist altogether.

Is that news?

For myself I know quite well what this little nation can achieve.

Unfortunately, I am too modest and cannot say aloud what it can achieve.

It's no small matter what this little nation has achieved!

When it wanted—it showed Christ and Christianity.

When it wished—it gave Marx and Socialism.

Can it be that it won't show the world some art?

It will!

Kill me if not.

How I Got to Know Peretz
1925[1]

From 1923, Chagall lived in France and was prominent in the French art establishment, yet he also kept contacts with the Yiddish cultural world. Y.L. Peretz (1851–1915) was enshrined as one of the three Classical Writers of Yiddish literature, along with Mendele Moykher Sforim and Sholem-Aleichem. All three appeared on the stamp issued by the Yiddishist Culture League in 1919, and their names were inscribed on Chagall's mural, "Introduction to the Jewish Theater." Peretz was a highly revered moral and ideological authority of the new, secular Yiddish culture, and in Warsaw he established a kind of secular Hasidic Court, which became a drawing point for the young modernist Yiddish writers. During the war, Chagall had illustrated a little Yiddish book with Peretz's story, "The Magician" (Vilna: B. Kletzkin, 1917). *Literarishe Bleter* (*Literary Pages*), published in Warsaw in independent Poland between the two world wars, was a central literary newspaper in the Yiddish world, promoting modern Yiddish literature and criticism. The editors invited Chagall to participate in the special Peretz issue, on the tenth anniversary of his death.

You asked me, dear colleagues, to write for the Peretz issue. You probably think it is enough to love something to be able to write about it—to write about Peretz. Can you be a critic if you love? Besides, I note with fear that I seem to have lost the talent for writing recently . . . The pen betrays me . . .

I didn't even know Peretz personally. Only when a publisher (I don't remember which) asked me to do drawings for one of Peretz's tales, "The Magician," did I start reading Peretz. I was surprised. You can certainly remember the impression when you walk down a street and turn into another street, and at that very corner, behind a fence, a Jewish moon with a dark horizon behind it suddenly leaps at your feet from the sky.

That's exactly how the poor and splendid Jewish images and figures float up from the little white pages. It is simple and new. It is that modest, hardly emphasized noble technique, those features that have been experienced for generations, which alone can make art national, independent of content. And really, from childhood on, haven't they dangled anxiously inside us—those tunes, Sabbath days, Friday evenings, velvet caps, your first loves, landscapes breathing with psalms, the last tones of the weary cantor, and Jews, Jews on the earth and in the sky.

I recall my strolls along the street on the riverbank. Past the sawmill and factory, far far beyond the other side of the bridge—there, you stop at a tree next to the graveyard. Peretz murmured to my feet from below. Swam in the clouds above. Rustled among the little houses—the tombstones of the cemetery, where pieces and crumbs of his tales in the folk manner were heaped up—various scraps of paper covered with writing. Wasn't the forsaken, hilly, half-alive place good for the stage of his play, *A Night in the Old Market Place*?[2]

I will not rest until the collection of his *Tales in the Folk Manner* is illustrated by me. A dream!

I am sorry, dear colleagues, that on the anniversary of his death, I cannot be in a corner in a synagogue somewhere—where Jews will remember Peretz. In such moments our lives and our works pass before our eyes . . . And years unknown are still there for us. And you think: even if our epoch be one of iron and cruelty, yet we have now rediscovered Peretz and Sholem-Aleichem. They were the first to lay their hands on you and bless you—the new generations of Yiddish poets and writers.

On Modern Art
1931[3]

In 1931, the first Mayor of the new Jewish city Tel Aviv, Meir Dizengoff, invited Chagall to visit and advise on the establishment of an art museum. Chagall spent almost three months in Palestine, visited the cities and kibbutzim, and was extremely impressed by this Jewish revival. In Palestine, he could afford openly to express his heresy and ambivalence vis-à-vis modernism, using his authority as a painter. Chagall did not formulate his positions in theoretical terms, yet he did have strong in-tuitions about the state and crisis of modernism at the time, combined with concerns about his own place in it and the nature of his own, stub-bornly figurative, culturally determined, and individualistic painting. Sometimes he talked down to his audience and taught them the history of art, misreading them as a Jewish *shtetl* crowd. But between the lines of the didactic tone is a real concern for the future of Western art (and his own place in it), from a position modernists might call "conservative," though it reflected the impasse and crisis of modernist art in France in the 1930s.

What I have to tell you about contemporary art is influenced, in part, by the present mood in European art. When I am here [in Palestine], I feel a vast difference between the moods here and there. Hence you must forgive me if you find a somewhat pessimistic tone in my words on art. Under this sky and on this soil, one could draw altogether different feelings from one's heart. Sometimes, you don't even want to think about the lot of modern art and its future. Sometimes, when I talk about art, a feeling of sadness, depression, displeasure, and even a sense of regret overcomes me. Don't talk. Don't explain. For inside me is a kind of skepticism, a lack of confidence in words. Not because I am hostile to the word, but because people don't pay attention to words, and especially to words from the heart. I would say that man is mostly the opposite of what is said and seen. Of those, just a faint trace will remain.

Therefore, in answer to questions, wonderments, and hesitations, I just smile.

And it seems that this art had little value after all, if right at its birth, words clouded its sky. Now I believe in the opposite. The great phenomena in art emerge almost unintentionally. But I don't say unconsciously. I myself never know in advance how a certain phenomenon will be reflected in me. Only after the fact is the right truth revealed. That is why I prefer silence. Wasn't I right to say that we have some measure of skepticism? Especially, since our youth has passed.

Some time ago I strolled through an exhibition with a visitor, and I asked him casually: Aren't you sad? Isn't it strange that after so many wars in the field of art, the question is still valid: what is the difference between the new art and ancient art, and is this question a sign of achievement? Nevertheless, the time has not come for various academicisms. All the talk about "naturalism" and "populism" is premature. The old did not produce the new. The life of the new is always different, that is, the new moves forward. New living forms with new contents appear. Hence, the treasures of museums and burial caves can serve us only as an example of wonderment, but not as a model for imitation. The real tragedy is in those waves of stylization that flood us time and again, in the turn to the distant culture of Egypt, to Bach, Offenbach, or Zola. It seems to me that no great artist—their number is small—ever returned back to look for his special way. Without borrowing, without stylizing, as if for the first time, a person shows the new face of his world and his time. This is what we need. And from this point of view we must be careful with the word "tradition." The culture of art does not leave us a heritage to use and benefit from. It is not something you can eat. And it is precisely the individual creators who express the spirit and essence of society. Only rarely is the road of modern art examined.

Actually, man lacks distance from the phenomena of his time. All that was said about some trend in art when it was still evolving, when it did not yet go beyond the boundaries of its own time, is of relative value. Only in moments of crisis, when events have passed through us, can we gradually recoup our strength and see the events themselves more clearly. As for me, I do not expect those motivations that exist outside of our being. And rather than express my opinion on the fate of art, I better listen to my own soul . . . Our inner "I" is much firmer than the state of the world outside us. For twenty-five years I have worked in art, and continue to hold the same ideas, even more stubbornly than at first.

The development of modern art began especially with Impressionism. The earlier trends and schools such as Neo-Classicism with the artists David and Ingres, Romanticism with Delacroix and Naturalism with Courbet—all those remained mainly in the domains of ideology, and this ideology is not much different, in my view, from the ideology of previous centuries of art. Even before the Renaissance, the primitive artist Piero de la Francesca created for himself a theory of light and shade, chiaroscuro. Without taking that into account, the Impressionists in the late nineteenth century renewed the nature of the picture, introducing a new concept of light. They turned a simple sketch into a picture, momentary impressions into a more stable image, as if they wished to mock the grand compositions of the academic masters before them. They purified the palette of colors and were liberated. Parallel to the discoveries of scientists about the rainbow colors and the separation of colors, the Impressionists, too, filled the surface of the painting with all the colors of the rainbow. This was young and fresh, faithful and new, but thin, and to my mind, shallow.

After the first impression, the creative imagination and scope of some of them does not seem very great. For example, the Impressionist Claude Monet is especially great as a professional. And this is not just my private opinion. His strength is that of a stubborn realist, an average French citizen. But, on the other hand, he did have an unusual eye. Cézanne himself admired Monet's eye. He was far from the transparent realism of Chardin. Edouard Manet, Monet's friend, was an artist of a higher rank, though not an official Impressionist. I place more value on the Jew Pissarro, who had one weakness: he did not believe in his own strength and followed the various directions taken by his friends, even the younger ones. On the other hand, this shows his extreme modesty. Apparently he considered his own personality more negligible than the search for theoretical truth of the art of painting, which he thought his friends had: Cézanne, Monet, Seurat. For Pissarro bore the elements of Cézanne's art even before Cézanne. In any case, he excelled in plastic depth found only in a very few. Not in vain was he considered a kind of patriarch of the whole Impressionist group, and they heeded his opinions. His only fault was that, as a Jew, he was assimilated. For I myself am in favor of a pure race, but that concept requires a special explanation, and this is not the place to elaborate on it.[4] Yet we must not forget that he was among the first Jewish plastic artists, in the pure sense of this word. In the revival of the new Jewish art he occupies first place. It is hard to consider the artists Renoir and Degas as Impressionists, unless we understand their Impressionism not as a conception of nature in a technical sense, but as an emotional impression which creates by itself a connection with nature.

Cézanne countered the thinness of the Impressionists, often returning to the dark painting of Courbet, Daumier, and the Spaniards. And though he claimed he wanted to give a new direction to the art of painting, to move it closer to nature, I think he was influenced mainly by the plastic art of El Greco, Tintoretto, and Chardin, rather than by the straight line of Byzantium, the primitivism of Cimabue, the black drawing of Goya. It is clear to me that, without all those sources and without this mixture, there would be no Cézanne.

The adherents of the so-called "tradition" will see this as normal. But I cannot see any merit in reflecting others and in heritage in general. I believe that the artist brings his own face from the beginning of his covenant, without mentioning any person before him. But Cézanne launched a painterly revolution in the nineteenth century, as El Greco and Tintoretto did in their time; with one difference—their plastic revolution was not felt in their own time. And it was not felt perhaps because in that period the formal aspect of art was not yet discerned, and technique depended on the spirit. No one yet proclaimed the kitchen of art. It was, no doubt, a happy time. Cézanne's theory of color and form is entirely separated from the spirit, in the sheer nihilist sense, without any connection to that humanism that reflects something of our unhappy soul. This system, which is the essence of Latin materialism, appears to my eyes, the eyes of an Oriental, as most cruel. Indeed, it would have been cruel if this system were the truth of life, though there are many kinds of truth. This cruel system fulfilled an annoying function in the further development of formal art, for it filled the hearts of those artists who were close to this system with a wave of sadness and joy. Now we can see that it was not necessary for everybody.

To be sure, I will be told that the mechanization of our time is valid in all disciplines of culture and life, and that all this was necessary and natural. But precisely because the mechanization was necessary, it does not follow that some opposite directions are impossible. Indeed, their time now came. As black is opposed to white, as Romanticism revolted against Classicism. Let us not dwell too much on mechanization, this atheism of our time; I myself refuse to see in it the humanism so needed for our soul, notwithstanding the fact that it brought us the blessing of modernism. Modernism—yes, but happiness—no.

The artist Cézanne was the first to take this road; others followed him: in their search for the formal side of art, they despised and discarded all the rest, including their thin soul, as a superfluous thing. Here, for example, are some names Cézanne gave to his pictures: five women, three apples, a saucer, etc. Indeed, all that exists in nature is valid for the artist's attention: a stick, a stone, a man—everything is alive and throbbing, but . . . The problem lies in this "but" whenever you say "but" there is something wrong. Thus an art for art's sake emerged, aestheticism, and so on, that dries the sap of our life. This aestheticism suits those poor of talent, who escape to it to cover up their paucity of talent.

The Spanish artist Picasso, who was most dilligent, understood the spirit of his time. When he first came from his homeland [to France], he was not especially original but was sharp and piquant, and he understood that the direction of the Spanish artist El Greco or the Frenchmen Toulouse-Lautrec, Steinlen, and Renoir, with all their humanism—would not award him a laurel wreath and he would be in danger of remaining in the shadow, as a somewhat sickly phenomenon, whose folk fluid had dried out. Hence he followed the formal side of Cézanne, his geometrical forms and gray colors. The French artist Braque helped him a great deal in that. The road to experimental art opened wide and the Chinese Wall is not too far . . . Yet I think there is no movement that would not bring some advantage, large or small.

Cubism discovered several plastic qualities in the field of form and line and in the search for the third dimension. Is it a little or a lot, or perhaps altogether superfluous? Who knows...

And I ask: what aspects of the human "I" require experimental art or purely abstract art? Art goes parallel to science and the discoveries of the scientists. But I cannot believe that the evil in man fulfilled a larger function than the good in him. Man is capable of evil—as shown by the last war, which swept over us with no rhyme or reason. You might conclude from this that art, in its own way, is linked to life, and the dissonance is revealed to the eye as soon as the heart actually stops participating in it [in the art]. To be sure, as soon as we abandon what our heart tells us, the age will punish us and our work and will turn it back a long way.

Cubism promoted a new decorative art, a geometrical architecture, but the picture stands at a crossroads, it was not vanquished, on the contrary, it takes revenge, smiles, and thinks of something else.

From the days of Cézanne, people began to adapt to Cubism. The awareness in the street, even in clothing fashions—this is the nature of fashion. But it turns out that somewhere inside, the geometrical line is alien to the straight painting, and the naked color turns into decorationism . . .

I shall say a few words about my own position in 1910, when Cubism appeared in art. This movement, with all its theories, like the movements of Impressionism and Naturalism that preceded it, did not provide an outlet for our inner world or for the essence of things. What would I have to do with the external aspect? I am not an aesthetician to be excited about it. Of course, art pleases the eye, but art itself has no eyes. It looks at you from its inner being, with its simple, bare face, and anyone who thinks that the technique of modern art achieved perfection is mistaken. For two hundred years artists have been busy improving it. Just look at the paintings of the Fauves, the sculptures of Negroes from ancient excavations, and you'll be struck by their amazing perfection. Our age was excited by those discoveries and even began to imitate this ancient art. It exaggerated the typical features of this art and thought it discovered a new expression. It turned out that art, reduced to the search of formulas, was not enriched by it; on the contrary—it was impoverished, and this revolution in art may be a shallow revolution after all.

It is clear that every personality brings with it the picture, the form, and the color, everyone for himself. And what is called a trend or a school is nothing but a group of imitators using up the freshness of the creative artist. Under the scientific cover and the theoretical rules it is easy to hide creative weakness. Art is not an institution collecting documents about various discoveries and experiments.

The question arises: what has modern art brought to our age? Did it enrich it with its technical treasures or impoverish its spirit compared to the art of earlier ages? Or, perhaps, mechanization appeared as the new religion in the world?

Even twenty or twenty-five years ago, when artists followed engineers and chemists, I myself wanted to hide in the ground, not to see it. For nothing can prove to me that great works of art are created on a scientific basis alone. Therefore—for example, the speeches of the strange French poet Paul Valery, the perfect imitator of Mallarmé's poetry, who wore Leonardo da Vinci's mask—his speeches about materialism as something without emotions, seem to me to be a kind of vengeance, a kind of incitement, as if he wished to destroy our fantastic house of cards of hopes and dreams. As if he didn't know that all life is, after all, a heap of stinging flies, and anyone who touches it is in mortal danger. He thinks that the raging spirit is the truth of life, and I think the opposite, that goodness, even misguided goodness—is the essence of life and art.

Even the work of an artist like Leonardo da Vinci, based on science, inspires a spirit of disappointment in the spectator viewing it in the Louvre. Depressed and amazed, we stand before his calculations.

Recently, the French artist Seurat also constructed his pictures according to rhythm and color. Colors became laws for him, and so his Pointilism was created. But by now, what he thought was the most important thing disappeared and what remained was the essence of his pure spirituality. And this should not be seen as an anachronism. To achieve absolute freedom, I think art must assume an illogical character, must plunge into new depths, and not just in its content, to shatter something inside and to change, to move art away from formal realism—either Impressionism or Cubism. Those trends did not, actually, change the old foundations of art, only the means have changed. All of French art—and I am speaking only about it—is built, after all, on a material base. Often it seems to me that it was my destiny to be alone in my dreams, which are melting like foam on the water. Yet I don't want to think about myself more than about the problems concerning society as a whole.

I talked about the materialism of French art. Thus, the artist Matisse, who wonderfully combines patches of color, in his youth used to break down the forms of objects for the sake of expression of the patches and lines, after he got excited about children's paintings. He could have been an excellent decorator, if Frenchmen were capable of that like some Oriental peoples. The artist Derain who admired the art of the Negroes in his day, and for whom the artist Paul Gauguin served as a model—now devoted himself entirely to the closed art of the museum. He followed the road of Corot, Poussin, and like them, limited his work to two or three tones, reminiscent of museum art rather than the surface of a variegated picture with a wealth of colors. Sometimes, when you see it, you are filled with both laughter and sadness, that such an adult painter, wise and rich in devices, would refuse to understand that, no matter how beautiful and pleasant the miracle, that borders on imitation of the old masters—it leads him to be an epigone. Thus three artists, Picasso, Matisse, and Derain, symbolize the essence of French art today. The other artists, like Rouault, Utrillo, Dufy, Vlaminck, etc. sing their own songs freely—though we know their songs, thousands of foreigners come to Paris to see and hear them, and often follow in their footsteps.

When I was a child, walking in my city Vitebsk, I often pondered: What is the thing that guides our life? When I saw the work of my teachers, the academic artists, I looked for something essentially different. I wanted to see and find something that would match the greatness of nature, though there is some immodesty in it—I know. I believe that my dreams had some basis, otherwise Expressionism and Surrealism would not be born, and the future will show whether they brought some fresh air to art as a whole. And now, or in the future, a new realism would come—it will be entirely new, formal art will not be resurrected so soon. This is happiness, for this will bring us closer to an age of free creators, as in olden days, when people were people and not calculating machines, and society immediately recognized the great creators and not their imitators.

I am not amazed that, in this respect, Jews perform a kind of purging function. We must forget the arguments of strangers (like the Russian critic Stassov) that Jews are incapable of plastic art. As soon as the Jews liberated themselves from the chains of tradition and dared to interpret in their own way the laws that forbade them to do plastic art—they appeared.

Artists no less talented than the most important artists of other nations. True, the first [Jewish] artists were still academic artists and fulfilled their mission without much consciousness, but after them came others who began to sing in a full voice—and their voice was heard.

With Bialik in Eretz-Israel
1934[5]

Chaim-Nakhman Bialik (1873–1934) was the recognized National Hebrew Poet in Russia, the towering figure of the Revival Period of modern Hebrew poetry, whose Biblical voice was revered by Jews and admired by prominent Russian intellectuals. An ambivalent and complex lyrical voice in the tradition of Russian nineteenth-century poetry, yet influenced by Symbolism, he also wrote vigorous Poems of Rage, confronting the Jews with their destiny in the language and spirit of the Prophets. He was seen by many as the Jewish national conscience.

In 1921, with the help of Maxim Gorky, Bialik left Soviet Odessa for Palestine, where he became the major cultural authority in the new Jewish city of Tel Aviv, and initiated important literary and cultural activities. Yet after Bialik left Russia he wrote almost no poetry ("Bialik is silent!"), which some interpreted as either the drying up of his muse or disappointment with the Zionist utopia in reality. It was certainly also the shock of the spoken pseudo-"Sefardi" Hebrew, which was alien to his language and his poetry, written in the Ashkenazi pronunciation of Hebrew.

Bialik often traveled to Europe and founded a Hebrew publishing house in Berlin in 1923. Chagall was in Berlin at the time and met him. In 1931, Chagall and his family traveled with the poet to Palestine on the

French ship *Champolion*. Chagall published this article in July 1934, after Bialik's death in Vienna.

When a King dies, the people shout: "The King is dead, long live the King!" But Bialik did not die, he remains alive, and I want to talk about him as about a living person.

I think I met him for the first time in a restaurant [in Berlin]. He sat facing me and ate. I must tell you that I love to eat, but rarely have I seen among Jews a person who ate as ardently as Bialik. The spoon, the fork, the knife trembled in his hands as hypnotized, as if they approached and retreated from his mouth accompanied by his effervescent voice. And when he told a Hasidic legend or a beautiful story from his [childhood] forests, the ringing plates resounded. It seemed to me that the delicate, humid words emerging from his mouth were wiped off with his napkin, and meanwhile he attacked another dish. To be a little like him, I fanned my own appetite. He continued to tell his marvelous legends, and I looked at him as at a legend. Finally, my friend Baal-Makhshoves,[6] who was sitting with me, introduced us. "Ach!" screamed Bialik, and jumped up to kiss me. He started to persuade us that he understood everything, everything in my art. On the contrary: everything was clear to him, and I had to illustrate his books...

Happily we went into the street.

Not long ago, I traveled with Bialik to Eretz-Israel [in 1931]. Bialik—for the nth time, I—for the first. I gazed all around, observed the sky, sought the features of the Land of Israel. On deck, with a tense face, Bialik strolled back and forth. He didn't seem to see anyone around him, he seemed to be alone on the ship. In a gray, wide, long suit, a bicycle cap on his head, he gestured with both hands—spread them wide, or clenched them in a fist.

Later, he argued, tried to convince the travelers. Because of Bialik, the whole voyage became Jewish. I asked: "Isn't it a Jewish ship?" And he answered: "We have no Jewish ships yet!" The whole sea seemed covered with Jewish letters, a Jewish Prophet was walking on the deck of a ship, speaking Yiddish aloud,[7] hurling thunder and lightning at the Jewish fate. His face was seared, his gray and blue eyes sparkled and swirled on the background of the blue sea...

We reached Tel Aviv and I discovered that Bialik was not only a poet but the spiritual regent of the city. Everything flows back and forth because over there, on that street, lives Bialik. All storekeepers, new and agile, turn over their merchandise, buy-and-sell, and read newspapers that say: Bialik spoke, Bialik wrote, Bialik is there, Bialik is here! If Dizengoff was late for a dinner, he probably met Bialik in the street and got lost in a conversation.

If you have to name a cow, you ask Bialik, if you need a name for a flower—of course, you call Bialik.[8] The workers are for Bialik, and even the young poets who are against him, are with him.[9]

On Friday evening you can come see him, hear him, converse with him, and on the Sabbath afternoon he talks like a Magid [popular preacher]. I cannot convey here what he said. I only want to say: If my father were still alive—he used to go to the Vitebsk Synagogue every Sabbath to listen to the "Green Magid"[10] and cry his heart out, along with all other Jews—he would have been happy if he could hear Bialik... That's why I know no better speaker, no better poet, than our deceased Preacher.

I had the great honor and the great pleasure to hear his long speech about me in Eretz-Israel. Unfortunately, I didn't understand it at all.[11] I listened and looked at him, while he tried—laughing, joking, palpably—to explain my pictures to the audience. At that time, I did not dare answer him. Only now do I say a few words. But Bialik doesn't need my words. I know: he remembers how excited I was about his poetry, and how I used to nestle in his eyes. But his eyes often spoke about something else: "You see my fame here, my street is named after me in my lifetime, my palace, but I write no more poems..."

And on the roof of his house, where all Tel Aviv can be seen, with all the Jewish courtyards,—I asked him: "Why don't you write anymore. For you must be happy now. Eretz-Israel is not a ghetto. And here you are the first Jewish poet. Jewish earth glimmers around you like gold. Suntanned boys and girls are looking at you. Bearded Jews walk by your house and wait for your word, your gaze. The aroma of the orange groves surely makes you groggy and reminds you of your first love... You just have to wander on the sea shore, as Pushkin used to do on the banks of the Neva [river in St.-Petersburg], and strophes will begin to stream in your mind. Why don't you write? For God's sake, write! And if you have to give up lectures and social activities for that—everyone would understand and forgive you."

He was silent. A sad thought crept into my mind: the Jewish people don't yet understand pure poetry, real art—it is still foreign to them. When we parted from Eretz-Israel, Bialik sadly told my daughter:[12] "Pray to God, that I write..."

We must talk now not about Bialik alone. He is a giant, he is way above, and will remain so for the Jews forever. True artists and poets burn up their lives in the name of the people, and they want only one thing: Love. And when the Jews, along with all of humanity, lost the old form of religion—what remained for us was art, poetry, and love...

I am afraid my words may evoke a smile. They will say: humanity is busy now with economic and political crises, one party strives to swallow the other, Jews fight with each other and have respect for nothing. Anti-Semitism, led by Hitler, persecutes us, and I am talking about love, poetry, and art, as about a new religion...

Bialik expired dreaming of a Jewish artistic ideal, and we love him for that.

On a Jewish Art Museum
1929, 1935

For many years, Chagall cherished the idea of creating a Jewish Art Museum. One influence may have been his major collector in St.-Petersburg, Kagan-Shabshay, who bought thirty Chagall works for that purpose during World War I. In his proposal for building an Art College in Vitebsk (August 1918), Chagall mentioned a Jewish wing in the future city museum, and in his eulogy for his first art teacher, Yury Pen, in 1921, he envisaged a Central Museum of Jewish Art. Now, living in Paris, far from the Jewish masses and cultural institutions, Chagall suggested this idea to the two emerging centers of secular Jewish nation building: in Yiddish, at the YIVO in Vilna (today: Vilnius, capital of Lithuania; at the time it belonged to Poland); and in Hebrew, in the first modern Jewish city, Tel Aviv.

In 1925, the Jewish (or Yiddish) Scientific Institute, YIVO, was founded in Vilna. (The term "scientific" in the European tradition indicates the serious, academic conception of the humanities as "human sciences.") The YIVO covered a wide field of research, from linguistics and literary studies to history, sociology, and economics. Chagall rightly claimed that the renaissance of Jewish culture was primarily verbal, based on literature (and ideology, one might add), while other fields of culture and art were lagging behind. For the first YIVO Conference in 1929, Chagall wrote a letter initiating the creation of a Jewish Art Museum, which materialized only in 1935.

Parallel to that, in 1931, Chagall was invited to visit the new Jewish reality in Palestine; he talked and corresponded with Meir Dizengoff, the first Mayor of Tel Aviv, about erecting an art museum in the first Hebrew city. But they came to public blows in an argument over artistic values, and the museum was opened without Chagall and without his high stan-dards.[13] The YIVO museum was officially opened by the seventy-five-year-old eminent Jewish historian Professor Simon Dubnov on the tenth anniversary of the YIVO, August 18, 1935. Between 1929 and 1935, how-ever, Hitler came to power in Germany; Chagall was banned there as a "degenerate artist" and his paintings demonstratively burned.

The museum was supported financially by "the first Jewish benefactor" of art, the Eitingon family of Lodz. An exhibition of Chagall's etchings and an exhibition of Jewish artists were launched at the occasion. Marc Chagall traveled to Vilna and delivered the opening address. The painter Jacob Sher, who greeted the delegates on behalf of the Vilna Jewish

graphic artists, said: "It is the greatest celebration for the young Jewish
artists to see Chagall. Chagall is the dream of every young artist. The
Vilna artists have lived to see Chagall with their own eyes and to hear him
speak in the international language, the Esperanto called Jewish Art."

A year later, the first issue of the Yiddish-language Journal for Jewish
Art appeared in Vilna, and three years later, in September 1939, World
War II broke out. Jacob Sher and most of his painter colleagues perished
in the Holocaust.

Speech at the World Conference of the Yiddish Scientific Institute, YIVO On Its Tenth Anniversary, Vilna, August 14, 1935[14]

Actually, you might think I am out of place here. For I am an artist and you
are scientists. But I am here exactly as you are, for we share the same
weakness, the same passion: Jews.

And precisely now, in this terrible and ridiculous time, in the time of
contemporary fashionable anti-Semitism, I would like to emphasize once
more that I am a Jew. And by this very fact, I am even more international
in spirit—not like those professional revolutionaries who contemptuously
shake off their Jewishness.

There are several reasons why I am here. I have known these little huts
and fences around you by heart for a long time. But your house, the house
of the Institute, though it seems to be as poor as a hut in one of my paintings,[15] is nevertheless as rich as Solomon's Temple. So I greet it and I greet
you who created it. I am filled with a special bitter joy by the thought that
without means, with no state support, with only enthusiasm and love, you
built a house with your own hands. In the future, in the period of our as-
cendance, this house will serve as a model of stubborn Jewish devotion to
the idea of culture.

There is also a personal reason why I came here. A few kilometers from
you, there is a land, actually just one city,[16] which I haven't seen in a long
time, and which won't let go of me. I used your invitation and came to me-
ander here a while. I admit that the older I get, the lazier I get, and I don't
move if I'm not called.

I don't know why, but between me and my homeland [Soviet Russia] there is a one-sided affair,[17] and nevertheless, such a land of genius, with such a revolution of genius, might have sensed what occurs in the heart of one of their own and not just listened to and believed in the words and declarations of the confession letters...[18] But the major reason for my coming here is to remind again not just you Vilna Jews (because you do do something in this respect), but the Jews of the whole world, that a Jewish Scientific Institute is indeed beautiful—but a Jewish Art Museum is just as beautiful and just as important.

Indeed, since the end of the nineteenth century and the beginning of the twentieth, Jews have strained at their fetters and stormed into the world with their art; and it seems to me that this cultural contribution is the most important Jewish contribution of recent times. But most people have barely heard about it. The masses and the intelligentsia don't see it, everything is splintered, not concentrated, and I even feel awkward talking about it because I am myself an interested party.

But what can you do? We Jews don't have our own Baudelaire, Théophile Gauthier, Apollinaire, who powerfully forged the artistic taste and the artistic concepts of their time. Can you help it? In our Jewish society, we don't have a Diaghilev,[19] a Morozov, a Shchukin,[20] who collected and organized the art culture with such ardor and understanding.

And the fact that the intelligentsia in general and the Yiddish writers in particular lack interest in plastic art indicates that art is alien and superfluous in their lives and work, and the world rests on literature alone.

If Yiddish poetry, Yiddish literature were intertwined with other branches of art in general and with plastic art in particular, it would have been richer, it would have strengthened its upward thrust both in spirit and in style. If we take, for example, Russian literature—the connection between Pushkin and the pseudo-classicists of his time, between Gogol and Alexandr Ivanov, Tolstoy and the itinerant Artists (Peredvizniki), Chekhov and Levitan, or in our literature, Peretz and his fine sensibility for the modernism of his time—we will surely find that this connection filled their literary creation with an intensive plastic actuality, with a new source of richness, with a great freshness. And therefore their language is also not ethnographic,[21] but universal in a pure artistic sense. This is a different problem, much more important than one might think, and perhaps also a scientific problem, so I hand it to the proper address, to you, scientists.

Simply, we the new Jews who, thousands of years ago, created the Bible, the work of the Prophets, the basis of all religions of all peoples, we also want to create great art that would resound in the world.

But I am not amazed at the relationship toward us on the part of strangers or enemies. No, what amazes me is the relationship of all layers of Jewish society to its own artists, their treatment of the artists as second-class political activists, who don't deserve even part of that respect we grant artists of the pen or the theater, who often have to be grateful to the graphic artists themselves. I am not talking just about the fact that Jews don't buy paintings,[22] don't support the artists, though this is also important in today's time of crisis. What is important is the attention, the interest. And if this appears sometimes, it is directed to the least talented and most tasteless "kitsch."

Indeed, the reasons for that situation are well known. The Torah which gave us the Ten Commandments snuck in an eleventh commandment too: "Thou shalt not make unto thee any graven image"...

Our monotheism was dearly bought—because of that, Judaism had to give up observation of nature with our eyes, and not just with our soul. On religious grounds, Judaism struggled with ancient idolatry, whose remnants are displayed today in all museums of the world, so that it remained with no share in the treasures of plastic art. We left nothing behind us in the world's museums except for Torah Scrolls and the abandoned synagogues which are no longer attended.

But we, the new Jews, have revolted against this, we no longer want to recognize such a state of affairs, we want to be not just the People of the Book, but also a people of art. This is the source of the birth pangs of our art, this is why its infancy is so sad. All this requires good organization and good will: to collect art among Jews and everything that is related to the history of art, to promote art not as a thing outside us, but as part of our internal life, and to encourage our artists

Collecting paintings must not be only a matter of the artists' philanthropy. Keep in mind that even canvases and paints cost the artist more than a pen and paper for the writer; but no one would think of asking for a writer's manuscript—whether valuable or not—for nothing. At a time when we seem to complain everywhere that we have no advocates in the world which persecutes us so much, and we dream of a congress where debarred lawyers[23] will appear, we forget that we have in our hands an immense shield—our cultural treasures must speak for us, must plead our case, and defend us.

The Scientific Institute is a valuable treasure, but we must also create an art institute, national art foundations, which will continue to nourish and build museums in the centers of Jewish life. You may say that this is an illusion, but the illusory and fantastic, as we often discover, are the most real. A proof is the YIVO. For the first conference of YIVO, six years ago, I wrote to you about creating a museum at the YIVO. I know how difficult it is. Better difficult than hurried, as they did in Eretz-Israel, where, despite my warnings, they brought together anything they could, and the leadership went to inexperienced and not-very-artistic hands.[24] The new Jewish people does not need a repetition of the Bezalels.[25]

We don't need to reach the goal right away. There is a whole series of preparatory stages moral and material: propagating the idea, training art historians and museum specialists, staging exhibitions in public institutions, workers' clubs, schools; organizing excursions to the European centers, to the great international exhibitions; instructing teachers, pupils, students in teachers' colleges and universities in understanding art; fostering their knowledge of art as you foster their taste in literature; publishing books and journals about art. For Jewish taste is horrible, backward; and their confidence in their own judgment is even greater. Young (and not so young) people, who travel to the great centers to study law, medicine and other professions which often don't quite feed the body, might have thought a bit about art culture, about art that at least nourishes our spirit.

I close with the feeling that all I have said and all I have not said should have been said at a conference of writers and artists. But artists as a social element practically don't exist, artists can hardly talk to each other. Therefore, others, all of you here, have to look at us actively from the side, organize sensibly, tactfully and with an internal empathy.

For a long time, I have wanted to say these few words about our role, about your role, about the role of all of us, not just artists, but scientists, and all Jews for the good of all humanity. In these days of crisis, not just a material but also a spiritual crisis, when world crises, wars, revolutions flare up over a piece of bread, and the Jews truly don't have the wherewithal or the where to live, there is still no sweeter mission than suffering and working for our goal, for our spirit, which lives in our Bible, which lives in our dreams about art, which can help bring the Jews to the true and right path, to achieve which other nations just spill blood—their own and others.

Artists and Jewish Artists
Lecture at a debate in the hall of the
Jewish Art Exhibit in Paris, April 10, 1939[26]

A Jewish pavilion, containing a wide representation of literature, books, and art, was established at the international exhibition in Paris. In the Jewish/Yiddish cultural field, there was a "Popular Front" coalition, including liberals, cultural activists, and Communists. Notwithstanding the debacle of the democratic forces in the Spanish Civil War, the Communists were seen by many as the only viable alternative to Hitler. In 1938, the Anschluss of Austria brought Hitler to Vienna, were the Nazis openly humiliated and persecuted the Jews. And in spite of the appeasement policy of Western Europe and the Munich accord, Hitler broke his promise, dismantled Czechoslovakia, and on March 15, 1939, his army marched into Prague. This was the context for Chagall's speech.

This is not a time for "Art." War hovers in the air, war which the enemies of man and culture want to provoke. Even more bitter is the lot of us—Jews. However, our "personal" account with the enemy is over[27]—for the general account has begun, and we should hopefully play our moral and physical role along with others.

But even before the conflagration, we gather to talk about our tasks in culture and art. Isn't it a sign of our ability to live? Nevertheless, I shall not speak of art in general, for even [in normal times] it is quite difficult [to speak about] our "profession." Is it, perhaps, something too personal and intimate, like love or other great things, that you don't waste too many words on? I know one thing: to be an artist and a Jew is a special and responsible matter. It is one thing to be an artist, and another—an artist and a Jew. For if this is not an idea in life—it is nothing, just a craft!

We [= the Jews] already have many fine and better-than-fine talents in painting; we often achieve the tone and style of quite decent painting—like many nations, and perhaps even more refined. I personally liked it when, some 25–30 years ago, errors were made, technical mistakes, no matter how primitive they may be. But "God protect us" from signs of an easy "Renaissance," of smooth and consistent academism, of easy "Maestro" and daubing.

All the prattle about the meaning of ostensibly "pure" painting—is nonsense.

An artist, a painter, is born in his mother's belly; then, fortunately or unfortunately, he is a Jew; and finally, in all generations, just a few artists remain of each period. And even that is fine—so it was in all times.

Talk about "national" art is premature; we are an ancient people—and yet so young [in art]. The national arts of Greece, Egypt, Assyria, Italy, Spain, Holland, Flanders—were constructed long after their "renaissance," hundreds of years later, when their art had cooled off, when they left behind many traditions.

And if we can—forgive me—talk about us in the same breath, we have almost no traditions yet [in art]. On the contrary: even before we started speaking our [artistic] alphabet—some people began imitating, though quite naturally, what others do, often even quite nicely, quite fitting, even with talent. Is there a danger in this? Indeed, in this we are no different from other nations, even the young French [artists]. And I believe that our situation, as modern Jews with an advanced taste, is worse and no more secure than that of the Jewish "Itinerant" artists in the past,[28] who had no idea of surface, color, and line, didn't hear and didn't want to hear about Cézanne and others, but searched for content only. And what happened to them all? We led a "Revolution" against the old ones, and scared them to death . . .[29]

But I said before, I won't get into problems of art, and Jewish problems at that. In any case, we cannot take the "easy way" in art. If the official academy is discredited—we must go through even a more difficult "apprenticeship," as in Raphael's time, and do it in light of today's social and psychological problems. With all that, we must consider the path of a Jew-artist, who was and still is a luftmensch [a man hovering in the air]. We cannot let ourselves be marred by raw work, mannerism, and daubing. If we do not give our all, our whole life to art, if we are not, in our own way, extreme maximalists in art—then we are nothing. It is not accidental that Israels and Liebermann, with all their talent, are merely bourgeois artists (Pissarro's luck was that he, less "bourgeois" [than the others], was in the revolutionary group of Impressionists, though he did not become a Cézanne or Seurat—who, by the way, were influenced by him). For in those Jewish artists, there was more of the dozing bourgeois than the revolutionary spirit in art of a Cézanne, Grunewald, Seurat, El Greco, Rembrandt, Goya, and Bosch.

Yes, today, we Jews-artists are like grass, even pretty grass—but on a cemetery. It pains me to utter this word, for basically I never was a pessimist, quite the contrary.

The Jewish artists (and I don't assume the right to speak in their name) are often paupers, with no fatherland, no friends, no "benefactors," quarreling with each other and with themselves, apparently with no respect for one another.

Do we forget that we have to set an example, as in other countries and times? Weren't the artists the first ones who provided the impetus for other cultural domains in life, for literature and theater?[30]

Did we Jews, in all times and countries, ever have any trace of a Tretyakov or a Shchukin in Russia,[31] of several [collectors] in France, a Barnes in America?[32] The bourgeois Jews, forgive me the expression, have the holy experience of their gefilte fish and . . . do not help us, or help just a little, from a distance. Sometimes they respect money and titles, and perhaps the person who holds a pen in his hand, lest he describe them for better or worse . . . I am seething, body and soul, when I see them and talk about it. Unfortunately, other, democratic, intellectual circles of writers also keep their distance. Perhaps it is our fault, everybody's fault, that our taste and attitudes are lower than in the same classes of other nations.

Indeed, today you have to be an angel to have an idea about art.

The situation of our Jews-artists in Paris is even more delicate, for this is the capital of art and we cannot unite in this country on a national basis. What can easily be done in Warsaw, New York, London,[33] is hard here in Paris, with some isolated exceptions. The role of Jews-artists is different in their activities among Jews and somewhere in other countries.

I would like to use this opportunity to appeal to the Jews of all countries to observe us closely. The Jewish artist, living today in a bourgeois milieu, must either work somehow or gradually disappear... The Jews have lost their old spiritual power, today they are losing their material capital, expelled by the enemies who "devour" them,—higher goals must awake in them, the impetus to defend our art and culture.

And those Jews who used to contribute to the "box" for buying land,[34] thus "saving" themselves for eternity—when will those Jews understand that aiding culture and Jewish art can also "immortalize" your name—and simultaneously help encouraging the art and culture, which are one of our achievements in the world.

THREE

World War II and the Holocaust
1941–1950

Some Impressions Regarding French Painting
   Address at Mount Holyoke College, August 1943/March 1946

At the invitation of the art historian Lionello Venturi, Chagall delivered
an address in French at Mount Holyoke College, followed by an English
translation.[1] Chagall used the same text when the war was over, on March
5, 1946, for a lecture delivered to the Committee on Social Thought at
the University of Chicago.[2] The new text included the earlier lecture with
several changes and several pages added in the beginning and the end.
The first text was written when France was under Nazi occupation and
Chagall expressed his worries about the destiny of French art and artists.
The second lecture occurred after the liberation, when Chagall had spent
five years in the United States, was hesitant about a possible return to
France, and expressed his gratitude to his host country. There are some
changes of order between the versions, which derive from Chagall's habit
of writing his text on loose pages and reshuffling them later.

   We reproduce here the English translation of the second version,
with minor corrections. The earlier passages omitted in this version are
restored in brackets, the new passages are in italics.

I will have to admit that speaking in front of an audience, and not in an intimate circle or to myself, is unfamiliar. I am a painter, and allow me the expression: "I am an unconsciously conscious painter."[3] There are many things in the realm of art for which it is very hard to find the key words. But why should one try so intently to open these doors? It sometimes seems to me that they open themselves—without effort, without vain words.

First, I would like to speak of my impressions of America. Above all I am impressed by the greatness of this country and the feeling of freedom that it gives me. But one has to be free oneself to appreciate that freedom. Perhaps during these past few years I have come to know a little of the air, the clouds, the trees of this country; perhaps I have learned to understand the great "silent" traits of Americans, perhaps I have been able to let all this pass into my art. I have breathed this stimulating air—though I may not have assimilated this or that local trait, the "reproduction" of which has never constituted art in itself.

In short, I have strengthened myself quite naturally on this hospitable air of America without my art being disloyal to anyone or to anything. I have lived and worked here during a time of universal tragedy for all men. I lived in America, and I didn't grow any younger as the years went by.

Here I would like to state that one of the primary foundations of art (if we speak of painting) is a right sense for painting (une dose juste de peinture). *But the human environment which surrounds the painter, with its living conditions, if unfavorable, can finally weaken or even destroy in the painter this right sense for painting—if it ever existed. Blessed be the country and its nature which give the painter something with which to develop and vary his natural gifts. The rest depends on the gradual development of that "human atmosphere which is as indispensable as a frame is for a picture."*

Finding myself in this new world, in this hospitable America, I think of France where I have lived for thirty years of my life.[4] I left the country of my birth in 1910. At that time I decided that I needed Paris. The soil which had nourished the roots of my art was Vitebsk, but my art needed Paris—like a tree needs water—otherwise it would have withered.

Russia had two artistic traditions: the popular and the religious. I wanted an art of the soil, not an art solely of the head. I had the good fortune to be born of the people; but popular art, although I have always liked it, did not satisfy me. It was too exclusive. It excluded the refinements of civilization. And I have always had a decided taste for refined expression, for culture. The refined art of my native country was religious art. I recognized the quality of some great creations of the icon tradition—for example, the work of Rublev. But this was essentially a religious, a [Christian] Orthodox, art; and as such, it remained strange to me. For me, Christ was a great poet whose poetical teaching had been forgotten by the modern world.

In order to achieve a fusion of refined expression with an art of the earth, I felt that I had to draw from the source spring of Paris.

I would like to say that my moves from country to country have always been dictated by artistic considerations. As the son of a worker, basically I had no other reason for leaving my native land, to which I believe (despite everything) I have remained faithful in my art. As a painter and a man of the people (and I consider the common people the most sensitive class of society), I felt that plastic refinement of the highest order existed in France. Here was the source, perhaps, of my dualism and my climactic maladjustments throughout the years.

What did I find on arriving in Paris and of what art was I dreaming then—although this was a time when dreaming was not considered right? Painters were then absorbed in their purely technical researches. One did not speak out loud of these dreams about art—unless it was a question of fleeting theories which quickly followed one after another. In those best periods of technical discoveries, the painters seemed to be silent. Was the soul silent out of modesty, or from other motives? I do not know. Even he who combined in himself the painter and the inventor[5] remained discreetly obstinately silent, while provoking others to noisy ramblings.

I arrived, then, in Paris as if driven by destiny. From my mouth flowed words which came from my heart. They almost suffocated me. I stammered. The words forced their way out, anxious to shine with this brightness of Paris, to be adorned with it.

I arrived with the thoughts, the dreams, which one can have only at the age of twenty; yet, perhaps, those dreams have stayed with me for a long time. Ordinarily, you do not go to Paris, so to speak, with your baggage already packed. You go empty-handed in order to study, and you leave with baggage—sometimes.

I could, of course, express myself in my faraway native town, in the midst of my friends. But I wanted to see with my own eyes that which I had heard so much about from afar: that visual revolution, that rotation of colors which spontaneously and cleverly melted into one another in a stream of thoughtful lines, as shown by Cézanne, or freely dominant, as shown by Matisse. One did not see all this in my homeland, where the sun of art was not shining so brilliantly as it was in Paris. And it seemed to me then (and still seems to me) that there do not exist greater and more revolutionary "appeals to the eyes" *(plus grandes revolutions de l'oeil)* than those which I observed in 1910 on my arrival in Paris. The landscapes, the figures of Cézanne, Manet, Monet, Seurat, Renoir, Van Gogh, Fauvism, and many other things over-whelmed me. These attracted me to Paris like a phenomenon of nature.

I was far from my native country, where the fences stood out in my imagination against the background of the houses. I saw there none of Renoir's colors. I saw instead two or three dark patches. And with these I might have lived a life without hope of finding the emancipated artistic language which breathes its own life as a man breathes.

In Paris I visited neither academies nor professors. I found my lessons in the city itself at each step, in everything. I found them among the small traders in the weekly open-air markets, among the waiters in cafes, the concierges, peasants, and workers. Around them hovered that astonishing light of freedom *(lumière-liberté)* which I had seen nowhere else. And this light, reborn in art, passed easily onto the canvasses of the great French masters.

I couldn't help thinking: only this *lumière-liberté* (more luminous than all sources of artificial light) can give birth to such sparkling canvases, where technical revolutions are just as natural as the language, the gesture, the work of the passerby in the street.

I was then in my twenties, and vaguely I felt why I had seen nothing comparable in the other countries I had visited. Perhaps I did not see this with the eyes of reason but with the eyes of the soul. And this soul was newly and differently opened up in those "academies" which the markets and the streets of Paris provide. There I saw still-lives richer, newer, more pictorial than the still-lives of Snyder—in fact, I saw the still-lives of Chardin and Cézanne. There I saw some landscape paintings of the Ile-de-France as it unfolds beyond the gates of Paris, not the heavy land-scapes of the museums (like those of Hobbema and of Ruysdael), but sensitive and throbbing with the spirit of the times (like the landscapes of Van Gogh, Monet, Seurat). These spontaneous landscapes were living and whole, as in Cézanne, Renoir, and the others. Things, nature, people, illumined with this "freedom of light" seemed to be bathing in color. Never before had I seen such pictures. It was the crowning of an epoch which found unique expression in the art of this time.

From the streets, the squares, the fields, one enters the French rooms in the Louvre, where this pictorial revolution looked for its sources, only to go beyond them afterward. One day a friend[6] with whom I had come to Paris said to me: "Poor us! What can we do, what can we accomplish here? Everything has been said and said again. Let's buy a ticket and go back [to Russia]."

But I remained, and I remained myself. I answered: "Why take anything from anyone else?" I had been inspired by what I had seen, and my enthusiasm returned to its starting point. Participating in that unique technical revolution of art in France, I returned in thought, in the soul, so to speak, to my own country. I lived as if I were turned back to front. The doubts, the dreams, which had already tortured me in my native town now left me no respite.

Exactly what sort of painter would I have liked to be? I don't say "could I have been?" I was still very young and did not picture art as a profession or a job. It did not seem to me that pictures were destined solely for decorative or domestic purposes. I said to myself: "Art is in some way a mission—and don't be afraid of this old word."

And whatever may be the technical, realistic revolution, it has merely scratched the surface. Neither so-called "real color" nor "conventional color" really colors the object. It is not what is called "perspective" which adds depth. Neither light nor shadow lightens up the subject—and the third dimension of the Cubists does not yet allow a vision of the subject from all sides.

Perhaps I spoke of a kind of "world view," of a conception beyond the subject, beyond the eye. If you think this way during a technical, realistic period of art, you will be accused of falling into "literature. " I admit that when I heard this word pronounced by young painters and poets I grew a little pale. I grew pale—not from shame, not from fear on account of myself—but rather for the others, for those who said it.

I saw myself as in a mirror, different and strange.

While being fascinated by the "eye" of the French painters, by their sense of measure, I couldn't help thinking: perhaps there exists another eye, another vision, a vision of different order, differently placed.

For instance, the trees painted by Monet are good for Monet. But perhaps these trees are waiting to be shown yet again. Perhaps other dimensions exist—a fourth, a fifth dimension, not only of the eye. And this dimension is by no means just "literature," "symbolism," or what is called "poetry" in art. Maybe it is something more abstract, not in the sense of being unreal but of being more free. Maybe it is something which intuitively gives birth to a scale of plastic and psychic contrasts, piercing the eye of the spectator with new and unaccustomed concepts.

This, in short, was the feeling which had got hold of me in Paris in 1910. Was not I, myself, escaping from "literature," from symbolism in art?

It was precisely "literature" I saw, not only in the great compositions of the old "Romantics" but in the simple still-lives of the Impressionists and Cubists, since the "literature" in painting is *all* that can be explained and narrated from beginning to end. It seemed to me that only in some way by "killing" a still-life or a landscape (not merely deforming their surface) is it possible to give new life to that same still-life or landscape. Thus a sort of dualism took form in me: on the one hand, I was enthusiastic about those brilliant examples of a formal art (sometimes by Delacroix, sometimes by Ingres, sometimes by Chardin); and, on the other hand, my soul was, in spite of all, plunged into a certain sadness, thirsting to find a way out.

In my doubts I turned to my friends of those days—to the poet Blaise Cendrars and, later, to Guillaume Apollinaire. Cendrars, at that time, was only laughing in impulsive bursts of his tempestuous youth. He read his verses to me, his verses free as open windows; and gazing upon my paintings as he read, he consoled me in a rich and incomprehensible way.

As for Apollinaire, I was a little embarrassed in his presence—unnecessarily, since he was gentleness itself. [This is what I said about him in my book *My Life*:

Apollinaire, that gentle Zeus. With his verse, figures, and ordinary syllables, he paved the way for us. He would emerge from his corner room, a smile spreading all over his broad face. His nose grew sharper and his gentle, mysterious eyes sang of sensual delights. He bore his belly like a collection of Complete Works and his legs gestured like arms...]

At that time he had entirely plunged into cubism. On his throne sat Picasso. How, during those years of the triumph of cubism, could one dream of attracting anybody's attention, above all Apollinaire's? I only wanted from year to year to exhibit in the Salon des Indépendants. This was not at all difficult, since the salon was open to everyone. At this period the Salon des Indépendants was the most revolutionary, the most disinterested, of schools of art.

But Apollinaire, despite everything, came to see me in my studio. It was there that he pronounced for the first time the magic word "supernatural." "Supernatural"—he said it as if catching his breath. He himself blushed before the canvases. To be honest, I little understood this word myself at that time.

[One day in Apollinaire's office at the *Soirées de Paris*, I heard him advise Mr. Herwarth Walden to organize an exhibition of my paintings in his gallery, Der Sturm, in Berlin. He immediately introduced us to each other.

Walden was a German with a long nose.[7] That nose seemed to help him find his way around the most extreme trends of art of that time. His manner, which was essentially Germanic, struck me at once; it was a manner that proclaimed the German Expressionism he defended in his country and in which I was later mistakenly included. He was not particularly trustworthy. I paid dearly for that.[8]]

The period up to 1914 has commonly been called the "heroic epoch of French art." Like the heroic period of Italian art in its time, like the best period of Spanish art, it was heroic by reason of the decisive brilliance of its formal realizations. In France, this burst of technique dominated; and unlike art in other countries, and strange as this may seem, this burst was originally reflected in society, in the social life of the country, while the decisive brilliance of technique was a reflection of society. This period of technical researches had been achieved by a revision of the earlier artistic procedures, with the help of techniques of many painters of preceding generations and of the art of primitive peoples.

Thus were submitted to examination and often to "stylization" the primitive art of cavemen, Egyptian art, Assyrian and Negro art, the newly discovered art of Piero della Francesca, of Pallajuola, of Paolo Uccello, of Masaccio, of El Greco, of Goya, and so many others. In this "revision" of the ancients could be discovered a certain convulsive search after the aging or absent gods. In it also could be seen the yearning for an innocent, newborn language which, little by little, in the course of two thousand years, had lost its freshness.

This continual search reveals the tragedy of humanity, which had thought to attain in art an apogee, a fulfillment, of its language, technique, and means of expression. And yet humanity in that period when old religious and other ideas were waning, was still hopeful of mastering this language of perceiving a new shaft of illuminating light, a new meaning of life.

Is this not, likewise, the mission of art?

In this heroic period of French art it finally became evident that an enormous plastic, technical revolution had really occurred.

Think, for example, of Delacroix. He exaggerated (one might say) certain liberties, stressing, even to the point of fear, the plastic dream-pictures of Rubens. And he did this to such a daring degree that the white tone alone in the studies of Delacroix surprises because of its unexpected character—without speaking of his brush stroke. And this was even before Manet, whose brush never dreamed of it either.

What a spectacle! Simultaneously, they painted and drew with the brush; and Van Gogh definitively invites us to feast upon his touch—which is not without the influence of Japanese engravings. The appearance of Courbet, apparently revealing a great master of secondary greatness, has, in my opinion, not so much demonstrated a new moral ideology or social naturalism as a plastic ideology. Cézanne understood this in its primary meaning when he worked and applied colors with his knife. It might be said that this is what allowed Cézanne "to air his forms and his painting" and afterward, at Aix, to leave the white canvas as a contrast, painting that canvas like an unfinished water color. The Impressionists themselves took, for example, the allusions of a yellowish light and of the grayish shadow of Piero della Francesca and, having become aware of the scientific theories of Helmholtz, opened the doors of art so wide that it is impossible not to consider impressionism as one of the most remarkable technical discoveries in the history of art.

To all this, Cézanne added the lessons of Tintoretto, recognizing fully the not purely symbolic value of this master's blacks and Venetian red-browns and his spasmodic layers of paint. Add to this the lessons of El Greco, the Byzantine frescoes, and those tendencies which, as a Latin, Cézanne had toward geometry. The genius of Aix has done the rest: the painting of Cézanne.

With Cézanne there began a kind of atomic explosion of plasticity and of form, an explosion on a geometrical scale, abstract—a fact which sometimes links his plasticity of form with the tradition of certain French primitives of the school of Avignon, Chardin, the brothers Le Nain, and Fouquet.

Cézanne drove the Cubists into cubism. But, while Cézanne took his cubism from nature, the Cubists fell more and more into stylization and thus detached from nature; they have left behind—for the most part—only a series of processes. For this very reason, cubism entered into the decorations of everyday living. And this has always seemed to me to be a terrible, prophetic omen.

Manet, like Cézanne, has brilliantly studied the art of Goya, discovering there the value of his black tones and the polish of his patches of color.

To this obviously incomplete but illustrious group of masters I could have added a series of living masters. Thus has been handed down (from one master to another, like divine gifts) those and other elements which together have formed that unique and almost miraculous gallery of art in France. To create this miracle, these masters have given the fullness of their strength, their whole lives. Yet other times were already approaching, years full of responsibility, which also demanded definite decisions, demanding one's whole strength, one's whole life.

[The relatively quick acknowledgement of specific movements in painting has always seemed to me rather strange. Cubism, for instance, and other movements, achieved that acknowledgement more easily than Impressionism. One instinctively recalls that Rembrandt, El Greco and others waited a long time for a definitive acknowledgement. It seems strange that Art, which by its technique and essence, aspires to be on the walls of a museum, should have so many premature charms. On the contrary, really great Art does not have this facile prettiness. For instance, Rembrandt, Goya in some of his works, Chardin, Cézanne, Van Gogh and others. A language which is both simple and plastically varied is already sophisticated in itself, while a language that lacks simplicity becomes decadent and finally fades away.]

Then the first World War broke out. I left France and returned to Russia. The war of 1914 seemed to me not only a school of life but a school of art. Back in Russia, I saw once more the sky and the landscape of my native land which are, perhaps, not so picturesque as the skies and the landscape of France. But now I saw them differently.

Far from the salons, the exhibitions, and the cafés of Paris, I asked myself: "Is not this war the beginning of a certain 'settling of accounts'?" The recent forms of the self-styled realistic schools (including impressionism and cubism) seemed to me outmoded. Then there began to come to the surface that which many have contemptuously, lazily, labeled "literature."

Men were dying on the battlefields. They were fighting for something which they did not yet clearly perceive. The war, it appeared, and what was to follow it in life, took upon itself the formation of that "complementary" deformation of nature[9] which the painter could hardly realize in a realistic, technical medium. Life itself entered the arena and began to create additional psychological and, as it were, "illogical" elements which, previously, had been lacking in art. Life created "contrasts" without which art is unimaginable and incomplete.

The Russian Revolution broke out and added more new strains. All this came all of a sudden—although well prepared for—with that popular spirit compared with which the actions of the individual (with his repressed Freudianism) often appeared emaciated, a kind of aestheticism or, at best, symbolism.

That revolution disturbed me with the prodigal spectacle of a dynamic force which pervades the individual from top to bottom, surpassing your imagination, projecting itself into your own interior, artistic world[10] which seemed to be already like a revolution. The double shock of these two revolutions is not always very happy.

The years which I then spent in Russia breathed that forgetfulness of self which often seizes you when you constantly see and find entirely new things. Who among us can see his way in its entirety, the way of his life and of his art? Who can foresee where it will end? Destiny, one might say, has always pushed me from place to place. Yet I have to be grateful to destiny for my stay in Russia during the decisive years of war and revolution as well as for my life in France prior to these crucial days.

When I returned to Paris in 1922,[11] I was pleasantly surprised to find a new generation of artists, the surrealist group, which, in some sense, redeemed the pre-war term "literature." And that which had been harmful in 1910, one was now almost inclined to encourage. Sometimes among certain artists this took on a symbolic character, and sometimes it was truly literary.

It is to be regretted greatly that the art of this period should have shone much less with the natural and technical mastery which the masters of the heroic epoch before 1914 had possessed so abundantly. Since, in 1922, I had not yet become fully acquainted with their art, I had the impression of finding in them what I, myself (between 1908 and 1914), had felt obscurely and yet concretely. But why, I thought, is it necessary to proclaim this so-called "automatism?"

However fantastical or illogical the construction of my paintings may appear, I should be horrified to think of them as having a mixture of "automatism." If in my picture of 1908 I have painted death in the street and the violin player on the roof, or in another picture of 1911, entitled "I and the Village," I have painted a little cow with a milkmaid in the head of the large cow, I did not do all this by "automatism."[12]

Even if automatism has helped some to paint good pictures or to write good poems, still this does not permit us to set up automatism as a method. Nor can all those who have painted trees with blue shadows be called "impressionists." Everything in art must spring from the movement of our whole life-stream, of our whole being—including the unconscious.

I'm afraid that as a conscious method automatism generates automatism. And if I was right in saying that the realistic period of technical rebirth was declining, then the automatism of surrealism is laid bare.

Some people are wrongly afraid of the word "mystical," to which they give a meaning that is too religiously orthodox. We must strip this term of its obsolete and musty exterior and understand it in its pure form, exalted and untouched.

"Mystic!" How often have people hurled this word at me—just as they had accused me earlier of being "literary." But without a mystical element is there a single great picture, a single great poem, or—even—a single great social movement in the world? Does not any organism (individual or social) wither and die if it is deprived of the power of the mystical, of feeling, of reason? Sadly I answer myself. It is unjust to set upon mysticism, when it is precisely a lack of mysticism which almost destroyed France. But we should distinguish between different kinds of mysticism, and this war through which we have just passed should have the final purpose of insuring victory over a misconceived mysticism, exploited for evil, cruel and one-sided—the mysticism of the enemy.[13]

Recently, I had occasion to remark: "The good old times have passed when art nourished itself exclusively on the elements of the external world, the world of form, lines, and color. We are interested in everything, not only in the external world, but also in the inner world of dream and imagination."

I cannot forget the emphatic, ponderous declaration of an artist with modernist pretensions: "You know, sincerity is not fashionable." If he is right, then everything is very simple.

All the phrases about so-called "pure art" and about bad "literary" art have quite easily led to the very shaky positions of these last years. Lack of "humanism" in art—don't be afraid of that word—was a sinister presentiment of a sinister present. The example of the great schools and the great masters of the past teach us that a true and genuine quality in painting is not in harmony with the antihuman tendencies displayed in certain works of the so-called "avant-garde" schools.

What was gratifying about the young movement of French painting after the First World War was its eagerness for the new. But this drop of new blood was poured into an old organism with little vitality.

In other days French painters like Corot and Poussin went so far as to leave their own country to search in foreign lands for new revelations—which they were later to develop on their own soil. In those times the banners of crude nationalism did not wave over our heads, and each journey was beneficial for the painter.

[I would like to say here that my moves from country to country have always been dictated essentially by artistic considerations. I will not say that, like some other foreign painters, I could not adapt. On the contrary, in France, I had the signal honor of being invited to participate in international exhibitions in the French pavilions. And—forgive such presumptuous comparisons—would Van Gogh have been Van Gogh if he had stayed in Holland, Picasso in Spain, or Modigliani in Italy? In France, I was fortunate enough to get close to a man like Ambroise Vollard, whose whole life consisted of encouraging certain artists, myself included, to create new works, always newer, although he himself—alas!—abandoned those works to the mercy of fate.[14]]

I should like to recall how advantageous my travels outside of France have been for me in an artistic sense—in Holland or in Spain, Italy, Egypt, Palestine, or simply in the south of France. There, in the south, for the first time in my life, I saw that rich greenness—the like of which I had never seen in my own country. In Holland I thought I discovered that familiar and throbbing light, like the light between late afternoon and dusk. In Italy I found that peace of the museums which the sunlight brought to life. In Spain I was happy to find the inspiration of a mystical, if sometimes cruel, past,[15] to find the song of its sky and of its people. And in the East I found unexpectedly the Bible and a part of my very being.[16]

I venture to insert here some personal data.

There are no stories in my pictures, no fairy tales, no popular legends. Maurice Denis has said of the French synthesists of 1889 that their paintings were "surfaces covered with colors arranged in a certain order." For the Cubists a painting was a surface covered with forms in a certain order. For me a picture is a surface covered with representations of things (objects, animals, human beings) in a certain order in which logic and illustration have no importance. The visual effect of the composition is what is paramount. Any other nonstructural consideration is secondary.

Before the war of 1914, I was accused of falling into "literature." Today people call me a painter of fairy tales and fantasies. Actually, my first aim is to construct my paintings architecturally—exactly as the Impressionists and Cubists have done in their own fashion and by using the same formal means. The Impressionists filled their canvases with patches of light and shadow; the Cubists filled them with cubes, triangles, and cones. I try to fill my canvases in some way with objects and figures treated as forms... sonorous forms like sounds... passionate forms designed to add a new dimension which neither the geometry of the Cubists nor the patches of the Impressionists can achieve.

I am against the terms "fantasy" and "symbolism." Our whole inner world is reality, perhaps even more real than the apparent world. To call everything that appears illogical "fantasy" or fairy tales, etc., is really to admit that one does not understand nature.

Impressionism and cubism are comparatively easy to understand because they present but one single aspect of an object for our consideration—simple contrasts of light and shadow. But a single aspect of an object is not enough to make up the complete subject matter of a picture. Every object has diverse aspects. I am not against cubism; I have admired the great Cubists and I have profited from their work. But I have discussed the limitations of its viewpoint, even with my friend Apollinaire, the man who has really given cubism its place. For me, cubism seemed to limit the possibilities of pictorial expression. I needed greater freedom.

Later when I saw the tendency toward expressionism in Germany, I felt that I had been somewhat justified; and even more when I saw the birth of surrealism in France. Surrealism was the most recent awakening of the desire to liberate art from traditional modes of expression. If it had been more profound in its internal and external expression, it might have crystallized into an artistic movement comparable to the periods immediately preceding it.

Concerning the so-called "literature" in my work, I sometimes feel that in the use of pictorial elements I am more abstract than Mondrian or Kandinsky— abstract, not in the sense of unreality. Abstract painting of this kind is to my mind more ornamental and decorative and always limited in scope. What I call "abstract" is something that rises spontaneously from a gamut of psychic and plastic contrasts, bringing to the picture and to the eye of the spectator realizations of unknown objects. In the case of the headless woman with the milk pails in one of my pictures, painted in 1910–11, it occurred to me to separate her head from her body because I found that I needed an empty space in that particular place. In my painting, 'I and the Village,' I painted a small cow and a milkmaid in the head of a large cow because I needed that kind of shape in that place for my composition.

I have used cows, milkmaids, roosters, and provincial Russian architecture as a source of form because these are a part of the country from which I come; and these things, without doubt, have left a deeper impression in my visual memory than all the other impressions I have received. Every painter is born somewhere; and even if later he responds to the influences of other surroundings, a certain essence, a certain aroma, of his native land will always remain in his work. Yet, don't misunderstand me: what matters here is not the subject in the sense in which pictorial subjects were painted by the ancient academicians. These first influences determine, as it were, the handwriting of the artist. This is evident in the character of the trees and the card players in a Cézanne, born in France; in the winding horizons of a Van Gogh, born in Holland, in the almost Arabian ornamentalism of a Picasso, born in Spain; or in the sensitive quattrocento lines of a Modigliani, born in Italy.

[After talking for so long, I notice that in fact I have said very little, and above all, have I made it clear what is bothering me, what I wanted to say? No doubt, it is best to judge a painter by his works; his words, I fear, only cloud the issue. What haunts me and what I fear most is the deficiency of language, of language which is frequently only an approximation. How many cannons and murders do we need before language becomes more miserly, more tragically alive, and thus more responsible? I noticed this irresponsibility of language just after the "heroic" times of World War I. And yet, since then how many veils have been lifted! What horizons have not been discovered between those two wars! I would not want you to think I am fighting for some distant ideology.[17] Not at all. But humanity wants something new. It wants to return to the originality of its own tongue, similar to that of the primitives, those who opened their mouth for the first time to tell only their own truth.]

Often what disturbs me in the periods of art since the impressionists is the inadequacy of artistic language, a language which is often only approximate. How else can we explain the artistic "excursions" in search of new styles and content? Man seeks something new; he must rediscover the originality of his own language—a language like that of the primitives, of men who have opened their mouths for the first time to speak their one single truth. Mankind wants to rediscover this language, however, without reverting to stylistic imitation.

We used to be against "literature," but have we enriched ourselves with another language and another content?

Wars and revolutions arise, perhaps, because man wants to forge for himself a new clear meaning. Once we have found this new meaning, a new artistic language, a new form, will emerge.

When France has recovered from its cruel ordeal, I do not know (and who can foresee) what external and internal forms the French art of the future will assume. Will there be a gradual rebirth of the former wondrous vision and its emphasis on form? Or, instead of this former vision, will a new inner vision spring up, a new conception of the world with new moral and social foundations? And all this not only in France. After the closed circle of its great masters, France will again, I am sure, fashion new miracles as in the past.

Let us keep faith, as ever, in the spirit of France. With our whole soul we look for that rebirth, which will be at the same time that of the whole world.

James Johnson Sweeney
An Interview with Marc Chagall, 1944[18]

One of the better known European painters whom the war and Nazism have driven to refuge in the United States is Marc Chagall. Chagall was born in Vitebsk, Russia, in 1887. In 1907 he took up painting.[19] From

Vitebsk he went to St.-Petersburg to study there under Bakst. In 1910 he moved to Paris. Shortly before the outbreak of hostilities in 1914 he returned to Russia for a visit. He remained there until 1922 when he returned to Paris[20]—this time definitively, he hoped—only to be forced out of France by the Nazis in 1941.

Perhaps the most striking characteristics of Chagall's work are the persistence of certain images, apparently based on rural and religious reminiscences of his childhood, and the anecdotal illogicality with which they are arranged on his canvases. In his most recent work we still find roosters, fiddling cows, floating brides, decapitated women carrying milkpails, rabbis clutching the Torah tight in their arms, and half-clocks slung from giant pickled herrings, very similar to those of his Vitebsk period, twenty-five years ago. His earlier work seemed predominantly idyllic in character. But since his arrival in this country he has painted a large canvas, the *Revolution* and a *Descent from the Cross* which have stirred up questions regarding Chagall's point of view—his political, aesthetic and religious ideologies—questions which, for the most part, have hitherto gone unanswered by the artist himself due to his reluctance to speak or to write about his work.

Chagall: A painter should never come between the work of art and the spectator. An intermediary may explain the artist's work without any harm to it. But the artist's explanation of it can only limit it. Better the understanding that grows from familiarity and the perspective that will come after the artist's death. After all, it is better to judge a painter by his pictures. His words, I am afraid, do nothing but veil the vision.

Sweeney: But your work is well known to the art-public in this country. It has enjoyed an extremely wide appeal. You are regarded as one of the leading fantastic illustrators of the present century—a reactionary from cubism and abstract art, a sympathizer with the emotional emphases of German expressionism and a forerunner of surrealism in its irrationality and dream-character. Thanks to the exhibition of major work such as *I and the Village* and *Paris Through the Window* and to large retrospective exhibitions in New York, your name brings to mind at once certain images. The constant recurrence of these images had both fixed them in the public mind and whetted its curiosity. In them it sees a suggestion of nostalgia for the surroundings of your childhood, a fairy-tale atmosphere or the illustration of some folk legends of your native Vitebsk. It sees them as private symbols—using the term symbols to signify an image used as an analogy for an abstract idea,—a dove, for example, to represent peace. Your friend and admirer, Raissa Maritain, apparently also sees them in a similar light in her recent appreciation of your work. Yet the critic Florent Fels in *Propos d'artistes* once quoted you as stating very flatly: "in my composition there is nothing of the fantastic, nor of the symbolic."

Chagall: That was many years ago, 1925, still it is just as true as ever. There is nothing anecdotal in my pictures—no fairy tales—no literature in the sense of folk-legend associations. Maurice Denis described the paintings of the Synthetists in France about 1889 as plane surfaces "covered with colors arranged in a certain order. " To the cubists a painting was a plane surface covered with form-elements in a certain order. For me a picture is a plane surface covered with representations of objects—beasts, birds, or humans—in a certain order in which anecdotal illustrational logic has no importance. The visual effectiveness of the painted composition comes first. Every extra-structural consideration is secondary.

Just as before the war of 1914, I constantly had the word literature, or "literary painting" thrown at me, now I am constantly said to be a maker of fairy-tales and of fantasies. As a matter of fact, my first aim is to construct my picture architecturally, just as in their day the impressionists did, and cubists did—along the same formal paths. The impressionists filled their canvases with spots of light and shadow. The cubists with cubic, triangular, and round shapes, I try to fill my canvases in some fashion with objects and figures employed as forms—sonorous forms like noises—passion-forms which should give a supplementary dimension impossible to achieve through the bare geometry of the cubists' lines or with the spots of the impressionists.

I am against the terms "fantasy" and "symbolism" in themselves. All our interior world is reality—and perhaps more so than our apparent world. To call everything that appears illogical, "fantasy," fairy-tale, or chimera—would be practically to admit not understanding nature.

Impressionism and cubism were relatively easy to understand, because they only proposed a single aspect of an object to our consideration—its relations of light and shade, or its geometrical relationships. But one aspect of an object is not enough to constitute the entire subject matter of art. An object's aspects are multifarious.

I am not a reactionary from cubism. I have admired the great cubists and have profited from cubism. But I have argued the limitations of such a view even with my friend Apollinaire, the man who really gave cubism its place. To me cubism seemed to limit pictorial expression unduly. To persist in that I felt was to impoverish one's vocabulary. If the employment of forms not as bare of associations as those the cubists used was to produce "literary painting," I was ready to accept the blame for doing so. I felt painting needed a greater freedom than cubism permitted. I felt somewhat justified, later, when I saw a swing toward expressionism in Germany and still more so when I saw the birth of surrealism in the early twenties. But I have always been against the idea of schools and only an admirer of the leaders of schools. Cubism was an emphasis on one aspect only of reality—a single point of view—the architectural point of view of Picasso—and of Braque in his great years. And let me say in passing, Picasso's gray cubist pictures and his *papiers collés* are in my opinion his masterpieces.

But please defend me against people who speak of "anecdote" and "fairy tales" in my work. A cow and a woman to me are the same—in a picture both are merely elements of composition. In painting, the images of a woman or of a cow have different values of plasticity,—but not different poetic values. As far as literature goes, I feel myself more "abstract" than Mondrian or Kandinsky in my use of pictorial elements. "Abstract" not in the sense that my painting does not recall reality. Such abstract painting in my opinion is more ornamental and decorative, and always restricted in its range. What I mean by "abstract" is something which comes to life spontaneously through a gamut of contrasts, plastic at the same time as psychic, and pervades both the picture and the eye of the spectator with conceptions of new and unfamiliar elements. In the case of the decapitated woman with the milk pails, I was first led to separating her head from her body merely because I needed [to fill in] an empty space there. In the large cow's head in *I and the Village* I made a small cow and woman milking visible through its muzzle because I needed that sort of form, there, for my composition. Whatever else may have grown out of these compositional arrangements is secondary.

The fact that I made use of cows, milkmaids, roosters and provincial Russian architecture as my source forms is because they are part of the environment from which I spring and which undoubtedly left the deepest impression on my visual memory of the experiences I have. Every painter is born somewhere. And even though he may later respond to the influences of other atmospheres, a certain essence—a certain "aroma" of his birthplace clings to his work. But do not misunderstand me: the important thing here is not "subject" in the sense of the pictorial "subjects" that were painted by the old academicians. The vital mark these early influences leave is, as it were, on the handwriting of the artist. This is clear to us in the character of the trees and card players of a Cézanne, born in France,—in the curled sinuosities of the horizons and figures of a Van Gogh, born in Holland,—in the almost Arab ornamentation of a Picasso, born in Spain,—or in the quattrocento linear feeling of a Modigliani, born in Italy. This is the manner in which I hope I have preserved the influences of my childhood not merely in subject matter.

Sweeney: I know you have frequently stated "art is international, but the artist ought to be national." Nevertheless, on your return from Russia in 1922 after an eight years' sojourn there you came to the realization that your native land—the Soviet no more than Imperial Russia—had no need of you. You stated "To them I am incomprehensible, a foreigner." Does this mean that you regard racism as more important than nationalism and that you, as a Jew, were a foreigner even in Vitebsk?

Chagall: Race? Not at all. As a native of Vitebsk I was still as close to
Russia and to the soil as the day I left. But as an artist I felt myself just as much a stranger to the official, aesthetic ideology of
the new government as I had been to the provincial art ideals of
the Russia I left in 1910. At that time, I decided I needed Paris.
The root-soil of my art was Vitebsk, but like a tree, my art needed
Paris like water, otherwise it would wither and die. Russia had
two native traditions of art, the popular and the religious. I
wanted an art of the soil, not one uniquely of the head. I had the
good luck to spring from the people. But popular art—which I
always love for that matter—did not satisfy me. It is too exclusive.
It excludes the refinements of civilization. I have always had a
pronounced taste for refined expression, for culture. The refined art of my native land was a religious art, I saw the quality
of a few great productions of the icon tradition—Rublev's work,
for example. But this was fundamentally a religious art and I am
not, and never have been religious. Moreover, I felt religion
meant little in the world that I knew, even as it seems to mean
little today. For me Christ was a great poet, the teaching of
whose poetry has been forgotten by the modern world. To
achieve the combination of refined expression with an art of
the earth, I felt I had to seek the vitalizing waters of Paris.

I would like to say that my moves from country to country
have always been dictated by artistic considerations, Son of a
laborer, I had organically no other grounds for leaving my native land, to which I think in spite of everything I have remained
loyal in my art. As painter and man of the people—and the people I consider the class of society most sensitively responsive—
I felt that plastic refinement of the highest order existed only
in France. Here is perhaps the source of my dualism and my
climatic maladjustments through all these years. Still I would
not say that I have been less able to acclimatize myself in Paris
than other foreign artists.

Neither Vitebsk nor St.-Petersburg offered me what I felt I
needed as a young painter setting out on his career in 1910.
Similarly, after an eight-year sojourn in Russia between 1914
and 1922, I found the ideology of the Soviets provided no better
place for my ideals of what an art expression should be.

The Revolution had not replaced the atmosphere which had proved so unsatisfactory to me in my early years in Russia with a more congenial one. The ideal it proposed to its artists was to become illustrators—to transport the ideology of the revolution onto the canvas. Its aim was a pictorial photography, not a poetry of forms with logic of associations relegated to a secondary level. My ideal was still a picture above all—without subject, without "literature," as always.

But again do not misunderstand me: there has never been a true art but that has not been addressed solely to an elite; and equally there has never been an art truly great which has not been addressed solely to the masses. The fact is, an elite which is truly elite keeps in mind its bonds with and roots in the masses. In the past the proprietor classes possessed not only the great works of art of their period but also possessed the faculty of immediately comprehending them. The masses held themselves apart. This is one answer to the question your Dr. Coomaraswamy of the Boston Museum puts forward as a title to an essay, *Why Exhibit Works of Art?* The artist has lost his old public. The new public has not yet found the artist. While it may be contended that artists of earlier days were more fortunate in having in sight the specific function in a church house or communal building for which their work was destined, today it must be admitted that exhibitions in their real aspect serve an important end for art in educating a new public.

The year 1922 saw me back to the well-spring in Paris. And I can freely say today that I owe all I have succeeded in achieving to Paris, to France, of which the air, the men, nature were for me the true school of my life and of my art—the waters which fed the soil in which my art had its roots. In this way I found the international language in Paris and have scrupulously striven to maintain the strength of my root soil in Vitebsk.

Sweeney: On your first visit to Paris Guillaume Apollinaire the poet-critic from whom the term "surrealism" has been reputedly adopted, already pointed out a *surnaturel* character in your work; do you feel this movement an important factor in recent art development and do you feel your work has had any relation to the surrealist point of view?

Chagall: Surrealism was the latest awakening of a desire to lead art out of
the beaten paths of traditional expression. If it had been a little
more reliable, a little more profound in its interior and exterior
expression, it would have crystallized into an important movement after the example of those of the periods immediately
preceding it. You ask me if I make use of the surrealist approach.
I began to paint in 1907 and in my work from the beginning
one can see these very surrealist elements whose character was
definitely underlined in 1912 by Guillaume Apollinaire.

Again in Russia during the First World War, far from the
Salons, exhibitions and cafés of Paris, I began to ask myself:
doesn't the outbreak of such a war call for a certain auditing of
accounts? The recent forms of the so-called realist schools,
which for me embraced both impressionism and cubism,
seemed to have lost their vitality. It was then that that characteristic which so many had treated disdainfully and lazily as
"literature" began to come to the surface.

On my return to Paris in 1922, I was agreeably surprised to
find a new artistic group of young men, the surrealists, rehabil-
itating to some degree that term of abuse in the period before
the "literary painting." What had previously been regarded as a
weakness was now encouraged. Some did go to the extreme of
giving their work a frankly symbolic character, others adopted
a baldly literary approach. But the regrettable part was that the
art of this period offered so much less evidence of natural talent
and technical mastery than the heroic period before 1914.

As I was not yet fully acquainted with surrealist art in 1922, I
had the impression of rediscovering in it what I myself had felt
at once darkly and concretely between the years 1908 and 1914.
But why, thought I, is it necessary to proclaim this would-be
automatism? Fantastic or illogical as the construction of my
pictures may seem, I would be alarmed to think I had conceived
them through an admixture of automatism. If I put Death in the
street and the violinist on the roof in my 1908 picture, or if, in
another painting of 1911, *I and the Village*, I had placed a little
cow with a milk-maid in the head of a big cow, I did not do it by
"automatism."

Even if by automatism one has succeeded in composing some good pictures or in writing some good poems, that does not justify us in setting it up as a method. Every thing in art ought to reply to every movement in our blood, to all our being, even our unconscious. But every one who has painted trees with blue shadows cannot be called an impressionist. For my part, I slept well without Freud, I confess I have not read a single one of his books; I surely will not do it now. I am afraid that as conscious method, automatism engenders automatism. And if I am correct in feeling that the technical mastery of the "realist period" is now on the decline, then surely the automatism of surrealism is being stripped rather naked.

Unity—Symbol of Our Salvation[21]
Speech at the Conference of the Committee of Jewish Writers, Artists, and Scientists, February 1944

"Unity"—*Eynikeyt* was the name of a Yiddish biweekly journal published in New York during World War II, for which Chagall was both author and the subject of several articles. There were not many actual Communists in New York Yiddish circles, and their cultural impact depended on attracting sympathizers from both the left and the liberal center, especially writers and artists. The slogan of "unity," instrumental in this move, was a continuation of the "popular front" in France in the late 1930s (in which Chagall also participated). Calling for the unity of all Jewish forces had a special appeal for Jews in those bleak times of daily news about the Holocaust. At the beginning of World War II, the Moscow Yiddish news-paper changed its name from *Der Emes* (*Truth*, the Jewish *Pravda*) to *Eynikeyt* (*Unity*), organ of the Jewish Antifascist Committee, founded in Moscow in 1942, which aimed at mobilizing all Jews around the world in the war against fascism and in support of the Soviet Union. The Antifascist

Committee was, at the same time, the only separate Jewish organization in Stalinist Russia and became a rallying point for Soviet Jewry. In response, a Committee of Jewish Writers, Artists, and Scientists was established in New York, with Albert Einstein as Honorary President, the Yiddish novelist Scholem Asch as President, the German novelist Leo Feuchtwanger and Marc Chagall as members of the Board.

In the middle of the war, in September 1943, representatives of the Moscow Jewish Antifascist Committee arrived in New York. They were the Chairman of the Antifascist Committee, Chagall's old friend and Director of the Moscow Yiddish theater Shloyme (Solomon) Mikhoels and the splendid Yiddish poet Itsik Fefer, who made beautifully sounding, fresh poetry out of the simplest language (and who was apparently also a colonel in the NKVD). Though boycotted by the anti-Soviet Yiddish cultural elite in New York, their visit had a mass appeal: It was a combination of nostalgia for the old country, belief in the utopian Soviet propaganda from a distance, and gratitude to the Soviets who saved at least a million and a half Jews from the Nazis. The visitors called for "unity, " and "unity" became a code word for supporting the left. The New York *Eynikeyt* (*Unity*) was founded in that context.

Just as an artist approaching his creative work, instinctively clings to the most important forms, so a whole nation must instinctively clutch those important movements that make life worth living.

Just as there is no good art that does not look forward, so will a nation wither if it won't drink from the throbbing, forward-flowing springs.

What was it that once made artists great and important, artists with an internal drive like Daumier, Courbet, Cézanne, Baudelaire, Tolstoy,

Pushkin, or Gorky, a musician like Musorgsky, or Mendele, Peretz, Sholem-Aleichem? They all went forward body and soul—with the trends of their age, thus heralding new times.

We Jews, like other nations, irrespective of our accidental troubles, have been an unusual people until recently—and have gradually been weakened. Gradually, the miracle of Hasidism, which was the people's poetry, fantasy, religion, died out. The subsequent charm, the blooming of Yiddish classics in literature and the force of struggle with which the old Jewish popular parties had once shattered the Jewish street—those gradually subsided too.

In the European Christian world, the new schools of art were gradually exhausted, as in France, for example—after a century of heroic art movement. And finally, such weakened people's organisms were powerless to resist those microbes that attacked them—Fascism with its ugly war. The rest of the Christian world somehow survives, it lives in its own home. But we Jews—a people with a strange conception of external form—have remained mostly in the old world[22]—without any form altogether. So this terrible microbe has attacked our people's weakened body, and insanely attacks our soul too.

Meanwhile, the enemy jokes, saying that we are a "stupid nation." He thought that when he started slaughtering Jews, we would all in our grief suddenly raise the greatest prophetic scream, and would be joined by the Christian humanists. But, after two thousand years of "Christianity" in the world—say whatever you like—but, with few exceptions, their hearts are silent . . .

Meanwhile, a new sun has risen, red as blood and teeming with life—the great Revolution in Soviet Russia.—And the world looks at this sun, whose red color drives you crazy and irritates the enemy. But isn't this sun our hope? The Jews will always be grateful to it.

What other great country has saved a million and a half Jews from Hitler's hands, and shared its last piece of bread? What country abolished antisemitism? What other country devoted at least a piece of land as an autonomous region for Jews who want to live there?[23] All this, and more, weighs heavily on the scales of history.

We Jews were not and will not be able to create something important again, if we are not just scattered around the world, but also scattered [ideologically] of our own will, and are not united with the heart of our whole people, as it now confronts a change of the whole path of its life. I cannot and should not get into political discourse. It is enough for me if can at least say a word as an artist, for color is not our only material, life itself is also the material of art.

Today, locked up in your home, the soul and body not united, you cannot create anything. How united? With the pulse of the whole people—the people of every day, of yesterday and tomorrow. And only a blind man cannot see where the true pulse throbs today, and whose pulse it is. It is, first of all, the great country with its building efforts, its liberating war; where, along with all other nations, our Jewish heroes and partisans are fighting. Those are the stubborn settlers in the Kibbutzim (in Palestine); and those are the Jews in the ghettoes of Poland, who have risen in their uprising and their courage, who will stay alive; along with all the other fighters everywhere in the united nations. This is the beginning of our new history, and they call us all to follow them in unity.

A couple of great Jews recently came from there to ignite us and call us.[24] [For a moment,] there was more light here, but they left and it grew darker. True, we no longer follow the old roads, the roles have changed. The Lubavicher or Gerer Rebbes[25] don't have the same influence on us as in the past. The Jewish partisans and settlers [in Eretz-Israel] are singing different songs. They are the new Hasidim.

Mikhoels and Fefer came here to the Jews with a new call for battle, they said that we want to live and we will. And though the enemy has killed several million Jews—one day he will go crazy on our old-new Jewish content, which he cannot kill. A united people he cannot kill. We Jews grieve for our diminished "quantity," but we must not forget our "quality." Today unity is the best symbolic formula for saving our Jewish nation. Today it fills the air everywhere as the indispensable medicine for all nations and races of the globe after the present catastrophe.

I picture the following scene: in my distant home, in the enemy's hands, my father lies in the earth—a poor worker—he worked hard his whole life in holy silence. But he gave me hands that must talk and a mouth that cannot be silent.

I see: the artists in Christian nations sit still—who has heard them speak up? They are not worried about themselves, and our Jewish life doesn't concern them.

But often I ask myself. Why am I asked to speak, when I am scared about how little everybody—close friends and distant ones—cares about the content of the words. Apparently, words like deeds must come. The call for unity was a call to deeds. A new, unified Jewish life must begin to write a new chapter in Jewish history.

But those who are cold to the call of unity, who are sceptical, who continue quarreling among themselves and with others—are cold to the destiny of the people.

Not by accident did the call for unity come from the land of the great Revolution, and it must be the beginning of our own, internal "Jewish Revolution."

I wish you and all of us happiness.

To My City Vitebsk
February 1944[26]

As the Red Army advanced westward, the daily Orders signed by Generalis-

simus Stalin listed the victories and commended heroic people or cities.

Your name seems to be mentioned twice in a lifetime: in time of war, and when people see my pictures. Today you are especially mentioned for your heroic struggle, and I feel like talking to you.

I haven't seen you in a long time, my dear city, I haven't heard from you, haven't talked to your clouds, haven't leaned on your fences. As the gloomiest wanderer, all those years I carried only your breath on my pictures, and thus spoke to you and saw you in my dream.

My dear one, you never said in pain: Why? Why did I leave you many years ago? You thought, the boy seeks something, seeks such a special subtlety, that color descending like stars from the sky and lending, bright and transparent, like snow on our roofs. Where did he get it? How would it come to a boy like him? I don't know why he couldn't find it with us, in the city—in his homeland. Maybe the boy is "crazy," but "crazy" for the sake of art.

You thought: "I can see, I am etched in the boy's heart, but he is still 'flying,' he is still striving to take off, he has 'wind' in his head." On your soil—I left my homeland, my soul—a mountain with dead parents, stones scattered on top of them. So why did I leave you for so long, if in my heart I am always with you, with your new world, the bright example in history?

I did not live with you, but I didn't have one single painting that didn't breathe with your spirit and reflection.

Sometimes I am very sad when I hear people talk about me in languages I don't understand and cannot really communicate with them. They are talking about my relationship toward you, that I seem to have forgotten you. What do they say? Aren't my artistic suffering and difficulties enough—do I have to suffer as a human being as well? Not in vain did I dream long ago, that the human being in me would not be seen at all, only the artist . . .

In my youth I went far away from you—to learn the language of art which Paris had then. All the artists of the world wandered to Paris. After hundreds of years in Rome, in Toledo, in Amsterdam, Art settled in Paris. I cannot say whether I learned anything in Paris. Whether my language of art was enriched, whether I achieved something myself, whether my childhood dreams led me to anything good.

Yet, somewhere, specialists said and wrote that I contributed something in Art. So that way—I did contribute something to you. And still, all those years I didn't stop doubting: Do you understand me, my city, do we understand each other?

But today, as always, I want to talk just about you. Is there anything you didn't go through, my city? Suffering, starvation, destruction, like thousands of other sister-cities in my homeland. So I am happy for you, for the great heroism you displayed against the greatest enemy of the world. Happy for your new people, for their creativity, for the great meaning of life you have built. You are giving it not just to me, but to the whole world.

I would be even happier—to wander in your fields, to collect the stones of your ruins, with my elderly shoulders to help rebuild your streets. The best I could wish for myself is—if you said I was and remain forever faithful to you. Otherwise, I wouldn't be an artist. For you won't tell me: I am too fanatic, incomprehensible. For in your depth, you are yourself like this... Those are your dreams—I only brought them out on a canvas, like a bride to the "khupa" [wedding canopy]—I kissed you with diverse colors and lines, and don't say now that you don't recognize yourself.

I know I shall not find the tombstones or even the graves of my parents anymore, but you, my city, for me you yourself will become a big, living tombstone, and all your newborn voices will resound more beautiful than the most beautiful music, for they call for new creations, for life. When I heard that your heroic fighters were approaching your gates, I got excited and wished to create a big painting, where the enemy crawls even into my childhood home on "Pokrova Street" and fights you from my own windows. But you bring him the death he deserved, because, through death and punishment, he may perhaps, hundreds of years later, bear a human face on his shoulders.

And if in the past a nation would beatify a person, today all humanity should beatify you, my city, along with your older sisters: Stalingrad, Leningrad, Moscow, Kharkov, Kiev and more and more, and call you all: holy.

We, human beings, cannot and must not live peacefully, create honestly, and leave the world, until the sinful world is cleansed by the holy punishment. I look at you from afar, my city, as my mother would look at me from the door when I went into the street. The enemy is still inside you. It wasn't enough for him to take my painted city on my pictures, robbing wherever he could,[27]—he also came to burn my real house and my real city. I hurl back in his face the recognition and fame, that he once gave me in his country.[28]

His "Doctors of Philosophy," who wrote "profound" words about me, now came to you, my city, to throw my brothers from the high bridge into the river, bury them alive, shoot, burn down, rob, and with their crooked smile, observe it all through their "monocles."

I don't need my own house any longer, even if you save it for me. My home is in all your hearts, your breath is a balm. And I would be happy if I could produce something new, as you bring new things to the world.

Two Kinds of Art-Poetry
Speech at the Chagall–Fefer celebration, New York, April 30, 1944[29]

Despite a massive emigration from Russia, in 1897, over five million Jews still lived in the Russian Empire; almost 98 percent of them declared Yiddish as their language. A modern Yiddish literature had developed there since the end of the nineteenth century, yet only after the October Revolution did the masses (mostly secular by then) join high culture. Modernist Yiddish poetry flourished in Russia on the threshold of and just after the Revolution, mostly sharing Chagall's equation of "Revolutionary

Art" with a "Revolutionary society"—that is, working with the imagina-
tive, "incomprehensible" rhythms and metaphors of modernist poetry.
The clash between art and politics was bound to come: a new, simple,
"straightforward," proletarian poetry, refreshing in its language and into-
nations, could better appeal to a mass readership. Itsik Fefer was its
prominent voice. The paradoxical relation between "Super-realist" and
"simple" art concerned Chagall as it did concern his friends, the French
Communist writers and painters. Naive Chagall, talking to a Communist
assembly in New York, assumed he was talking to "the masses."

Itsik Fefer (1900–1952) was a volunteer in the Red Army, fought on the
fronts of the Civil War, and became a standard bearer of Yiddish proletarian literature. Chagall met Fefer when Yiddish writers visited the Jewish
orphanage in Malakhovka near Moscow in 1922, where Chagall lived
and taught, and again in New York in September 1943, when Fefer and
Mikhoels came to America as representatives of the Jewish Antifascist
Committee in Moscow and appeared before a mass audience. Two books of
Fefer's new Soviet-style poetry appeared in New York in 1944. *Heymland*,
illustrated by Marc Chagall, was published by ICOR (the Jewish Coloniza-
tion Organization, supporting the settlement of a Jewish autonomous
region in Birobidjan, in the Soviet Far East). Yet Fefer himself was not
allowed to come to New York for the celebration. On August 12, 1952,
Fefer was executed during Stalin's liquidation of Soviet Yiddish culture.

This speech was read by Chagall at the ICOR assembly, held shortly
after the anniversary commemoration of the Warsaw Ghetto Uprising of
April 19, 1943.

It is especially pleasant for me that in the days of Jewish mourning for the heroes—the fallen fighters of Warsaw ghetto—we are attending today an event for a poet—a living fighter for a new land which strikes our mutual enemy—a fighter who sings heroism, courage and hatred to the enemy.—I thank you all for your good words. But at the same time I think: it is too much honor for me to be the only bridegroom at this event. I am very happy to be together with you and celebrate the appearance of Fefer's book, though I am despondent that I am here alone without Fefer. First of all, his presence would have made us all jollier, secondly, I would not feel as a kind of "usurper," for the singing poems of the book were sung by Fefer in his full, youthful voice... —so the whole honor is deserved by him. I only, how shall I say it, whistled to the song.

We owe warm thanks to the publishers of Fefer's book—ICOR and [I.A.] Ronch, who composed the book with a lot of love and effort.

Yet it is essentially not just Fefer's evening. It is an evening for all those who want to transport themselves at least in thought again and again to his and our great homeland, that shows today the greatest art to be above art.

But speaking thus, I ponder: if people perhaps don't understand my art of color,[30] which, it seems to me, is my "profession"—how will they understand words, that are not my profession? So I am most greatful to my friend and great writer Sholem Asch[31] and the fine Jewish art critic Dr. Kloomok[32] and others who explained my art to you and even to myself...

For me it was a double pleasure to draw something for Fefer's book. True, very little, as I said, and in a hurry, but in that hurry which rushes to express again and again my feelings to the people and the land about which Fefer sings his songs. I met the poet Fefer for the first time in Moscow in the heat of the Revolution—in the yard of the "Jewish State Chamber Theater" where I worked at the time, and in the Malakhovka Colony, where I taught children.

Along with the writers Dobrushin, Nister, Hofshteyn,[33] and others... there I heard a new name that announced: "Hush, all you hovering people [luftmenschn] and hovering artists—We are coming with simple words."[34] I looked at the writers around me and no one was "afraid"...

Over twenty years passed. I was steeped in all the griefs and perhaps also joys that are destined for an artist of the twentieth century, through Paris—the capital of art. And when my old friend the great artist Shloyme Mikhoels came here [to New York] together with Fefer, we discovered in him a true Jew—revolutionary from his birth, and a true poet—a poet set in the general Yiddish poetic tradition, yet with a new chapter as new as the land that bore him is new in its content. Not that country [Tsarist Russia], where I, for example, hid under a bed when a Gorodovoy [policeman on the beat] walked by our windows in the street. If in my imagination, my country was as large for me as our courtyard—for Fefer it spread from "sea" to "sea" [the whole Soviet empire]. And he walks and sings and travels over it as free as other young people like him.

Why do I love Fefer? As when you want to know a painter you start with his sense of color, and to know a musician—with his quality, his voice and his harmony, the same holds for a poet. Today (as always, by the way)—true plastic and poetic quality go together with the life-path and the striving of the man—the artist. Therefore it is hard for a hesitating artist, for it means that his quality is shaking together with him.

Yes—I, who, according to some, is probably a crippled artist in his style, content, and what not[35]—it is I who love the poet Fefer, about whom they, probably, think that his poetic path is, on the contrary, entirely "straight."

Today there are two kinds of poetry-art. One is a super-realistic art,[36] and in the Soviet Union the Jew-Russian, the poet Pasternak is a fine example for that. The second kind of art-poetry is the so-called straight-line writing and clarity of a Fefer.

But as the super-realistic art-poetry, when it is authentic, is essentially straight-lined and simple—so is the so-called straight-lined and simple art and poetry, in its authenticity, super-realistic. This occurs when both of them have pure word and form material in themselves, when both directions are in the ultimate stages of their movement. Only those who did not reach such peaks in art—as in life, are limping and tormenting themselves and us.

I love "contrasts" in which the harmonic truth is hidden. I have in mind one of many examples, when different poles in art meet somewhere. Here is the classical realist Pushkin with his profound, chiseled rhythm and the ardent Romantic Baudelaire, enveloped in dreams of enchanted poisonous flowers—in their final authenticity they meet. I remember the last art experiments in Paris [before the war], where next to a painting of an old medieval primitive Giotto can hang a Picasso; and next to him can hang the pre-Renaissance artist Mantegna; and next to our [i.e., Jewish] Modigliani can hang a Byzantine icon; and several paintings by the artist—naturalist and revolutionary—Gustav Courbet, who in the time of the Paris Commune hurled the Vendome Column to the ground, can hang with the magic artist of the Renaissance period—Giorgione, and so on. And this is not "eclecticism"—on the contrary.

But I don't want to get far into these problems, and be closer to the book.

In my artistic work for books, I always dreamed of merging with literature, both ours and of other nations. Starting with the Bible, La Fontaine, Gogol, Peretz, Sholem-Aleichem, up to the living today. I meant to do it not as an "illustrator," literally, but as a sign of art-proximity. For, in addition to every art having its own laws and means, there is a certain heart-line between them, which finally unites them. Whether I succeeded a little in that, either with Christians or with Jews—is a different question. Once, for example, in the year of Peretz's death [1915], I tried to make something for Peretz's *Tales in the Folk Manner*. The person who came to me and asked me to do it was a good Jew, a scholar—Nokhem Shtif.[37] But his aesthetic taste and the "largesse" of the publisher allowed them to make of my drawings with the text an edition of a few pages on cheap packing paper, that costs a penny. Naturally, of such an "edition" and all my efforts no trace remained long ago. I don't know if I had better luck with Lyesin's poems,[38] with many drawings for him, which he begged me for years to make for him—but let it be enough for today.

Look at the poor Eretz-Israel—nevertheless, in war time, published several of my books with drawings on beautiful paper . . .

Of course, it is a pleasure for me to illustrate Fefer. For in his verses I felt the fire of those heroes.[39] They exude like smoke, like heat from the earth, and they carry in themselves the new man. I am always glad when I see a person in life, and in him I see not just him but, through him, a whole country, a landscape, a people. Fortunately, here and there I found such people in my lifetime. Indeed, why were thousands of Jews here excited when they saw Mikhoels and Fefer?[40] For through them you could feel a land, a nation, a soul.

And I hope today that those, in whose hearts is deeply engrained the destiny of the suffering Jewish people, wherever it may be, will devote a lot of energy together with all friendly united Jews—to save the people. I want to hope and believe that the power of that great land, with its fighting Jews [the Soviet Union], along with other nations there, will be stronger and more confident to help the Jewish national survival everywhere, even in

Eretz-Israel[41]—more than those others with their old promises, never kept, and their "White Papers"[42]...

When I was very young, I wanted to conquer worlds. Now I want to conquer only one world in art: to create several paintings. And this is very hard, because they have to "hover" in the air, because only then can they simply walk on the ground, and even then they are not understood, for it is too simple...

It is happiness to walk the road which our fathers walked inside their souls. It is almost a "via dolorosa" with all its smiles... And if not everybody liked it—what can one do. Those who sparkled too much upon our poor eyes and souls, let them go on sparkle.

For an artist today it is hard to remember that he is merely an artist. And though sometimes I have a pen in hand and want to say a word—but often I think: perhaps it is better to keep my mouth shut.

Many years ago, before the war, I said: "Do only artists have to search to justify our life in art, to show a way in art? And other people, don't they have to show also their 'collective life art'?

Isn't it enough for an artist to sit home and work, and thereby be useful to humanity and to his people? Why, what force pulls him today from his place?

Isn't it enough that our art speaks from the canvas to our eyes and to our heart?"

But art was like a bride enveloped in veils. She dreams in palaces and "is bought for money"...

And how can one sit quietly and write and paint "fantastic" pictures and books, when life is even more fantastic?

And speaking many years ago about our culture, I said:[43] "Our culture is not only Spinoza, Freud, Einstein, Mendele, Peretz, Sholem-Aleichem and Bialik, Israels and Pissarro—today those are also our Jewish folk people and the workers in all countries, with their sharp vision and their fists, who resist and will resists our enemies[44]—for our insults. And I would like just one thing: to be in their rows at that time.

Our enemies, rather than draw the light from our ancient spirit, want only our blood, to get intoxicated on it and draw courage for their lowly exploits.

And as an artist, I do not mean that we must become experts in art. Let our life assume the discipline that governs true art. Internally and externally, let at least one ray of such beauty descend on our words and deeds, on our whole life, for its lack has bent our backs for thousands of years..."

Perhaps I have no right to talk like that, for you must always demand more of yourself, for sometimes you blush seeing your own weaknesses.

It is not a time for art today. War in the world. Still, in the fire, people come to speak about culture, poetry and art, for all these are also our weapons.

The official academies have been discredited long ago. And artists still have to go through a harder "apprenticeship" than in freer times. And all this in the light of many contemporary social and psychological problems, especially when you consider the path of an artist who was and still is a person hovering in the air [luftmensch]. Lightness, mannerism, and casual daubing cannot stick to us—if in art we don't give of ourselves our whole life, if in art we are not "extreme maximalists" in our own way.

"Yes, we Jews-artists[45] are today like the grass, perhaps pretty grass— but on a cemetery. And it pains me that I have to utter such words, for in essence I was never a pessimist—on the contrary.

[Jewish] Artists are often lonely, with no friends and no benefactors, quarreling with each other and with themselves. But weren't the artists some times the first to provide a push for other [genres of] culture, literature, theater?[46]

And those Jews who donate to the 'box'[47] in order to 'save' themselves for eternity—when will they understand that by helping culture and art you can also immortalize your own name and help the growth of art and culture, which are one of our achievements in the world."

I recall that thus I talked many years ago. And I ask myself: what for did I talk? What has changed since then? The time came, came long ago, the time for deeds. Therefore my heart melts when I hear the music of those heroes who bury the old world with our enemies together... and call us to a new life. We, artists and writers, must be the first to hear it. We need it for ourselves.

And why must we wake up together only on the barricades and in the ghettos, before death? And why not while we are still alive? Why do we have to show today our genius and talent for survival primarily in the resistance in the ghettos? While in life, when the axe is not hanging above our heads—we are enemies to ourselves [and to others, so that often I am in despair...].[48]

Dozens of years of flying in the sky convinced me about what is happening on the earth. Is there really no person among the Jews, whose word has any worth for them ... As that word, once upon a time, in the old religious

life, as the word once uttered by old fighters in the party... [49] In the meantime, the Jew is scattered, in his trade up to his neck, in his lowliness and
hiding. And our so-called "authority" of the artist and culture creators is
worth a penny in his eyes.

It is terrible how the enemy beats us. More terrible, how the nations are
silent... But even more terrible it is to see how we weep over the graves
of the martyrs but do not scream to each other: "This is the time to give
a hand to each other, to see in each other a brother, to prevent our total
demise."

Our enemies observe our eyes from afar—as a "termometer. " Today,
shining are only the eyes of the heroes in the battle-fields, in the ghettos,
in Soviet Russia, of the pioneers (halutzim) in Eretz-Israel. And everywhere, if we demand more of ourselves, will get more from others. What
we shall give—we shall get. True, there are other nations who have the
"luxury" of not giving much and getting a lot. This is not our destiny.

I think of that kind of "oil" which softens our hearts, when the screws
stop screetching and the voyage is smoother... We artists, writers, need it
more than anybody. Without that "oil" our creative style is dry, the writing
is dry, the paint is dry. And if so, what do you finally see before your eyes:
no ideal worth to live for...

I would like to finish my overly long speech with a "prayer"—not to God,
whom I did not yet paint, not in a synagogue, which I did paint, but to myself: that, the older I get, may our steps hear our voice change from the
new-old content, and our eyes begin to see that confident new-old path, [50]
which we ourselves and all together must always seek and build. And this
will be felt and seen on our faces.

Today I was so surprised, that I have to tell you about it. I opened Fefer's
book, wanted to leaf through it, and the book opened on the following
verses. And since I think they will tell you much more than what I wanted
to tell you, I would like to read them: [51]

> I know: I did not cross all thresholds yet.
>
> In my eyes, the same fever is alive
>
> And the same curiosity, and the same desires
>
> That I carried for a long time under the high sun.
>
> And the same freshness dwells in my eyes,
>
> *And the same smile was folded inside...*

To the Paris Artists
   December 1944[52]

I send my word to you, my painter-colleagues of the Salon of Liberation.

Thirty-five years ago, as a very young man, like thousands of others, I came to Paris to fall in love with France and study French art.

In recent years I have felt unhappy that I couldn't be with you, my friends. My enemy forced me to take the road of exile. On that tragic road, I lost my wife, the companion of my life, the woman who was my inspiration.[53] I want to say to my friends in France that she joins me in this greeting, she who loved France and French art so faithfully. Her last joy was the liberation of Paris.

In the course of these years, the world was anxious about the fate of French civilization, of French art. The absence of France seemed impossible, incomprehensible. Today the world hopes and believes that the years of struggle will make the content and spirit of French art even more profound. The world hopes and believes that the art of France will more than ever be worthy of the great art epochs of the past.

I bow to the memory of those who disappeared, and of those who fell in the battle. I greet you, Picasso, Matisse, Bonnard, I greet you Raoul Dufy, André Lhôte, I greet you, the old and the young, who all fought with so much courage. I would also like to greet my friends the French writers who are so worthy to bear that name, Jean Paulhan, Jean Cassou, André Malraux, Paul Eluard and so many others. I bow to your struggle, to your fight against the foe of art and life.

Now, when Paris is liberated, when the art of France is resurrected, the whole world too will, once and for all, be free of the satanic enemies who wanted to annihilate not just the body but also the soul—the soul, without which there is no life, no artistic creativity.

Dear friends, we are grateful to the destiny that kept you alive and allowed the light of your colors and your works to illuminate the sky darkened by the enemy. May your colors and your creative effort have the strength to bring back warmth and new belief in life, in the true life of France and of the whole world.

October 19, 1944

The End of the War
May 1945 [54]

This speech was delivered at a leftist assembly in New York in May 1945,
on the celebration of the end of World War II in Europe. Chagall pleads
for embracing three principles that would revive the Jewish people after
the Holocaust: to be illuminated by the rays emanating from the Soviet
Union; to be united; and to build a home for millions [sic] of Jews in
Eretz-Israel (the term *home* rather than *State* refers to the promise of the
Balfour Declaration to build a Jewish "Home" in Palestine, and was still
accepted by the Zionists as well).

The theme of unity ("our new Hasidism") runs through many statements
by Chagall on the Jewish situation (see "Unity—Symbol of Our Salvation,"
p. 87 in this volume). It may have been influenced by the Communist–
anti-Communist war in Jewish society in New York. Of course, the Zionist ideal was anathema to his hosts, for whom Palestine was a colonialist
outpost—until their line turned around 180 degrees when the Soviet
Foreign Minister Gromyko made a speech in the U.N. in 1947 in favor
of a Jewish state.

Thank you for your invitation to be with you at this assembly, I am just an
artist struggling with himself and his art. What can I say, I who want to
hear? Perhaps the folk proverb is right that silence is golden and the word
is silver.

But today it must be different. Keeping silent is not golden and there
are words that say nothing. For an artist, it is not enough today to live with
nature, with himself. He must also live with and feel the people.

Today my people are those who let their life's road be illuminated by the
young rays that emanate from our great homeland; [55]

My people are those who strive toward the unity of all its parts;

And like many of you—I want the realization of a just Jewish home for millions of Jews in Eretz-Israel, which must be dear to everyone.

Those are the three points without which a Jew is today only half a man and only half a Jew. The more I strive toward them simultaneously—the fuller is my personality as Jew and as artist.

With those three points, we bring our Jewish face to its ideal which is possible today. The splintering of the Jewish people has long led to its deformation and unhappiness. What Paris once was for those who sought art—I admire my great homeland for its achievements and ambitions. It saved the world. Jewish America should have become the great movement of Jewish unity.

Three Jewish worlds need each other. Together they must create the strength of Jewish creativity and culture, together the Jewish people will become whole, morally and physically. Unity is our new Hasidism.

I come to greet you as a simple Jew from the people, My father was from the people, a worker.[56] In his shul, he was for "unity";[57] when he heard the word Jerusalem, he cried. My father is my best academy.

A few days ago, the war in Europe ended. The remaining Jewish people rise emaciated, pale. They look around: what remains of the people? What remained are their pain and the scattered sacks of their limbs. I don't know if they will count the lost armies of our Jewish people. If only Moses were here, he would have presented a bill.

I want to hope that "on the waters of another river" a new child will be found—a Moses[58] who will heal the Jewish people both from fullness and from hunger, will straighten the crooked ways, and "twist" a bit the overly straight ones. He will put us on our feet so we will become a people of dawn and not of sunset.

Now is the time. No world conferences[59] can be successful until the Jewish people are taken down from the cross on which it has been crucified for two thousand years.[60] The world must do justice to itself. Temporary luck and wealth is not enough—a state, a land also has a conscience, a soul like an individual person.

The Jewish people emerged from the war like a ship at sea turned over on its head. We look in the water—torn legs and souls are floating, torn Torah scrolls dissolve like bright, childish intestines. From the abyss you hear no divine or prophetic voices. And as always, the sun burns above and colors us and everybody [all of humanity] with the color of red blood.

The war is over. But may peace not be like that painting that has every-thing except a soul.

I greet the Jewish folk masses.[61] I always wanted to feel like one of them, to fill myself with the people's breath, as once upon a time in my home. It is good to come to the people. As a man who knocks at the door at night. Let us just not think that the door is like a wall. To go to the people... Find in them a salvation from yourself, a way to a lost world.

I wish you and your children to seek not only a piece of bread, but primarily to strive to reach the source of Jewish and human culture, and thus we will attain general human value in our own eyes and in the eyes of others.

To the Jewish People in Paris
June 1946[62]

From one soul to the other, from year to year, from country to country . . . I am back here again, where I spent my youth in art. You, along with other peoples, brought me here.

Here is my beautiful and melancholy city. I still saw little of you. Just a few eyes, a few weary faces. I saw how similar you are to me, to my art—but through your eyes I saw more—I saw the gun that liberated us, but also the smoke of the burning ovens, the forests and the villages where you hid and fought,[63] and the heroism that is the greatest in our history.

It seems to me that you are standing before me, impoverished and naked, in tatters. But be calm, this reminds me of those paintings of Rem-brandt, where naked and barely covered figures appear, and are therefore as pure as gold... We lived to see that our life is like the torn tatters on those paintings of genius, but our spirit shines.

Only one woe. We lost our dear ones. Our house is empty, even when we are in it. We are crying and cannot cry them out of our system. We are seeking them up above in the clouds. We are seeking them down below in the corners. We are seeking them in ourselves... We touch ourselves and push ourselves away. It is only us—without them.

We are desolate, not just because we are missing our near ones, but because many "near ones" here and there look like strangers... We are amazed that the more we break through to light—the deeper we see the "shadow."

But where was the real "foe?" The barbarian who accidentally has a human face, who destroys a child and a woman and robs in broad daylight, cannot be called "foe." He could not present to us any important philosophical or moral proof—against our philosophy and morals. We won.

In my personal life, I want to see some consolation in that: that we will remain what we were before. We don't want to flee from the depths of our culture and belief, for through them lies the road to the world. And we still want to create our form and content.

And it seems to me that out of the fire, breaking the boundaries of factionalism, Jews will find a language of unity.

"Comfort Ye My People... "

Speech at a reception for Marc Chagall, organized by the Yiddish Culture League on July 8, 1946, at the Hotel Lutetia in Paris[64]

On June 4, 1946, one year after victory over Nazi Germany, Chagall arrived by ship from America to liberated France. It was his first visit to Europe, from which he had fled in June 1941. Now he was on the crossroads, hesitant between staying in America or returning to his adopted second homeland, France. He wrote the famous poem "My Land," as we can see now, not as an abstract metaphor about his imaginary land of art, but as an expression of his profound anxiety of homelessness. He conveyed this mood to his audience who, like him, lost their homes and world in Eastern Europe. Many Jews, Communists, and others, especially immigrants from Poland who lived in Paris without French citizenship, fought in the French Resistance. They, and the survivors of Nazi concentration camps, were in his audience at the Hotel Lutetia in Paris, which had served under the Nazis as the Gestapo headquarters.

When I walked off the ship, the following lines appeared in my mind:

> Only that land is mine, which dwells in my soul.
> Like a native, without papers, I walk into it;
> It sees my sadness and my loneliness.
> It puts me to sleep and covers me with a fragrance-stone.
> Orchards blossom in me, my invented flowers,
> My own streets.
> Only: there are no houses.
> They were ruined since my childhood ...
> Their inhabitants stray in my air.
> They seek a dwelling—they live in my soul.
> Hence I smile when my sun shines a bit,
> Or I cry, like a quiet rain at night.
> Once both faces
> Were covered with a love-shine
> Night and Space...
> Now I imagine:
> Even when I walk back
> I go forward to the road of high gates—
> Beyond them, wide steppes spread out,
> Where exhausted thunders spend the night
> And broken lightnings.

I am happy to be among you—representatives of the heroic Jewish survivors in France. Thank you for your reception.

I thought we had little time today for receptions, when so much injustice is done to the Jewish people that you want to hide somewhere to find the logic of all those illogical events.

Our admiration, all our thoughts and wishes have to go today to those who suffered in the ghettos and to the Jewish remnants in all corners of Europe, to the Jews and all the heroes of Soviet Russia—my great homeland—and to those who still suffer today and fight so tragically in Palestine.

So I am perplexed about why you said so many good things about me. I don't know if I deserved them for I do intend—and have not yet done it—to work so hard as to deserve the honor. I think the praise you showered on me belongs to all Jewish artists—those who are no longer alive, and those who are—to their ideal of creating a new art among Jews.

I would like to speak as little as possible about myself. I never thought I accomplished or achieved anything. All I ever wanted was not to be too close to the great world-masters like Rembrandt, El Greco, or Tintoretto, and others; but to be close to the spirit of our own fathers and grandfathers. To be essential, as they were, to merge with their wrinkles—as if I were hidden inside their garments—their souls, inside their sighs, worries and rare joy.

This was my "Art School." I felt and even saw that there was no difference between these fathers and grandfathers and those ancient Egyptian or Assyrian or other sculptures in the museums of Alexandria or Athens— both of them have the static and dynamic power of expression and humanity, a natural character, untouched by mechanical devices, as in our transitional period. I often thought that Vitebsk may not have been worse than Florence and Paris.

Perhaps I did not seek to paint entirely from nature, for nature is in us and everything in us is also nature, and in the recent past we saw that the so-called dream is even more than nature . . .

As I said, it is an honor for me to be with you, but it is also sad to be among people in general today, because—I don't know why—at every step I feel that, somehow, the human being is diminished, is even smaller than he was before this war and the one before. But one thing: the suffering and pain a human being can endure, and your resistance, make us think that there is still a mysterious power in human beings which will not succumb to the blind, selfish, evil powers.

And we Jews, whose suffering and voice are still unheeded by humanity—we are like the tic of an eyelid: now it closes, as before the end, and now it opens as for a new life. Sometimes we seem to be the barometer of possible world-happiness or world-calamity. It seems—does the world know it?—if it treats us justly, it can expect some happiness, if not, it will remain lying in history as in the dark. We are the innocence and the conscience, like the body of a newborn baby or of an old man, demanding respect and admiration as a father.

Many alien powers have tortured us, but sadly, there are also our own, Jewish elements who disturb our unity. Without unity, where is the strength we could master to oppose the enemy when he assaults us again?

Of course we know that art and culture—the true, high, and shining—was and finally will be the best content in life, and our new "God." The war is over and there is new talk about wars. But perhaps a new kind of struggle would have started, the struggle of cultural and spiritual humanity to forge artists, prophets—people with the weapons of justice, new cultural soldiers to march in cities and squares and countries, calling nations and governments to justice. Is it now a chutzpah to talk about justice, is it out of fashion?

Sometimes illogical traits in art and culture may be very beautiful, but when you encounter them in life, for dozens of years, they are disastrous for humanity.

I often wanted to tell my fellow artists, writers, and thinkers of many nations, that pictures and books are made not only with colors and words, but also with a pure conscience. Only a pure conscience of the soul can lead to roads of high and pure creativity. Millions of fallen and oppressed nations, especially the eternally oppressed Jewish people, weigh heavily on our conscience and can cause the decline of our art and culture. You don't need a genius to sense it. We ourselves must wage war against automatic and atomic evil in life and culture, against ruthlessness in life and culture, though it is disguised with ostensible "beauty" of form and pure "technique." And if you think it is a dreamer who says it, perhaps it is better. Dreams give rise to a new reality, but only dreams with their foundation in love and justice for all humanity.

And as long as we can prepare just strivings of life. I wish that we could breathe again, heal and calm our wounds, both physical and moral. May we find comfort in our stubbornness and in the spirit of our fallen, of those who left us, who beg us and pray for us. For we Jews live not only with the living but also with the dead. They protect us and fill us with new well-springs of love and resistance.

Art After the Holocaust
Speech at a banquet offered by the Jewish Writers Committee for the great Jewish artist, July–August 1947[65]

I am grateful for your friendship and sympathy. I hope that this is not a banquet for me but for Jewish culture. For me, this evening is an evening of culture, an evening of friends who think about and are concerned with the problems and tasks of culture. I would like to be a simple instrument in a cultural organism. I would like to stay in the shadow. Still, the most important reason I agreed to talk today is that I consider myself one of the many sons of the Jewish nation, a nation recently chased into the lime-pits and gas chambers by our inhuman enemies.

We came here to show that not all of us are dead and that we want to live and create. We came so that the eyes of our enemies, both the dead and those still living, can see that all their methods and theories of evil eventually turn on themselves. Although, alas, they destroy and darken the ideals of a better social life and the development of creativity. In the name of the dead and those who were burned alive, we say to our enemy that we shall neither forget him nor forgive him—neither in life nor in art.

We are not among those who think that the "poor" enemies of humanity must be helped and forgiven.[66] Forgiven, so to speak, for the sake of saving European culture.[67] If they, our enemies, have to save our culture—such a culture had better not exist anymore.

I think that the sins of the enemy cannot be expiated just by imposed agreements and their material reparations, but in baths of their own tears. The sins are expiated only in their own awakened consciousness. And only then can we talk about any relation to our culture. The doors of new creativity are locked for any ideas of evil and slavery.

At the same time, I am shocked that after the war we have gone through, we are still permeated with a feeling of war, which still continues. War is not only outside us, but in us, between us.[68] Tragically, the feeling that suffuses us does not foreshadow some new creation. No! These feelings, alas, do not fertilize our imagination, our art, but hang over us as in a stratosphere, an airless atmosphere, soulless, like a pall over our heads—under us and in us. It is strange, even terrifying, how the world of the prophets and all their baggage, the world of the great idealists and artists of humanity is apparently cut off from the present.

I am sad that I have so few words and feelings today that could lighten the gloom of our time, if only for myself. Especially when I occasionally see a kind of art that casts me even deeper into confusion and gloom.

When you see this art, you ask yourself: Have we gone through the whole cycle of hatred and evil, fostered, perhaps unknowingly, in the past by the same art?[69] If pictures can be painted automatically,[70] cold-bloodedly and heartlessly, under the motto: "Isn't it all the same?"—you may ask: Does this kind of art have any understanding of the tragedy of millions of people sent to the crematoria? When you see that those paintings don't project a simple sense of pity, but only carefully calculated combinations, cold-blooded, formal, and hollow, even though they are sometimes externally beautiful.

Many people thought, and perhaps many people still think, that artists sense the near and far future many years in advance and even break new paths. If today you can paint automatically, and coldly produce paintings with the words: "Isn't it all the same?"—we may ask: why were only 5 or 6 million sent to the crematorium ovens rather than 15, with the same words: "Isn't it all the same?" The very possibility of such comparisons and hypotheses is one of the signs of the tragedy of our spirit, art, and life.

It is good to see that the nations who remained alive, after unparalleled sufferings, still have a kind of understanding that keeps them alive, gives them some meaning. We may begin to see some glimmer of hope.

The world must not think that the Jewish nation is the same as it was before, in the ghettos. No! It is not the same. And it will no longer live in the ghettos. New, young people have emerged, and with them, a new consciousness. Just as a new art has emerged in the world, that is divorced from the old academism.

We would like to believe that the energy of Biblical epochs will be gradually revived by the young and the new. They will burn their light, and the fire of the crematoria will fan the flames more intense and hotter, and will also expand the shadow in the enemy's camp.

Nevertheless—as religion has aged naturally, humanity, striving toward a naked "power" in art, wants to use that naked power to evoke a "holiness" or a "superrealism" [iberrealizm] which we lack. People arm this mechanical power with mystical and speculative attributes.

Today it is clear to everybody that there is no longer an art with those melodies and harmonies of earlier centuries. Even the key to them is lost. The years of formalism in art could not revive them, and did not produce any important results (in that sense).

In the meantime, the so-called "powers" came to art with a lot of "automatism." Why this cult of the underlined power? Rembrandt, Van Gogh, El Greco, were not such a "power." Little boys ran after Cézanne. Van Gogh begged Paul Gauguin in vain for a continuous friendship until he cut off his ear. Rembrandt, unrecognized, "without power," closed himself in his Biblical vision. The Prophets and Christ himself walked barefoot, powerless, over the earth. Even Moses—lawgiver and stammerer—lay at the gates of the Holy Land—and couldn't enter.

But humanity was truly touched by the creators who touched its soul.

Art is not a newspaper editorial, nor does it have any special "mystique," as some think. It is a kind of plastic "texture."[71] It has as much "mystique" as a natural stone in the field. Such a similarity between the plastic texture of art and nature may amaze you. But what kind of similarity is it? For example, the texture of Cézanne's painting recalls the earth, the texture of Tintoretto's painting recalls dried blood. Rembrandt's texture—the rays of light. Vermeer of Delft recalls expensive stones, the texture of Van Gogh recalls objects and furniture of poor churches, after fiery sermons.

The art of our time chose to take the so-called "scientific," formal path. The so-called soul was declared to be just "literature." Until the soul actually evaporated, leaving behind just a pretty cover... No wonder the masses shied away from us, for lack of a spiritual contact.

Nevertheless, it is wrong to bring the masses closer to art by means of subject matter and illustrations. An artist is one who provides "texture" in his art—as natural as the earth. An expression of the soul, independent of the subject matter, which, by the way, must not be underestimated or neglected either.

So where is art today? Perhaps we now confront an artistic regression? In the Bible, in the chapter about Bezalel,[72] there is a description of the artist as a hakham-lev, he who has "wisdom of the heart." If an artist has "wisdom of the heart"—where is the art of his heart today?

The tragedy is that people approach the solution of life's problems as they enter an office. For this, as for art, you need talent. You must feel that the so-called religious ideology is perhaps not so obsolete as we are ourselves, as long as we ourselves are not steeped in awareness of the necessity to embrace each other and unite. You don't need talent to feel that you cannot paint a painting or write a poem without the feeling of love and unity with the whole nation and with all humanity. In the foundation of all the better revolutions—isn't there such a fantastic color of love and unity, which is like a yeast which opens up, liberates and develops all possible skills and elements. But where shall we get those talents?

Unity is the salvation. I would select those with less talent who are for unity over the so-called great talents who oppose it or make it peripheral. In light of history, the new Jews look ever more like partisans, not wandering like peddlers with a sack on their back over the roofs of cities. On their banners, in spite of their military countenance, we see words of unity and love.

Thus their fathers and brothers fought in the ghettos of Warsaw and other cities. And the "crucifixions" in the streets of Vitebsk and other cities take on the tragic look of the crucified Christ himself.

For thousands of year, the nation has been straying in the labyrinths of the world. It has actually been straying in its own head too. And there seems to be no God to hear their laments and see their pale faces. As the waves breathe in the depths of the sea, so does this poor nation breathe its own luck, and its breath disturbs both the world and itself.

But what did I say about the problems of our culture? I would like you to see why I don't dwell on details, for our problem today is one: unity. After the world tragedy, we must gather our remnants both physically and culturally. It is a time when we must start anew to lay bricks for the foundation—the foundation of art and culture. To shoulder the work with the greatest honesty. The [ideological] programs will emerge by themselves during and after work.

But as I talk—should I admit it—am also afraid. I sense that there is too much calm among us, people have got quiet and are hiding in corners. Again as long ago, I seem to be a little boy in my dark, unlit street,[73] stumbling into people in the evenings, and they are seared of my shadow. Let us light the lanterns and illuminate our faces. Let us start to count and re-count our assets.

May we soon become aware that, if we will create, we must unite today, using all means and opposing all those who are against it. The sharper we are aware of this, the sharper will be our art and culture, for the time of art behind closed doors is over.

At the base of art must lie the great plastic ideas. It is time to grant the carriers of real culture and real art a place of honor, a special place in the leadership of life—a life in which man seems to have lost his humanity. The war has destroyed not just cultural and material values, but also internal humanism. This was the "power" of evil and the calculated abstractions that left us lost and helpless. But there is another, creative power, a power of love and justice, realistic or super-realistic power. This means a power that can first save the human in the individual, and then rebuild the ruined cities and countries.

But why, when I speak thus, do I feel that someone is whispering in my ear: "You are spinning fantasies, you're talking in a dream." And immediately fall into a world where you don't know whether you are alive or not. I feel my parents and great-grandparents, quiet and honest folks, coming to console me and walking above me. I see the shadow of my bird flying toward me—asking me to stop my dream in the flow of my words.

I do not count my years anymore. Their dust makes my eyes gray. Sometimes I feel that we must put aside our brushes and pens for a while and call the heavens flowing quietly above us. But we can achieve this "power" when we are all together—and only then would you like to give your own years and your own art to the people and to everyone.

For the Slaughtered Artists: 1950

The poem was published as an introduction to an album-almanac, *Undzere Farpaynikte Kinstler* ("Our Martyred Artists"), edited by Hersh Fenster, Paris 1951. It is a memorial book for eighty-four Jewish artists who lived in France and were killed by the Nazis. There is a short biography of each artist and sample reproductions of their work. An additional list of 138 Jewish artists from Poland, Hungary, and Czechoslovakia, who lived in Paris and perished, is appended.

Did I know them all? Did I visit
their atelier? Did I see their art
close up or from afar?
Now I walk out of myself, out of my years,
I go to their unknown grave.
They call me. They pull me into their grave—
me—the innocent—the guilty.
They ask me: Where were you?
—I fled...

They were led to the baths of death
where they knew the taste of their sweat.
Then they saw the light
of their unfinished paintings.
They counted the years unlived,
which they cherished and waited for

to make their dreams come true—
not slept through, overslept.
In their head, they sought and found
the nursery where the moon, ringed
with stars, promised a bright future.
They young love in the dark room, in the grass,
on mountains and in valleys, the chiseled fruit
doused in milk, covered with flowers,
promised them paradise.
The hands of their mother, her eyes
accompanied them to the train, to the distant
fame.

I see them: trudging alone in rags,
barefoot on mute roads.
The brothers of Israels, Pissarro and
Modigliani, our brothers—pulled with ropes
by the sons of Dürer, Cranach,
and Holbein—to death in the crematoria.
How can I, how should I, shed tears?
They have been steeped in brine—
the salt of my tears.
They have been dried out with mockery, and I
lose my last hope.

How should I weep,
when every day I heard:
the last board is torn off my roof,
when I am too tired to make war
for the piece of earth
where I rested,
where I will later be laid to sleep.
I see the fire, the smoke and the gas
rising to the blue cloud,
turning it black.
I see the torn-out hair, the pulled-out teeth.

They overwhelm me with my rabid
palette.
I stand in the desert before heaps of boots,
clothing, ash and dung, and mumble my
Kaddish.

And as I stand—from my paintings
the painted David descends to me,
harp in hand. He wants to help me
weep and recite chapters
of Psalms.
After him, our Moses descends.
He says: Don't fear anyone.
He tells you to lie quietly
until he again engraves
new tablets for a new world.

The last spark dies out,
the last body vanishes.
Calm, as before a new deluge.
I stand up and say farewell to you,
I take the road to the new Temple
and light a candle there
before your image.

Paris 1950

Words in Jerusalem
Bezalel Museum, June 1951[1]

Chagall arrived in Jerusalem for his first, major exhibition in the State of Israel in the second half of June 1951. The exhibition traveled in four museums, starting in the Bezalel Museum (precursor of the Israel Museum) in Jerusalem. There can be no doubt about Chagall's great excitement on this visit.

Surrounded by my paintings, it is agonizing for me to speak not just with colors, but also with words. Do you think my halting words could add any explanation for either of us? For me, there are things and words here in Jerusalem that overshadow everything else.

It is Eternity, hovering here, hiding in the folds of our clothes, creeping into our soul. The air that filled the hearts of the war heroes[2] who had no weapons, who fought almost with their bare hands, who strove to take back our historical destiny after 2000 years. Stones are scattered here like chunks of flesh, and the dust, like the sand, is a remnant of our ancient forefathers.

So I came here, into a ready-made country, won by the hands of your children, bringing only the tears and smiles of our other forefathers in the Diaspora, who seem to leap off the paintings, kiss you, and wish you *mazl-tov.* And to my greatest happiness and amazement, my painting matches your faces and the same stones. I don't know why. I look at you as you look at me. I always look at myself. Perhaps that's why everything amazes me, and more than everything—my Jewish people, whose Bible made me a Jew.

And my parents, your parents surrounded me in the *Heder,* and when my rebbe held this Bible in his hand—I swam on clouds and felt why life was worthwhile. Art became my easiest and hardest road to the sky. Through the Bible—to you, to the world. And, with the years, I get tragically enmeshed among you, so that, to the last drop of my years, I shall flow and melt in the eternal Jewish river like a light for our future, for us and our children, and to enhance our heritage through Jewish art—for ourselves and for the world.

Now, to shift to reality... What could I say about art, if asked. It is simple: there is good art and bad art, as there is a good voice, or no voice at all. Sometimes I think: did I study? Where and with whom? And perhaps I walk at night to the field and look at the stars. I stretch my arms—and I fly, begging: "take me"... I see colors—blue, black, green, violet—all most precise in nature—they are in their full measure.

What shall I do? On my desk and on my shelf, the Bible and the Song of Songs. They are permeated by the same stars—From whom and where should I study art?

At long last, I want to walk outside and stop the first worker and peasant I meet. I shall look into his eyes, at his hands—to learn art. They are like trees, stones, pure and broad. And when you think of the great artists, such as Chardin, Tintoretto, Le Nain, Van Gogh, and many others—you must sense, where actually was their art school?

Our Jewish Academy must go through the hearts of the Jewish people and merge with our past and future.

To be an artist, to feel and understand the other—what do I feel and what do I understand? Perhaps I don't understand myself. And sometimes you think you live far away from the world. But, on the contrary, I am in the same world as in a bathtub. If I live, as it were, far from myself—then I live inside myself. I seem to live inside every good person, and therefore I am not lonely or sad. Only art remains difficult, with every year of my life—harder and harder.

As an answer to all the trends of art history in our time—I thought about my people. When there was Impressionism—I thought about Vitebsk;

when there was Cubism—I remembered my grandfather, who would sit on the roof and watch the city burning, or would just dream. I did not make pictures like a professional for walls. But I talked with my people, my roots, in an impossible and airy plastic language. As in a distant dream, yet close by. Then came Expressionism, later Surrealism. For only the last grade of freedom moves mountains. The freedom from yourself and from all that is in yourself and in you—this is the brightest and most transparent color, which alone can bring the soul to its highest expression.

Thus, you can approach art with light hands, with bare understanding, with trite fashionable theories. It is rarer than gold and pearls. But here, in this holy Land, I don't want to talk too much about art, or about my art.

I want to thank you for the great honor accorded me by the people, the government, the State, to come and appear before my brothers—the fighters—at the birth of the new Land. I would like to thank the former Minister of Culture Zalman Shazar for his invitation, the [Foreign] Minister Moshe Sharet for opening this exhibition in the Bezalel Museum, my friend the artist and Director of Art Mokady, the Committee of the Museums in the Land for organizing all the exhibitions in the Land, My friends Narkis, Shiff, the management and secretaries of the Bezalel Museum for the splendid organization of the exhibition, which gave me so much joy, and which closes today.

I thank you all for your sympathy and love. I hope that all this, along with the sky and the earth of the Land, will give me strength to continue, develop, and justify my life for the Jewish people.

To Israel
On My Exhibition in Tel Aviv, July 19, 1951[3]

I left, fled [the Jewish world in Russia] to the worlds of art, not to see a life with injustice surrounding me. But I calmed down when I saw your heroism, and for that it is worth living. This is my first impression, descending onto the Biblical earth. It is such a pleasure to come to you, after having gone first through the old Bible, then through the fields and mountains of our long Exile, which shone with such sadness until the last, heroic resistance. And finally to come to you here in a new State.

The Bible caught my imagination, for it is the highest form of idealism and art. Your struggle is the continuation of the Biblical spirit. To be a Jew means to have the honor of continuing the Bible tradition, this Bible, which the whole world adopted, and every Jew has to create in his own manner, to recreate this earth as an example of art and culture and a style of life.

There are struggles as pure as great art. But such struggles are rare. There are struggles demanding mountains of ammunition, weapons, and ornate propaganda. But rare are those struggles where you feel the presence of that very small thing that makes the difference between great art and small art, the thing called belief. For a Jew, there is nothing nobler than sacrificing his life for such an idealistic struggle and for the earth where the elements of justice and belief were born. And I dream of the day when this spirit of idealism and purity will impel humanity everywhere to conduct its battle for justice, and thus we will perhaps emerge from the epoch of "fear."

To win in the field of art and culture, you need a great spirit and a great form. If the form is authentic it shows there is a great spirit. For 2000 years, the form of life of the Jewish people was perhaps not up to their spirit. For the Jewish people was locked in ghettos. I know that there are many Jews who think that our land and our strength are only in our spirit— a kind of moral country. But I am sad thinking that the dream of our parents and our children may not become a reality. I am for the internationalism which will arrive some day. But every tree has to have its roots in its own earth, and only such a tree can give fruit of international quality.

My entire art consists in that, that I love with all my heart my Jewish people, represented for me by my father and mother. That means, your fathers and mothers too. They taught me art, Jewishness, how to behave in the world. My art is connected to the books I saw on the desks and cabinets in the synagogues, touched them with pale hands. All my colors— are the coloring of my parents. Pink, violet, green and blue—the colors that touched me so deeply when I watched my Bella and her girlfriends from near and far. Their skin and color are perhaps the same as Rachel's, Rebbeca's, and Leah's.

For a long time, I searched for my native city. But she exists no longer except in my paintings. [I wandered] from one country to another. And now I swam up to you, here in Israel. You also seem to be part of my palette, heroes of my paintings whom I would like to paint again—to admire your conduct in the battle for justice, not just for yourselves but for the world. I am sure you will demonstrate your life in culture and philosophy, rebuilt on the sands of the Biblical earth. They must let us. The youth will do it. Outside of the philosophy of our Bible and the prophets, and all other countries, great and small, that were inspired by them—the youth has nothing to copy for themselves.

Open your heart. The truth is in it. No Hitler can wipe out the spark of love inside you. You know what you want. And what you want—is not to deprive others of their freedom and not to kill the innocent. You want to grant life to yourselves and right to life for others, in friendship and peace. You want to raise your children on your own piece of earth. But even when we are disturbed in our way, you will burst in fire not just with weapons. But also with your soul, which is stronger than numbers, weapons, iron, and stone. Two thousand years in Exile have strengthened your body and soul.

It is enough to look into your eyes. The world begins to believe. The world, struggling in fear and doubt for tomorrow, wants to love children, freedom, and art, as a new religion. Here, in this Land, the engraving in Moses' Tablets sometimes shows that Love is the foundation of life, progress, and creation.

Farewell to Israel
July 20, 1951[4]

A few hours before embarking on the ship Kedmah, I hasten to express my feelings toward all of you for the warm reception that you, my brothers, gave me.

I thank the government of our heroic state for the invitation which gave me the opportunity to see all that I as an artist was destined to feel and see in this land after 2000 years... I saw Judea, Sharon, the Galilee, Har Efraim, the Emek [Jezreel Valley], traveled almost through the whole land which is gradually removing the stones from its body and is covered with greenery and life. I saw the vibrant temporary tents, every day overflowing with thousands of rescued Jewish persons, who were uprooted and grow every day to be equal human beings.[5] I saw the heroic spirit in the Kvutzot, the schools, the military barracks and factories.

I saw the same clouds that traveled through the sky in Biblical times and now they are hovering with the same rhythm above the cities of Tel-Aviv,

Haifa, Jerusalem and other villages, and cast a shade full of promise and prayer... A voice from somewhere tells us that it is worth continuing to fight, notwithstanding all difficulties. To fight for our sake and even for the sake of the neighboring peoples—together in a cultural, social, and peaceful contact.

I thank you for your interest in my art which I produced in the Diaspora with my trembling soul and hand, but never stopping to dream about our origins, our roots and soil. And for that reason I closely observed the problems of culture and art that are challenging the new land.

I saw the importance of developing a true Jewish architecture, harmonized with nature [crossed out: with properly matching material].

—the importance of planting here and there such temples, buildings, spots, or *Hekhaley omanut* ("Temples of Art,") as drawing points which will remain in history, as they exist in other cultural countries; so that, as in the Renaissance, the architecture will flow together with all other arts as a whole symphony.

—the importance of the treasures buried in every piece of the earth, which some call archeological treasures, but essentially those are real works of art that must be uncovered and can fill a whole national Louvre in Israel.[6] The development of Jewish art as well as the youth and thousands of tourists are waiting for it, to see the connection between the old and the new creative possibilities.

—the importance of a central art authority, made up of several pioneers, who have proved their pioneering work and their understanding. The society and other institutions in the land will have to accept their exclusive authority.

—the importance of a central academy, not in the sense of academies in other countries, but as a focus of Jewish atmosphere, so that young and old will not be drawn to other countries where art exists fitting their own traditions but not fitting for Israel.

—the importance of developing and building the museums of the country in various cities with a central national museum at the head.

I feel that all these factors and others which I encounter here in the Land are important for the development of the new state so that it could create and live not only normally but would justify its *spiritual drawing power* also for other countries which look and will look to Israel as a cultural, spiritual center. Of course, economic and other achievements are also important, but those one could see in other countries shining brighter.

I want to hope that I will have the strength to help and set foot on your soil again. Traveling over the mountains and fields, my heart was wrenched by helplessness and, in spite of the overwhelming beauty, stifled tears that you can hear at the Sea of Galilee where the summer heat reminds you of the turmoil before the entrance to the world's Garden of Eden. One wants to pray and build our share of happiness.

A. Sutzkever—Poet and Symbol
1950, 1955

Abraham Sutzkever (b. 1913) is one of the great Yiddish poets and a unique master of Yiddish verse. He spent his early childhood in Siberia during World War I; he returned to Vilna and was a leading poet in the "Yung Vilne" group of Yiddish writers in the 1930s. Active in the Vilna ghetto and a partisan in the forests, he wrote about the destruction and resistance of Vilna Jewry. In 1947 he immigrated to Palestine and, after the establishment of the state of Israel in May 1948, he founded the prestigious Yiddish literary quarterly *Di Goldene Keyt* (*The Golden Chain*), where Chagall published all his Yiddish writings: poems, essays, autobiographical chapters, letters. Chagall illustrated Sutzkever's masterpiece *Siberia* and the book of poetry *The Fiddlerose*, and corresponded with Sutzkever almost until the end of his life.

SIBERIA (1950)[7]

I consider it a great privilege to write about Sutzkever, for his name will shine among the figures symbolically linked with Vilna and Vitebsk, those heroic souls filled with powerfull imagination. Sutzkever is as dear and near to me as a brother, and he is particularly precious to me as a Yiddish poet, who created lines and forms with which he has reached out to the greatest heights of the Jewish soul.

We had not yet met personally when he approached me with the request to illustrate his poem, *Siberia*. Of course, I put all my other work aside at once, and set myself to tackle his world of Russian Siberia. Filling it in with dots and lines and shades and light, I wanted to show him and his friends[8] my love and respect for what they have done: they have raised high our Jewish banner and our Jewish honor.

The time has not yet come to assess the role of the Sutzkevers, the men of the Resistance; nor of Sutzkever the poet, whose poetry is not just Jewish; it is Jewish poetry of a new kind, modern in manner and subject matter, and free from the usual limitations of our poetry. As such it is distinct and outstanding. As an art form, his poetry appeals to the eye not only to the intellect, yet it avoids the pitfall of formalism.

When later Sutzkever visited me at my home in Vence, he tried to convey to me something of his life in the Vilna Ghetto. Listening to him I thought that I was listening to a boy of thirteen, with a pale face, from whose mouth sprang tongues of red flame. He spoke of his deeds which at one and the same time seemed to be illuminated and darkened by shreds of shadows born from a cold and broken moon, which envelop our ancient Jewish soul but cannot cover our catastrophe. When he told me of how he had prepared to jump from the high ghetto-wall opposite the church, drops of sweat appeared on his face across a thorny road they reach to the light. It is the same with his best poems—across a thorny road they reach to the light.

When the Jewish State received Sutzkever as "Jewishly" as it did, it also extended its hand to Yiddish literature beyond the confines of Israel.[9]

Considering such Jews as Sutzkever, I would wish us all to find within ourselves, now and in the future, our inner Jewish strength to preserve and to cultivate our purity of soul, which alone can and must lead us towards genuine human ideals. It alone has been in the past, and must be in the future, the basis of art, of social life and of culture, and only for its sake is our life worth living and our art worth creating.

POET AND SYMBOL (1955)[10]

I am happy to be among Jews and greet my friend and poet Sutzkever, who is not only a great poet, but also a symbol of that tragic and heroic time when our people still lived in their old homes. He was among those who, in the locked-up ghettos, fevered and fought our enemy. His young eyes saw that reality which we didn't know in our youth. Therefore, his poems, no matter with what color they are painted or what they sing about, often take on that tragic tone of our yesterday. While we dreamed once upon a time about such fantastic, sweet fires and crumbling *khatas*,[11] he saw ugly man in his physical and spiritual mire.

Therefore, I feel a kind of obligation to Sutzkever and his friends the other heroes. Moreover, Sutzkever the poet is also often close to me. Pieces of his young poetry remind me of pieces of my Vitebsk streets, when I walked over them, over the roofs and chimneys, believed that, outside of me, no one lived in the city, that all the girls were waiting for me, that from the graves in the cemetery, the dead were listening to me, that the clouds and the moon turned with me into another street.

But there is no more Vitebsk nor Vilna, and together with them, the Yiddish language has shuddered, and what not? Only a distant sound remained, such an unclear taste on the tip of your tongue. Sometimes the familiar tombstone with its torn Torah scrolls appears from afar—the thin Yiddish poet and painter who writes and paints. For whom, for what?

But if Sutzkever saw the face of that last day, on a happy day he started a new day. He hovered over to the land of the Jewish natural dream, to the biblical land. He lives in Israel. I cannot help but recall here my old friend the national poet Bialik, walking around the streets of Tel Aviv like a prophet and suddenly, quietly, on the side, asking my little daughter and my wife (apparently, he thought women were closer to God...) to pray for him to be able to write poems—he had in mind the city of Odessa, where he had previously created his monumental poems...[12]

My dear friends, you feel that the time has come for us Jews to be born again. We are not a people that dies. And may your art attain even more the new shine we have recently seen on the faces of the "sabras," born in our land. May you find the harmony of yesterday and today. I know it is difficult to find such a balm to heal and renew our body and soul. Perhaps this is a good means: to let your own diamond shine and illuminate freely, if you have one; let the colors sink freely inside you if you are born with them. And the form of a world will follow us like a shadow, but the shadow is not a shadow, it is the Jew in us. It becomes ever clearer that the freer we are—the more Jew we are; and the more Jew—the more man we become.

We are stronger now, though smaller in number, and may our enemies understand little by little that it is superfluous and dangerous to touch us. For our strength is our internal truth, a truth like the purest hue of a painting, as freedom itself.

Art, poetry is built on such a fiery base. It envelops the man and the people. May you so Jewishly stream into our people as into a river, a river that flows into the sea of the world.

Art and Life

Lecture delivered at the Committee on Social Thought, University of Chicago, March 1958[13]

I do not know how to express my deep gratitude to my friend, Professor John Nef, for his very kind invitation to come to Chicago, am also very grateful to his colleagues, the professors of the University, and to you all, for inviting me and for the welcome you have given me.

I am happy to take advantage of this opportunity to come back to your country with its generous hospitality which I experienced once before.[14]

At that time, I found in America a special kindness, a feeling of youth. (I saw it with my own eyes, and without asking anything for myself.) I looked at your countryside, at the big trees, at the gray and blue clouds floating in the sky.

I saw this continuous motion, the coming and going of machines and people, in search not only of material welfare, but of an ideal unknown to me. Here, where so many people speaking different languages are mixed together and united in the same youthful aspirations.

Often, while working in my studio, I listened to [Dvořák's] "The New World Symphony" on the radio, a piece which an old composer dedicated to America. Every time I listened to it, I thought of you, and of my stay among you. What a happiness it would be for another artist and for you, if he should erect a monument to your new world of today and of tomorrow. And I thought of the future of this country and of its freedom.

About ten years ago, I came to Chicago, at the invitation of Professor John Nef.[15] I was his guest. At that time his charming wife Elinor was still with us.

I talked here, I gave you my ideas and my feelings. It seems to me that some among you now were at that time my listeners.

It was during the days of this last sad war, which many have called "la drôle de guerre"; days when, it must be admitted, we were much younger, but during which the sky was stormy, and when so many relatives and friends left us forever. Cities, houses, families vanished like smoke and I tried to bring back their images on my canvases.

However it was a time when we were all filled with an almost messianic hope. I remember our reactions, our dreams; our eyes were trying to catch something far away.

At the invitation of the Museum of Modern Art in New York and of numerous friends, I had left France, Europe, where the enemy was hunting us down and driving us out. I spoke here of Art in general, of Art in France, of my life, of our life. Fantastic dreams which appeared to be realities... I spoke of an unreality which is real, of a reality that is not of the earth, but that is nevertheless the only possible reality.

Then as now, I do not feel at ease when I have to speak. It seems to me that each word is nothing but a repetition. At times I think "That's enough." But, maybe, the smallest word, a simple gesture, a glance may bring the most important things to light, make them clearer and more understandable.

One thinks, "Hasn't enough been said already, during and since the war?" Yet we, the artists, in our own realm, have to say something in a certain way, to make people feel, see and hear all at once. However, isn't it preferable, in times of doubt, to keep silent?

We live in a period when, although so many things have been said, it seems that something has to be added. And this needs to be done at a time when all about you people can say: "Brother, I have understood."

It seems to me that only such moments provide the hour for perfect paintings, for the music so long dreamed of, and even for the unhoped for peace.

Truly, there is somewhere within ourselves, a fear of birth and death, of hate and even of love. Often one turns to the authentic lasting works in the history of Art, to see in them one's own fate. I think that it is never given us to see and to know, to its real depth, our own value.

Perhaps what I do is worth something. Perhaps it is worth nothing. Maybe later, much later, it will become something valuable, something significant for us. Or nothing. I live however with the illusion of having a clearer view into others.

A strange thought comes to me, for which I ask your forgiveness. It is the involuntary recall of a great name, Mozart's, for example. He created while playing, went from city to city, here and there, like any boy, he wrote light-hearted and worry-free letters. While Haydn's music, so great also, was listened to with so much respect, at Mozart's burial, three or four people only were present. And now, we cannot listen to his musical sonority without tears. This very perfection reminds us of happiness, youth, a child's smile, angels, the light of the sun and, alas, also death. But Mozart prepared for himself a magnificent funeral when he wrote his immortal Requiem.

This is why it hurts to see often this useless stream of colors, this voluntary stubbornness or this musical difference, this hard work and sweat. With all that, one goes away from something the nature of which one does not know. It is something which reaches beyond Art itself.

No, I do not intend to think negatively about a certain professionalism. I only have in view what prevents us from raising ourselves towards things more unknown than the stratosphere itself. Those unknown poles are ourselves in the world or the world within ourselves.

Basically, we resemble one another in our world, and, perhaps we have nostalgia, not for what we would like to know and for things outside of us, but for our own dream, for our own swing towards a certain revolution in our inner life which is the discovery of purity, of simplicity, of natural self, such as we find on the face of children or in the voice of the one we are used to call Divinity.

If, at times, we are sad, it is because we often give the predominance to what in us is cerebral, rather than to our hearts where is to be found the right coloring, that is to say the coloring of Love.

I have often been asked why, in the periods of different classifications of Art, I do not stress, or do so only lightly, my role in such and such a period, for instance during the cubistic period and before the surrealistic period. Such a question reminds me of the visit Apollinaire paid me, in my studio in La Ruche, back in 1912. Looking at the paintings I produced between 1908 and 1912, he pronounced the word "surnaturalism." Of course I was not aware that, fifteen years later, the surrealistic movement would start. I like to keep silent on that point, as well as on others, and to leave people free to think whatever they like. One does not consciously look for an ISM. It comes by itself. Unconsciously, since 1908, I have looked for another realism.

If someone sees in my art only a pleasure-seeking art, he is entitled to his opinion. He is also free to consider the illogical and psychic construction of forms and colors as another reality unwillingly transformed in a symbol.

But within myself, I know that I was not born simply to seek pleasure; it is true that I formally wanted, and without all ISMS, to find a psychic form, another reason and other plastic means for the Art of our times. Those are researches, but not into the relationship between tastes and artistic ways among other people in different periods. It was not a question of imitating or taking from them their elements, their writings, under the pretense of stylization, but only to listen at great length to the messages of those people and of those arts. Listening to one's own voice, to the voice of one's own conscience, to one's own feelings, only that maybe, will satisfy, will quench... This is my way quite apart from others of seeing things and of building without borrowing and without copying.

Not one single authentic art, not the Egyptian, nor the Assyrian or the Greek, nor the Mexican or the Negro, nor the Byzantine, nor the Art of Masaccio nor that of Giotto, are construed consciously, according to a cerebral or scientific method.

This so-called scientism began around the 19th century, above all with the impressionistic trend, in relation with the theory of colors put forward by the learned chemist Chevrelle. But if the impressionistic school had not the plastic genius of a Monet, this trend would have been a dead thing. And romanticism would have suffered a similar fate without the plastic talent of Delacroix and naturalism without Courbet's plastic talent.

People often ask me: "How do you explain that hurrying on the part of today's youth, and even the more mature, toward a certain trend of today's Art which, as a matter of fact, is not older than about fifty years? In our present social state, young people as well as older ones, have to force their way through to be accepted, and that at any cost...

The other sign of our times—of those last twenty years especially—is that they want to be, as we say, "a l'avant garde," they want to belong, as they put it, to a more advanced party. Through belonging to this school, to this party, they feel stronger and more secure. This is true, not only of the artists themselves, but of those surrounding them. It seems as if they need some sort of an identity card. And if those young people, those cluttering around them, find it more suitable to belong to a party in Art, it is because our time is above all a time for parties.

Nobody paid any attention to us. Moreover, we were so few, we the young people before 1914, that it would have been possible to number us on one's fingers.

Bonnard, to mention but one, left his circle very early and, one of the most modest, always stayed outside the schools and outside the parties. He was frightened by the realism which came up later. In his paintings, the forms which are presently the most fashionable can be found, without imitators being able to hide their poor pictorial "chimie."[16]

It is true that we very often see a certain fabrication, a certain haste, a fear. One looks behind, as in a race when one is afraid of being passed.

On the other hand, we see here and there so-called technical or mechanical proclamations in Art; one forgets that our human hands cannot compete with machinery. Neither can machinery fully replace the hands of a man: let's take simply the example of furniture manufactured by a craftsman and that which is machine-made...

The mechanical and scientific technique is precious when it is well put to use for living; but our organic capacity is always limited. Art is the work of the hands, alone.

We reject any divinity, we even speak of its fall; but we are making an error. We are looking for something which could take the place of this divine sense. We are coldly and mathematically busying ourselves trying to improve the material situation and the fate of mankind. But with all that, we destroy often in ourselves and in others, Love or the Divine, call it what you will.

Since it is impossible to create a painting without love, in the full sense of the word, no social construction can be made by men without that amount of love. That is why we are turning around in a never-ending circle.

Genius! Yes there is genius. To almost any century, perhaps, to each generation, has been given, at the time of its birth, by nature, a portion of this genius. But it is not given to me to know where are those sensitive spots in our lives, in our nature, which prevent their regular bloom. We can only dream of that ... In the meantime, we strive for bread and material comfort.

This is a strange thing: the more theoretically strong the artist is, like Leonardo da Vinci or Delacroix, the less clarity there is in his works. Their paintings are almost black, while with an unaffected man such as Fra Angelico, for example, the paintings shine today as if they had been painted yesterday.

I have sometimes painted in the darkness, without light; but aren't the colors the products of one's own soul.

And I repeat that only the presence of a purity, a pictorial and chemical purity, saves the schools in the history of Art and in the ISMS.

As I have already said, the realistic trend has been important because of the chemical resources of the inspired Courbet, while the romanticist trend had less importance on account of Delacroix being less inspired. Impressionism owes its importance to the plastic genius of Monet. One could, carrying on the comparisons, reach as far as our present times.

It is possible that, in general, the art of painting does not shine, nowadays, in such and such a trend of plastic Art. Do you expect a blade of grass, dewy in the morning, to remain fresh and glittering, if over it are passing hundreds of engines and many other things?

In such times of doubt, rage takes hold of you. One would like to leave for a desert where everything would be sweet, sensitive, filled with an untouched genius. One feels that, all of a sudden, the doors have closed in front of one. What can one do to gain the strength to open the doors of this inaccessible paradise, which however seems to be so near?

I grant that it is difficult to feel what I am saying, often, in a rather unobvious way... But I believe that one eye only is needed, in the same way that one ear is enough for musicality.

A canvas can be covered in many ways, geometrically—even by splashing;[17] in a figurative way or any other, but, at the end, it will be judged according to the distinction and the nobleness of the matter: the colors or the chemistry, as I call it.

Of course, I am not concerned here with artistic criticism. We speak different languages: my language is the eye, I do not cross the threshold of an exhibit hall if my eyes encounter an impossible chemistry. I do not cross the door of any trend if my eyes reject the chemistry of such and such a painting, of such and such a school.

It is not my business to draw a list of those plastico-chemical values. There are, for that job, specialists. I am a moon-rider bound to another paradise. I am neither a statistician nor an historian of Art. I am not a museum builder. I do not give advice in the business of painting. I am just a man, like the others, to whom his parents have given the gift of fresh air, of drinking pure water and of smelling the spice of the perfumes, of being without any mixing with other elements. That also, perhaps, should be given at birth, as well as a voice to sing.

I repeat—this is why I can walk by quietly, and pass any ISM, if, before anything else, I am not attracted chemically. I am not attracted by the ISM if from it does not come this eternal thing, which is always the same through the centuries, this distinction, that nobleness of the covering which enables you to foresee the content of the work.

It is indeed very pleasing to think that in America and in the whole world one has begun to acknowledge that. A Toulouse-Lautrec, for example, does he attract by his satire, his sarcasm? No, but by the distinction of his scale. One also begins to appreciate Gauguin: is it for his anarchy, for his departure for Tahiti? No, but for his magic coloring. The same thing is true with Seurat. Neither for his Neo-impressionism nor for his fight against Impressionism, but for his tone which is not earthly.

The great poet Verlaine said: "De la musique avant toute chose,"[18] i.e. music comes first. The same thing can be said about the chemistry of the artist.

A complete exhibit of canvases, from the most remote period up to the most recent ISM can be organized and presented to the public. The same canvases can even be hung upside down. It does not matter. What matters is their chemistry. After such a judgment, very few things will remain, alas, and their number will be as limited as the number of those who have the feeling for it.

Wouldn't it be necessary to set up a school for the amateurs as well as for the artists, with the sole purpose of recognizing the chemical qualities, away from all ISMS.

Chemistry does not lie in the vigor, in the palette or anything of that sort. The chemistry of Henri Rousseau, for example, in spite of the fact that he was too poor to afford colors and canvases of superior quality, can be compared to that of the famous painting *Les Pieta d'Avignon* even more so than Cézanne's could. Seurat's chemistry, Gauguin's chemistry can be placed next to Giotto's or even Masaccio's. After that, I leave it to the others to speak or to say nothing about their literary or ideological message, about their ISM which, surely, has a certain historical value but which results, once more, from their chemical power.

Over the years, I have been asked many questions. I really would like to be able to give them all a logical answer. By answering questions, one also learns how to live and how to work.

I think it would be interesting to report here a few typical questions posed to me by some students in Vence. They asked me questions about the genesis of a work. Why such a subject? Why such a technique? For what purpose? Subjective impression or objective reproduction? Both? To what extent?

My answer was: I do not choose; life itself chooses for me the natural technique.

What importance do you give to the drawing, to the painting? With what goal in mind? (Answer) I don't know.

Under what influence from other masters? What is Chagall seeking? (Ans.) What I look for: work as a medium to make life meaningful.

Do you paint a dream born in you all of a sudden, or is the colorful expression of that dream the result of an elaborate and organized vision? Has it ever occurred to you to re-transcribe a dream? (Ans.) Not a dream, but life itself.

Do you believe in work or in inspiration? (Ans.) We are what we are, as soon as we come into life.

What part has Surrealism played in your work? Have you completely rejected its impact on you? (Ans.) I went through the so-called Surrealism from 1908 on. Surrealism has existed as an ISM since 1925.

Does composition play a primary part in your painting? (Ans.) In pictures, there must be something of everything.

Do your dreams carry any weight in the realization of your canvases? (Ans.) I have no dreams.

In front of a landscape, are you more sensitive to the light or to the lines? (Ans.) Each landscape stirs in me an emotion, but that emotion is just as deep when I face a man or certain life events.

An intellectual asked me the following questions:

What is the relationship between Art and Life? (Ans.) Of course I can enjoy many things which are being accomplished in our life and in our present culture. And we cannot enumerate here all that is talked about in the newspapers ... If I was a sociologist, I could, eventually, throw light on that state of things using material motivations. Sometimes, one withdraws into oneself with sadness to avoid hearing, and to avoid seeing. And one thinks of such and such a prophet lying on the sand and prophesying for himself and for the passersby who were ready to listen to him.

He also asked me: Have the natural sciences taught me anything useful for my art? (Ans.) Art, in the last resort, is not something consciously scientific. An artist without his instinct is like a pendulum.

He also asked me: "Is religious faith necessary to an artist?" (Ans.) Art, in general, is an act of faith. But sacred is the art created above interests such as glory, fame or any other material consideration. We don't know exactly what kind of men Cimabue, Giotto, Masaccio, Rembrandt were. But very fortunate is the hour of our life when, facing them, we are moved to tears. For me, even Watteau is religious, with his flowers, his lovers, his bushes. If his paintings were placed in a religious temple, instead of being in the Louvre, the emotion felt would be even greater.

In the course of these last ten years, I have worked a great deal. Joy came to me in the form of [illustrated] books being published, and among them, the Bible. I have chosen to paint: to me it has been as indispensable as food. Painting appeared to me like a window through which I would fly away to another world. Speaking of that, you will excuse me for recalling the biblical image of Moses who, in spite of his stammering, was haunted by God so that he would do his duty. In the same way, we are all, in spite of our stammering, pursued by someone so that *we* will perform *our* duty.

I see again the poor house of my youth where, it seems to me, on the door and in the sky, until night, shone also a burning bush. But I was then only in the house of my parents. Around me there were, haunting me, the bustle of the household, my parents' worries, my life when I felt so lonely and saddened by my father's tiredness (my father fed and raised with difficulty his nine children[19]). My head started to turn at the sight of his calloused and chapped hands, of his worn-out look. Haunted by all that, I left by another way which is, maybe, the same way as my father's who, on looking then at my drawings, thought that they were a continuation of the wall.

Since that time, I have traveled a great deal. I have seen many countries, have taken different roads looking for colors, looking for light. I have thrown myself into a certain observation of ideas, of dreams. But along that road, I have come up against wars, revolutions, and all that goes with them ... But I also have met exceptional people: their creations, their charms, and their contact have often quieted me down, reassured and convinced me to carry on.

More clearly, more precisely, with the years, I have come to feel the relative righteousness of our ways, and the ridiculousness of anything that is not produced with one's own blood, and one's own soul, and which is not saturated by love.

Everything is liable to change in life and in Art and everything will be transformed when we pronounce, unconstrained, this word Love—a word which indeed is wrapped in an envelope of romanticism (but we do not have, for the time being, another word). In it lies the true Art: from it comes my technique, my religion; the old and the new religion which has come to us from far distant times.

Love should also be the basis of true politics which could bring real peace.

All the other things are a sheer waste of energy, waste of means, waste of life, of time, and can take us nowhere but to the limit which is close to disaster itself.

Art, without love—whether we are ashamed or not to use that well-known word—such a plastic art would open the wrong door.

What is color, what is painting? So few people know what it is. True art in painting is not reached when either the canvas or the picture, depending on the subject, is abstract or figurative; but how scarce are those who could answer that question.

Prophets have been but few in history. Artists, composers, authentic painters are likewise but few, and religion and Love, rare.

Let us rejoice whenever we see signs of this somewhere and let us try to feed that flame, for it is the source of true Art and of Culture.

There cannot be any plastic message or, indeed, any other message, without humanistic values or without what we often call Love-Color. Outside of that, there is no value whatsoever. Greatness is to be believed in only at that level. Thus Titian, in spite of his religious subjects, thus Gauguin, in spite of his anarchism, thus Monet, in spite of his belonging to the bourgeoisie of the time.

When we look at the first works produced by certain inquiring artists, it is striking to find that, if they do not reach a certain plastic level, as far as quality is concerned, it can be concluded that whatever they have rushed into in the hope of discovering later, something else, is likewise to be not up to par as far as quality is again concerned.

It was not the same with Van Gogh. His early works can be compared with certain of Rembrandt's. Cézanne's debuts, in spite of their affiliation with Manet's and Pissarro's, are important too; likewise Seurat's, Gauguin's and those of a few others.

We are living on this planet only, and all the signs of our life, of our behavior, are for this planet only. No cerebrality, however great, be it da Vinci's, Mantegna's, Signorelli's, Cézanne's or that of any other can kill the values and the essential reason of our life on earth, which is, basically, like the joy of a plant and its natural growth.

That's why I speak often of certain qualities measured as if they were pharmaceutical products, exactly weighed. Such is the measure of life. But what is that measure?

This goodness and this Love of which I am speaking are in my own terms color, light.

It is possible to be gifted in the handling of lines, even on the architectural level. But what is most important is the blood, and the blood is, for the artist, color. Color and all its distinctions are the pulses of the organism. Color is the pulse of a work of Art. The line, the architectural composition of the pictures may often look like the attributes of dummies. They can be lengthened, modified, distorted according to the mood. In my opinion it is simply unfair to call that drawing. But the best drawings are so-called unconcerned things, such as Rembrandt's. Those by Bonnard, for example, give the impression that he did not know how to draw and I have almost never seen any drawing by Monet.

The predominance of writing, of drawing, is the sign often of a certain weakness in the painting, of its lack of depth.

No speculation, no skeleton-like scheme can change the disposition and the flow of the born colors; thus a butterfly or a flower in its simplicity or its natural beauty.

I am often asked: what do you call color and its chemistry? The same can be said about color as is said about music: "The depth of color goes through the eyes and remains within the soul, in the same way that music enters the ear and stays in the soul."[20] It is interesting to remember Cézanne's words about Monet. He said: "Monet is an eye, but what an eye!" In the same way we can, very simply, seeing a piece of material over somebody's shoulders, gauge its quality, without considering the cut or the fashion... Thus the Greeks, the Ancients, wore their robes freely, without shaping them, so full of distinction were their tints, their qualities.

Everybody knows that life will end one day. But this is not a good reason for us to let destructive elements take the lead in us. The more we criticize and reject this life, after the manner of some philosophers, writers and artists, the less we live ourselves—the number of years counting for nothing, of course—and the less life we give the others through our works.

Life is indeed a miracle. We are parts of that life and we pass, the years adding to the years, from one stage to another stage of life.

When I came first to Paris, I was instinctively against the realism which I saw everywhere. Upon my return to France, at the end of the war, I had the vision of glowing colors, not decorative and screaming ones, and I rediscovered Claude Monet, with his natural source of colors.

Now I feel the presence of a color which is the color of Love.

Never will a man be able, technically or mechanically, to learn all the secrets of life. But, through his soul, he is bound to the world, in harmony with it even unconsciously. Let us not torture the world, our soul and the others.

I am ashamed at times to speak this way. But if you would read the Bible and the Psalms, you would find everything, even the best thesis on Art and on Life. I would not like to hear people say, while listening to me speaking of Love in the realm of Art, that I am pursuing a theological or social idea. No. Underlining those elements, with Love in mind, I have no ISM in sight. But, simply, just as during the ancient times or during the impressionistic period, color-light was emphasized, I underline, today, color/love exclusively, above all plastic and not literary.

In our times when a great deal is said about the decay of religion, Art itself is transformed into a stream of technicalities, in a matching series of ways and, in spite of all that, it does not have the strength to bring about a miracle, that is to say to give us in exchange another message.

Those techniques, those ways are parts of today's Art. Basically, it is the same ancient realism. Only, instead of copying all the accidents and details of faces, bodies, trees, objects, as the old masters did, one copies now, with less precision as a matter of fact, the different graffiti of the accidents, the details of materials, on the walls, on the pavements, in the streets, and even through the microscopes. But it is still the same realistic method.

I spoke before of this revolution we must accomplish within ourselves; it is only then we will see that it is not enough to knock at a closed door when in fact it is already open. Everything depends on us, on the genius which is in us.

What is genius? We think that we know what it is. But if we know it, why do we go in the opposite direction, why do we turn our backs to happiness? Where is the driving power, the will, this miracle which will lead us on this way if it is not within ourselves?

Nobody can be deaf, or blind to authentic Art. It is perhaps presently the only thing that should be looked at and listened to in order to bring life and culture to their fullness.

The Erasmus Prize[21]
Response by Marc Chagall, 1960

In 1960, Marc Chagall and Oskar Kokoshka were awarded the Erasmus Prize of the European Cultural Foundation in Copenhagen, in the presence of Prince Bernhard of the Netherlands, who read the address to Marc Chagall, and the Prime Minister of Denmark. Sir Kenneth Clark read an address entitled "Two Human Painters in the Age of Abstraction."

Your Majesty, Royal Highnesses, Excellencies, Ladies and Gentlemen.

First, I should like to thank you all, and especially H.R.H. Prince Bernhard, for your kind words and your warm welcome.

I should also like to thank you for having founded the Erasmus Prize, which bears witness to the idealism of those who, together with the members of the Fondation Européenne de la Culture, wish, in our troubled times, to encourage people whose lives are spent in search of an ideal.

I think it was a very happy idea to have named this prize after Erasmus, who was himself an idealist, thus commemorating his name and his thinking.

I thank you for your choice, and am deeply appreciative of the honor you have done me.

On a day like this, I cannot help reflecting on the future of Art.

A few weeks ago, I was in Italy. All of you, I am sure, have seen there works by Titian, especially the "Descent from the Cross" and the "Miracle of San Lorenzo." How strange it is to think that Titian and Erasmus were almost contemporaries.

Except for Rembrandt, I wonder whether there was ever a greater master, and at the same time a greater man, than Titian, who is so much in keeping with our own period and our own artistic preoccupations.

For, after so many revolutions in the plastic arts, do we not seem to be orphans, lost in a planetary solitude?

Fifteen years ago,[22] when I returned from America, to which I had emigrated, I was amazed to discover Claude Monet. He fulfilled my dreams, for in him I found a source of chemically-pure color that proceeded from the soul.

But it seems to me now that he indulged in a brilliant form of plastic chemistry; as Cézanne put it: "Monet is no more than an eye—but what an eye!"

Today, when the world, like ourselves, seems to grow old, we are looking for some deeper meaning. In the course of our search, we come upon Titian, a man who has been neglected by the fashion of the past two or three centuries. He seems to us to resemble nature, and his grandeur is written upon his face. He is like a God. A child of nature, he dedicated his art to nature.

In fact, when we are in a mood of doubt, we can always find aesthetic satisfaction in contemplating the Art of nature herself. But if we turn to gaze on the creations of man, we hope to find there the cosmic prolongation of nature.

How bitter we become if we find all kinds of things in that creation, but fail to be permeated by the natural chemical grandeur, the majestic rhythm with which Titian expresses himself.

It is the meaning of Art and of life that communicate a certain tranquility, a feeling of love. I do not forget that, beside the Titians I saw, were hanging a Crucifixion by Cimabue, frescoes by Giotto, Masaccio, and Carpaccio.

One of them heroically freed himself from Byzantinism, while another began to pave the way for Realism.

Titian quietly took his place in the Renaissance, which, I may say in passing, forced upon him the humanistic ideas of the period.

But these are mere historical details. What links them is man and nature.

All those who, like Tintoretto, and even Michelangelo and Caravaggio, did something to accelerate the tranquil and natural greatness of the human race, have now withdrawn into a certain twilight.

I have always thought, and even more so latterly, that man is theoretically weaker than, let us say, God Himself. But if man "sings," he is comparing himself to God in some way.

Of course, there are various keys of song: there are Leonardo da Vinci and Bach, and there are Mozart, Watteau and Schubert. There are Rembrandt, Vermeer, and Titian, or, in our own day, the Douanier Rousseau and Paul Gauguin.

It is exceptional for theoretical discoveries to be completely satisfying; in the long run, mankind has rarely rejoiced over them.

One feels like saying, in the silence: "Let us be simple, let us not hide our faces." But it is very difficult to be simple.

One would like to say to oneself, again: "Our unhappy life on this earth is not a masquerade, so there is no need to wear a mask. Those who do are wasting their time."

We cry at birth and we weep when we leave this life.

The only thing to us is to be as simple as a tree or, as Mayakovsky, the Russian poet, said: "simple as a cloud."[23]

It is up to us to shorten the duration of all types of inflation, be they cultural, artistic, social. or physical. It is up to us to bring joy to the hearts of the coming generation and those who wish to live worthily.

For in this inflation, that had lasted so long, there is neither love, nor religion, nor values, nor freedom, nor peace: there is nothing but an existence of frightened sleep-walking.

Sometimes one feels it better to be a voice in the wilderness than one of those multitudes who howl their approval from fear of seeming late for something.

"Late for what? For whom?"

But they forget, not to be late for themselves.

Let us not play at being geniuses, pretending that, before us, the world did not exist.

Mankind, today, is living in fear and even in a certain apathy.

In our childhood, we did not know that fear; and our father's house, despite the family's slender means, was intact.

Today, the family roof has, as it were, been torn apart for the children. We parents coddle our children, and even spoil them.

What effects will this have on Art and Culture?

Many people have quite consciously fled in Art from the visible world, or have deformed the world until it is unrecognizable. The result is a total divorce.

It is no excuse to say that the visible world with all its forms of humanism is going bankrupt unless man—God help him!—ruins Nature for a long time to come.

Why, then, should a part of nature—that is to say the human race—be going bankrupt?

As far as I can see from looking about me, the animals are *not* bankrupt!

Truly, man can be brought to despair by the realization that cultural and scientific discoveries do not exclusively better the circumstances of his life, but may also frighten him, or even destroy him for the so-called benefit of future generations.[24]

Truly, man can be brought to confusion by foisting an outlook upon him, or even a new ideology; not because of its moral strength, but simply by show of force.

Truly, man can be saddened by the sight of one or other of his fellow human beings behaving unworthily.

But I have no wish to continue with these themes, which could lead us very far. May I, in closing, express a wish? Let us remember the life of Erasmus, whose memory we honor here with the members of the Erasmus Prize Foundation—that seeker after truth who dreamed of a better life for men: let us, like him, express our belief in the genius of Man.

On Ceramics
1952[1]

Ceramics are the work of the hands and the heart. The theories only come afterwards, when the work is done. They result from the work, but they are not its source... The ceramic art is nothing more than the alliance of fire and clay. If what you offer is good, the fire will give you something in return; if it is bad, everything is smashed, nothing remains and there is nothing you can do about it. The test of fire is pitiless.

*

These few pieces, these few samples of ceramics are a sort of foretaste: the result of my life in the south of France, where one feels so strongly the significance of this craft. The very earth on which I walk is so luminous. It looks at me tenderly, as if it were calling me. I have wanted to use this earth like the old artisans, and to avoid accidental decoration by staying within the limits of ceramics, breathing into it the echo of an art which is near, and at the same time distant. It suddenly seems to me that this earth, so radiant, is calling from afar to the deaf earth of the city where I was born—Vitebsk.

But this earth, just as the craft of ceramics, does not give itself easily. The fire returns my efforts at the oven door sometimes gratifyingly, sometimes in a grotesque and ridiculous form. The fire and the earth remind me only too well that my means are modest.

Marvelous examples of this Western and Eastern art often occur to me. During these threatening times, one is especially eager to attach himself to this earth, to mingle with it.

Whether I am speaking of ceramics, of engraving, of sculpture, or of painting, all my words are centered on the material, which, because of its very characteristics, is abstraction, provided it maintains a certain aloofness. But even if this material were imbued with an excessive sensitivity, is it not better to devote oneself to this, rather than to be lost in a world where automatism and prideful insensitivity prevail?

On Engraving and Lithography
1960[2]

It seems to me that something would have been lacking for me if, in addition to color, I had not, at one time in my life, worked at engraving and lithography.

Already, in my earliest youth, when I first began to use a pencil, I looked for this thing that would be capable of spreading out like a great river towards inviting, distant shores.

When I held in my hand a lithographic stone, or a copper plate, I believed I was touching a talisman. It seemed to me that I could entrust them with all my joys, all my sorrows... Everything that has crossed my path, throughout the years: births, deaths, marriages, flowers, animals, birds, poor working people, my parents, lovers at night, the Prophets from the Bible, on the street, in my home, in the Temple, in the sky. And, as I grow older, the tragedy of life that is inside us and all about us.

When I handle all these tools of the trade, I feel the difference between lithography, engraving, and drawing. It is possible to draw well and yet not possess in one's fingers the lithographic touch; this is a matter of feeling. Not to mention the fact that, in general, there should emanate from each line a particular spiritual quality that has nothing in common either with "knowhow" or with knack.

But I shan't go into this at length.

It is real suffering for me to speak of myself. And yet my friends the publishers have asked me to say a few words. But for me, it's the same thing as walking on water...

The longer I live, the less I like to talk about myself.

Not because I have "nothing to say," but because I have nothing I want to underline, nothing to ask for. Nor shall I try to persuade, especially in a book that contains works of mine.

However, I should like to take this opportunity to express my cordial appreciation to all those who first commissioned me to make engravings and lithographs.

In the past, in Berlin, they were Paul Cassirer and Walter Feilchenfeldt. Then, in Paris, Ambroise Vollard.

Later, Tériade, with whom I have made an entire series of publications, as also with Aimé Maeght.

I should mention too the firm of Fernand Mourlot, which took me into the encouraging atmosphere of its ateliers, where I found such devoted collaborators as Charles Sorlier, Georges Sagourin, and many others.

But before putting the final little black dot at the end of this preface, I say to myself that, in reality, I owe this spirit, which I have tried faithfully to mirror, to the training received both in the schools and academies I attended; that is to say, to my home and to my parents.

The Stained Glass Windows in Jerusalem
At the Opening of the Synagogue with Chagall's Stained Glass Windows in the Hadassah Medical Center, Jerusalem 1962[3]

"A stained glass window has a different fate from a painting. Because of the setting, the eye does not look at it in the same way as a collection of paintings. The eye of a man at prayer is simply part of his heart. For me a stained glass window is a transparent partition between my heart and the heart of the world. Stained Glass has to be serious and passionate. It is something elevating and exhilarating. It has to live through the perception of light. To read the Bible is to perceive a certain light, and the window has to make this obvious through its simplicity and grace."
—Marc Chagall

How did the air and earth of Vitebsk, my hometown, along with thousands of years of Diaspora blend with the air and earth of Jerusalem?

How could I have known that it was not only my hands and colors that would lead me in my work, but also the dear hands of my father and mother and of others and yet others, with their mute lips and closed eyes who whispered behind me as if they wanted to take part in my life.

It seems to me that your tragic and heroic resistance movements in the ghettos, and your war here, in this country, have merged with my flowers and animals and fire-colors...

Insofar as our age refuses to see the full figure of the world and is content with a very small part of its skin, my heart aches when I observe this figure in its eternal rhythm, and my will to go against the general stream is strengthened.

Do I speak like this because, with the advance of life, the outlines surrounding us become clearer and the horizon appears in a more tragic glow?

It seems to me that the colors and the lines flow out, like tears from my eyes, though I am not crying. And do not think I am talking here in a moment of weakness. On the contrary, the more years I pile up, the more certain I am of what I want and what I say.

I know that my life's path is eternal and brief. And I learned, back in my mother's womb, to walk that path more out of love than out of hatred.

The thoughts have nested in me for many years, since the time when my feet walked on the Holy Land, when I prepared myself to create engravings of the Bible.[4] They strengthened me and encouraged me to bring my modest gift to the Jewish people—that people that lived here thousands of years ago, among the other Semitic peoples.

And what is now called Religious Art I created when I recalled also the great and ancient creations of the surrounding Semitic peoples.

I hope that, thereby, I stretch out my hand to the neighboring peoples, their poets and artists, to whom human culture is dear.

I wish to express my thanks to the Women of "Hadassah" and especially to Mrs. Miriam Freund, for choosing me for this work, to the atelier of Jacques Simon, Charles Marq and Brigitte Simon, where I worked, for their great devotion, and also to the Government of Israel for inviting me here.

I have concluded two years of labor, creating these twelve stained glass windows for this synagogue in Jerusalem. My hope is that the synagogue will please you and that it will overflow with harmony even as I have prayed.

I saw the mountains of Sodom and the Negev; the shadows of our Prophets in their garb the color of dried bread, shine from those mountains. I heard their ancient words...

In their words they marked the path for behavior on the earth and pointed out the moral essence of our life.

I draw hope and courage from the thought that my modest work will remain on their—your land.

A Crisis of Color
1963[5]

My friend, Professor Nef, asked me to come to you, listen to you, and say a few words to you.

In truth, I would have preferred to listen to you, for all my life I have preferred to listen to what others say, to learn something from them, as far as I can.

Not for the first time do I come to you, for it seems to me that the idea of your association deserves much interest.

Rationally, I should have stayed at work in my atelier, for this is the main goal of my life, when I am daring enough to hope that work not just for myself. But it is good to think that people in our time come together to share their thoughts about the main goals of life.

What can be more moving in our society, on this planet, than the striving to listen to the human heart, to hear in it the pulse of a world, the sighs and the dreams.

For hundreds and thousands of years, it was morally easier for a man to live. He had this or that moral ground, deeply anchored in himself. His life and his creative activity were the deep and precise result of his world-view. We see it clearly sealed in the works of distant epochs of the past.

Gradually, however, in the course of time, those old conceptions became powerless to inspire a living breath in people and fill them with an internal life, not only for their creativity but simply for their life.

I am not sad at all when I speak about it, and I'm not a pessimist. There are no such forces that could influence me not to believe anymore in the human personality, for I believe in general in the greatness of nature.

But I also know that human will and human behavior often result from cosmic influences of that nature, just like the unfolding of history and human destiny. Yet we cannot refrain from always asking the same question: why are we so sad in recent years?

The more and the more boldly man liberates himself from his chains, the more man feels alone, and among the masses he is left alone with his destiny.

As always, however, I shall shift to art.

With Impressionism, a window opened for us. A bright rainbow rose on the horizon of our world. And though this world was different and more intensively colored, it seems to me that, on the whole, it was narrower than the Naturalistic world of Courbet, for example. Just as the Naturalism of Courbet was, in his time, narrower than the world of Romanticism of Delacroix. And the world of Delacroix was more declamatory and narrower than the Neoclassical world of David and Ingres. I don't want to go on...

After Impressionism came the Cubist world which led us into the geometrical underground of things. Afterward, abstraction led us into a world of tiny elements and matter. Thus we see the diapason and the size of the stage growing narrower and narrower. Going on, you have the impression that you are going toward a constantly progressive shrinking. What did happen? Let us see what is authentic in our life-baggage.

The world belongs to us from the moment we are born, and it seems to us that we are prepared for it from the very beginning of our life.

For about two thousand years, a reservoir of energy has nourished us, supported us, given us a certain content in life. But in the last century, a crack has opened in that reservoir. And its elements have begun to fall apart.

God, perspective, color, the Bible, form, lines, traditions, the so-called humanistic theories, love, loyalty, family, school, education, the Prophets, and Christ himself.

Perhaps I was once skeptical? I made pictures topsy-turvy. I decapitated my characters, cut them to pieces, and in my paintings they hovered in the air. All this in the name of a different perspective, a different construction of paintings, and a different formalism.

And gradually our world appeared to us as a small world where we small people hover in the air, grasping onto the small elements of our nature, until the moment when, through very small elements of nature, we approached the atom itself.

This so-called scientific control of nature—doesn't it limit the source of poetry, doesn't it empty the soul? Doesn't it deprive man of calm, even of purely physical rest? Doesn't all this deprive the organism of the moral concept of life and creation?

In recent years, I have often spoken about the chemistry, about authentic color, and about the painterly matter as a barometer of authenticity.

A particularly sharp eye can see that an authentic color and an authentic matter contain in themselves every technical possibility as well as the moral and philosophical content.

If there is a moral crisis, there is also a crisis of color, of the moral material, the blood, and of the elements of the word, of sound, of all the components of art and life as well.

And even if you may have mountains of color in a painting, if you see something there or not, if there are lots of words and sounds—it does not yet mean that the work is also authentic.

In my opinion, the color and the matter of Cimabue itself stimulated an upheaval in the art of the Byzantine period. In the same way, another color of Giotto, also absolutely authentic—and I emphasize this word from a chemical point of view—stimulated a different moral and artistic upheaval. Just as later, it was done by Masaccio and others...

I repeat: it is not the world view, that is a literary or symbolic issue, that brings this change, but the blood itself, a certain chemistry of nature, objects and human concentration itself. You can see the conception of this authenticity in all domains.

How was it born, how is it built up, this chemistry through which art is created, the true conception of the world and of life?

It consists of elements of love and of a certain natural attitude, just as nature itself which cannot stand evil, hatred, indifference...

If, for example, we are seized to the quick by the soul of the Bible, it is primarily because, even chemically, the Bible is the greatest work of art in the world, which includes the highest life-ideal on our planet.

Let another chemical genius come, and humanity will follow him as a new world view, a new light in life.

I don't pretend in these few words to reveal to you the various other values of our history.

But those who think this chemistry can be found somewhere in scientific laboratories, in a factory are mistaken, nor can you learn it in ateliers or from theories.

No, it is in us, in our hands, in our souls, it is both inherent in us and the result of education.

Not to remain with general meditations, will tell you what I am doing now:

I intend to continue the biblical series planned for a building—not a church, not a museum—a place for people seeking this new plastic spiritual content I talked about. It seems to me that there are people among us seeking it. Perhaps today you, tomorrow—others...

Though I don't sense in myself any philosophical mission, I cannot avoid sensing what currently stifles art and culture, and sometimes even life itself.

On the other hand, precisely in a time of constant sapping of religiosity—not to go into the reasons for that—we must see how the art of the nineteenth and twentieth century up to now has been a weak reflection of scientific discoveries. Whereas, before this period, including the Renaissance, art always mirrored the religious spirit or, at least, illustrated the religiosity of its time.

I cannot refrain from saying that art of a scientific nature or art for enjoyment's sake, like nourishment, is not a living value. Historically, such art may gradually wither. They say that a "good" man can be a bad artist. But there is not, and never will be an artist who is not a great and indeed good man.

I know that certain people today discredit nature. After Cézanne, Monet, Gauguin, there seems to be no genius who would reflect it.

Today, it is common as far as possible to avoid nature; this looks to me like people who avoid looking into your eyes. I am afraid of it and turn my gaze away from such people.

Certain revolutionaries wanted, scientifically, to introduce order into the social and economic life of the world. But after a certain time, these scientific theories are contradicted in part by other theories.

Perhaps the change in the social order, as well as in art, would have been more certain if it also emerged from our soul, not just from our head. If people read more deeply the writings of the Prophets, they could have found there some keys to life.

Are there no other revolutionary methods aside from those we experienced?

Is there no other basis for art aside from the decorative art to please, or the experimental art, or ruthless art that wants to scare others? It is childish to repeat the long-known truth: the world in all its domains will be saved only through love, without love it will gradually decline.

If we could add love to the theoretical and scientific sources I spoke of, their result could have been more valuable and just.

It seems to me that, in our atomic epoch, we are approaching certain boundaries. What boundaries? But we don't want to fall into that world-abyss.

I had to live for many years to see many mistakes in life, and to understand that it is easier to climb Mont Blanc than to think you can change man.

As to art, I often talked about color which is love.

Joyfully I think about young people among whom we hope to find a resonance.

I think that you too think about the same things.

And I love to dream that it won't be a voice crying in the wilderness.

The Ceiling of the Paris Opera[6]
Remarks at the Inauguration of the Work, 1964

Two years ago, André Malraux asked me to paint a new ceiling for the Paris Opera. I was troubled, touched, and deeply moved.

Troubled, because I dread working at someone else's behest, dreaming all the while of doing monumental works, and touched because of André Malraux's confidence. I doubt myself, my work. Certain opinions only reinforced my doubts, until one day my wife said: "Try to make a few sketches and you will see." I doubted day and night. I thought about the whole building and Carpeaux's inspired sculpture.

I wished to reflect, as though in a mirror high above, in a bouquet of dreams, the creation of actors, of composers, to recall the colorful movement of the audience below. To sing like a bird, without theory or method. To render homage to the great composers of opera and ballet.

Sometimes, what one thinks is inconceivable is possible, and what seems strange is obvious. Our remote dreams are only starved for love.

I wanted to be among and with those of today, to pay lasting homage to Garnier.

I labored with all my heart, and I offer this work as a gift, in gratitude to France and her School of Paris, for without them there would be no color, there would be no freedom.

I sincerely thank those who have helped me: Charles Sorlier, Charles Marq, Roland Bierge, Paul Viersteeg, Rostain, Lefebre-Poinet, Richard Padchel.

I thank M. Bourdon and M. de Mouy, the Opera's architects, and the whole great staff of the theater.

I owe special thanks to Bernard Anthonnioz whose perseverance made the realization of this work possible.

The Circus
1966[7]

For me, a circus is a magic show that appears and disappears like a world. A circus is disturbing. It is profound.

I can still see in Vitebsk, my home town, in a poor street with only three or four spectators, a man who had come with a little boy and a little girl.

Before starting his act, he laid a dirt-colored rug on the ground, raising a cloud of dust. He produced a ten- or twelve-foot pole which he held propped against his belt.

The boy, completely naked under his pink leotard, climbed up the pole. When he got to the top, he bowed over like a snake. He did not smile, and his face had a grayish tinge. You might have thought he hadn't shaved for a long time, even though he was still far too young.

Below, costumed as an acrobat, the father held the pole against his belly, then hoisted it up to his face, than into his mouth where you caught a glimpse of yellowed teeth. The boy came down. Then it was the little girl's turn to climb up: a child with two small pigtails, in a multicolored dress, so tiny and tired-looking...

She slid down the pole and nothing moved in the street, nor at the height she'd come from, I don't know if anyone gave them so much as a penny.

And it seemed as if I had been the one bowing and bowing up there...

Another time I saw another little girl. She looked to me like a bareback rider without a horse. In the nakedness of the courtyard her transparent body stocking glistened. I was struck dumb with fear, dreaming of her at night. These visions have transfixed me, although the transparent girl, as well as the boy, evaporated long ago. Where can they be? Where will they end their days? Like them, I add up my age, year by year.

These clowns, bareback riders and acrobats have made themselves at home in my visions. Why? Why am I so touched by their make-up and their grimaces? With them I can move toward new horizons. Lured by their colors and make-up, I dream of painting new psychic distortions.

Alas, in my lifetime I have seen a grotesque circus: a man roared to terrify the world, and a thunder of applause answered him.[8]

A revolution that does not lead to its ideal is, perhaps, a circus too.

I wish I could hide all these troubling thoughts and feelings in the opulent tail of a circus horse and run after it, like a little clown, begging for mercy, begging it to chase the sadness from the world.

Yet, if I have made pictures, it is because I remember my mother, her breasts so warmly nourishing and exalting me, and I feel I could swing from the moon.

It is a magic word, circus, a timeless dancing game where tears and smile, the play of arms and legs take the form of a great art.

But what do most of these circus people earn? A piece of bread. Night brings them solitude, sadness. Until the next day when the evening flooded with electric lights announces a new old-life.

The circus seems to me like the most tragic show on earth.

Through the centuries, it has been the most poignant cry in man's search for amusement and joy. It often takes the form of high poetry. I seem to see a Don Quixote in search of an ideal, like that inspired clown who wept and dreamed of human love.

I have drawn lions, on King Solomon's throne, at David's feet, on the arch of the Temple. I have seen their image on the robes of the high priests, on palace carpets.

All my life I have drawn horses that look more like donkeys or cows, I saw them in Lyozno, at my grandfather's, where I often asked to go along to the neighboring villages when he went to buy livestock for his butcher shop.

At the sight of horses, who are always in a state of ecstasy, I think: are they not, perhaps, happier than we? You can kneel down peacefully before a horse and pray. It always lowers its eyes in a rush of modesty. I hear the echo of the horses' hooves in the pit of my stomach. I could race on a horse for the first time and the last time, to the brilliant arena of life. I would be aware of the transcendence, of no longer being alone among the silent creatures whose thought of us only God can know.

These animals, horses, cows, goats among the trees and hills: they are all silent. We gossip, sing, write poems, make drawings which they do not read, which they neither see nor hear.

I would like to go up to that bareback rider who has just reappeared, smiling; her dress, a bouquet of flowers. I would circle her with my flowered and unflowered years. On my knees, I would tell her wishes and dreams, not of this world.

I would run after her horse to ask her how to live, how to escape from myself, from the world, whom to run to, where to go.

Dialogue in the Louvre with Pierre Schneider
 1967[1]

Marc Chagall took the walk we are about to begin fifty-seven years ago for

the first time. It was the day after he arrived in Paris in 1910.

I hurried at once to the Salon des Indépendants (the Salon d'Automne was for successful artists). I went quickly to the moderns, at the far end. There were the Cubists: Delaunay, Gleizes, Leger... And then, I raced to the Louvre. A magic name...
  Why to the Louvre?
  I felt that the truth was there. The moderns hadn't passed the test yet. There, it was serious.
  The test of time?
  No, not time. Something else...
  Fifty-seven years ago, but the memory is still clear:
  Way up, in the Grande Galerie, I discovered Bassano's big painting. A mixture of people and animals. I sensed that it was very important.
  Beyond a doubt, the Louvre had shown him, as a welcome, a kind of Chagall. The dream of the self-educated adolescent from Vitebsk, then, did have an equivalent in the pictorial tradition of the Latin West. The undertaking became possible. The museum as a school? It does not seem so:
  I go to the Louvre to fortify myself, control myself. One hopes to learn something, but it is no use. Nothing helps us. There are no assurances, no certitudes.

Learn? He laughs. *Nothing! One does not learn how to paint. I am against the well-drawn, the well-painted. Cézanne had no draftsmanship, nothing.*

Is not that precisely what the Louvre is? Here, time and place no longer exist; there are no more fathers, sons, or brothers, no more causes, or effects. He says:

It is the cemetery for genius.

But what he means by that is that the work, behind the frontier marked by the museum, is snatched from history, released.

Death helps one to see a great deal.

Thus the adventure would be very simple. A dream, so intimate that it occurs in the margin of history, encouraged by the encounter with a work that owes nothing more to time, materializes. A symbol of such a conjuncture: at this very moment, Chagall is being exhibited at the Louvre.

In fact, he seems to have foiled the ravages of time, like a refugee who has eluded a hundred police round-ups. This man of eighty years and more is possessed of a stupefying physical vigor and mental vivacity. His eyes are now mocking, now tender, his smile ready, his step and speech rapid. There are people who polish themselves little by little until they become their own myth. What makes Chagall a legendary being—passersby recognize him and ask for his autograph—on the contrary, is that he simply has not changed. An uninterrupted childhood, because nourished exclusively by his dreams. All attention to his interior monologue, as Harpo Marx, whom Chagall resembles a little, is silent in his films. Angels do not age.

Simple, too simple. Chagall's eyes are wide open.

I see things. I am a terrible, a formidable critic. Ever since 1910, I have rarely been wrong. Except about Rouault: he bored me.

I admit that I was skeptical at first: criticism must be able to bite. But as we wended our way along the quays, our conversation convinced me: the angel has teeth.

Bonnard? A beefsteak that has been handled too much. "Finger painting." A little bourgeois. A man who does not look you straight in the eye. Matisse, yes! That rousing anarchy, that dash!

You have never been wrong, you say?

Yes, of course. I believed in Gleizes too much. I saw in him a sort of Courbet of Cubism. Today, I have a higher opinion of Delaunay at the time when he was modest than later, when he was pushing himself. He used to reproach me: "Chagall, you don't know the tricks of the trade." But he knew them. And yet, today, I notice, his work is falling apart. On the other hand, I used to think: La Fresnaye, he is a nice artist; now, he has gained scope.

This is because then Chagall was immersed in history, which is always unjust:

I saw the chemical difference between Picabia and Leger very clearly, but it didn't matter much. The closer you get to your times, the less close you feel. Even Corot seemed too realistic to me during that period. Monet, I did not want to look at him. I discovered him after the war, on the boat that brought me back from America. There, on the ocean, I asked myself the question: whose color really pours forth naturally? And I answered: Monet. Today, for me, Monet is the Michelangelo of our times, from the chemical point of view.

History's attenuation liberates clear-sightedness, as one can only see that a lamp is lighted after sundown. On the condition, naturally, that it is burning.

I can tell you if you were born with a voice or not. There is no professionalism. The technique employed means nothing. Dadaism is not so great, but Schwitters made some marvelous works.

Chagall has a name for that lighted lamp, that critical mind:

In our own times, the eye does not work very well. We do not see the differences. We do not see the chemistry. But later we see it automatically. Because it alone exists. Watteau endured for us not because of his figures, but because of chemistry. Pater has the same figures, but he has not endured. Today, for me, there is chemistry. All the rest—realism or anti-realism, figuration or non-figuration—no longer matters.

Well, then, why can we not see clearly right off, why not turn on in art that second lighting which extinguishes everything that is not what Chagall calls "chemistry?" Because it is not possible.

To arrive at that, at the Louvre, I told myself that we had to overthrow what was before us, which was the realisms.

The road to lucidity necessarily passes through its opposite. A god is only omnipotent in relation to man, and the atemporal is born of time. The lamp of second sight can only light itself at the blinding fire of history. Despite his personal, historical, geographical and cultural distance from the Parisian milieu which greeted him in 1910, Chagall at once and instinctively understood this: before going to the Louvre, he ran to the Salon des Indépendents. A simple phrase, spoken in passing, says more on this subject than lengthy explanations:

I am the same age as Juan Gris.

At five minutes to ten, outside the great Denon Door, which is the main entrance, the crowd is already forming,

The Louvre, what a magic word! Going to the Louvre is like opening the Bible or Shakespeare. Of course, there are some boring things. Guido Reni is a pompier but a pompier of great class.

Is there a spirit of the place?

Without any doubt. Transport the Louvre to the Trocadero and it would lose everything. The Louvre is a magical thing, It has to do with the proportions, the architecture of the galleries. Even its shadows are propitious. The walls are extraordinary. At the Metropolitan Museum, at the National Gallery in Washington, you won't find this magic. At the Hermitage, yes. A large part of the fascination that the Louvre has for artists comes from this.

There are those, however, who dream of burning it down.

What for? Those who are inside it are just people like us. They had the good luck, or the bad luck, to get into the Louvre; that's all. Anyhow, half of them might have to get out again. The risk of destruction is not there.

Where then?

In the "museographic" hanging, which smacks of vandalism. I don't like the way the Louvre has been reorganized very much. It is no longer recognizable. I loved those paintings that used to climb in serried ranks up to the moldings. Everything was on a par. It was intimate. Now the tendency is to put a single painting on one wall. They impose what should be seen, they emphasize. The isolated painting, set apart, says: respect me. I like to look, to find.

And Chagall informs me that while he has never stopped going to the Louvre, ever since 1910, it has always been by chance—or at least seemingly so. The other day, when I suggested that the two of us make the visit, he answered:

Yes, but I don't want to go on purpose.

I was a little annoyed, I admit: the demand seemed to me not only impossible to satisfy but also gratuitous. But was it? In the form of a game, Chagall was presenting me with the problem that had been his own: how does one cultivate ingenuousness? The paradox was a parable. And indeed the solution did exist since, at that very moment, we were entering the doors of the Louvre.

Chagall pulls me up the staircase opposite the one dominated by the WINGED VICTORY and along toward the enormous suite of rooms on the second floor that harbors the juggernauts of French painting. Surprise: without the slightest hesitation his gaze travels to the canvases of a painter I imagined would be at opposite poles from his own nature, Courbet:

He is an artist I am passionate about. Of the same breed as Masaccio, as Titian.

His eye wanders around the immense hall, stopping for an instant on THE RAFT OF THE MEDUSA:

Yes, even STAGS FIGHTING, which is a little academic, touches me more than Géricault and his technique. Of course, it is eloquent; and Gros, too, with his BATTLE OF EYLAU, is quite something. But I don't feel like endorsing him, all the same. In the whole room, Courbet is the one who stands up.

Why?

I don't know. He moves me. To tears almost. He is the artist of life.

He is standing before THE STUDIO:

Somewhere, there, is the tragedy of death.

Against their background, a fog of variable density, are light or dark groups, like pulsation:

Time, which comes, which goes, like a wave. We are shadowy. That is our sickness.

Now Chagall is before THE BURIAL AT ORNANS. Chagall? I have trouble recognizing him. The voice is neutral, the speech precise, the eye active. He speaks, falls silent, steps back, moves closer, says something more, as an artist returns to his easel to place another brushstroke on his canvas:

That sickliness, that execution, those faltering yet solid forms... I think of Braque: he could not do a bird properly, he would add some white, but that white!... Courbet's whites; the dog, the hats are vivid spots. And the blue of the man's stockings in the foreground: it is apart, not linked to the rest. It is very modern... The enormous poetry of our times... Courbet is a naturalist, and yet he is a great poet... The idea of death is everywhere in Courbet: it is not in Delacroix and Géricault, although he treated the theme of death.

After a fairly long silence, during which, at Chagall's suggestion, I think about the strange marriage of energy and decay in Courbet, he says:

Perfection is close to death. Watteau, Mozart...

And then, as we are heading for the transitional rooms where the paintings from the Beistegui Collection are hung, Chagall adds:

Courbet was right when he turned toward reality. As for myself, I do not understand myself. I only know one thing: my paintbrush is guided from my belly. It is the guiding of the paintbrush that counts.

Now we are before LUCRETIA by Rubens, another in the family of vigorous, exuberant artists:

He is a pig, but he is a great artist.

He does not linger at all. David, on the other hand, attracts him. Here is the unfinished NAPOLEON:

I like it when paintings are left empty... David has a delightful touch.

His gaze shifts to the Ingres portraits, very close by.

It is better than Ingres. A nobility. It is not dry, like Ingres.

He indicates the PORTRAIT OF MADAME DE VERNINAC:

A delightful gray. What softness in the background!

We come to the thick-set MADAME PANCKOUKE by Ingres:

He is more secretive, antinatural, abnormal. David is normal. Ingres disturbs me. There is something overstuffed about him. There is a sort of impotence in his portraits. They seem overworked, chiaroscuro. One thinks of Magritte. A pause. If one has an academic soul, one has had it since birth.

In front of Delacroix's PORTRAIT OF CHOPIN:

A great work. The great Delacroix is there. It is almost a Soutine.

And at Delacroix's SELF-PORTRAIT:

One really senses that Manet will come. What intelligence!

A glance at the Chasseriau that happens to be there on a temporary basis (they have removed several paintings by Ingres to send them to the Centennial Exhibition):

A sort of La Fresnaye. He began with tricks.

He hastens over to Géricault's MAD WOMAN, which also replaces an Ingres portrait:

There, this is the great Géricault. When Géricault painted reality, he was a great madman. When he made THE RAFT OF THE MEDUSA, he was carrying out a plan... One has to have a great deal of strength to sit down before a head and make a study of it.

Farther on, the halls leading to the Grande Galerie occupied by the foreign collections. Chagall does not want to go there. He seems to prefer the French school today. I lead him, almost by force, to Goya's LA MARQUESA DE LA SOLANS, framed by Davids and Ingres:

It is like a Watteau—but no: it is not from our country. Like Velásquez. One can weep before Courbet and Watteau, but not before Velásquez or Goya. They are gods, but foreign gods. Zurbaran perhaps—such freshness! And Greco—but he was Greek. There is always that bullfight quality: this Goya succeeds like a moment of truth.

He turns away immediately to look at MADAME DE VERNINAC again:

That yellowish liquid, what nobility! It is the café crème one dreams about in foreign countries. I like that gray better than Goya's superb gray. That is what I left Russia for.

This preference for French painting, since the beginning of our tour, is full of significance. Transposed in time and space, it re-enacts the young twenty-year-old's choice in leaving Vitebsk for Paris.

My training has been French. I detest the Russian or Central European color. Their color is like their shoes. Soutine, myself—all left because of the color. I was very dark when I arrived in Paris. I was the color of a potato, like Van Gogh. Paris is light.

Chagall's attraction to French painting, so steady, so positive, may seem strange. His temperament should have carried him to Vienna, Munich, or some Tahiti closer to the Dnieper than to the Seine. In fact, his first canvases, painted under the influence of Western works known to him only through reproductions in magazines, illustrate his affinities for a subjective art. Yet, instinctively, Chagall chose the opposite, because it was the opposite. When, thanks to a scholarship procured for him by a deputy to the Duma, Vinaver, he arrived in Paris in 1910, those who attracted him and soon surrounded him were Cendrars, Apollinaire, Léger, La Fresnaye, Delaunay, Lhôte, Gleizes—in other words, the defenders of an objective, formalistic art.

The painters of thirty years ago were absorbed in purely technical pursuits, he said about them. *One did not talk out loud about one's dreams.*

Why seek out that which goes against you? Why, when you are in love with Bassano, run all the way to the farthest room at the Indépendants? Necessity. So *I arrived in Paris as though driven by destiny*, Chagall wrote further. *From my mouth flowed words straight from my heart. They almost suffocated me. I stuttered. The words came hurrying out, anxious to be illuminated by that Paris light, to be bathed in it.*

Elsewhere, Chagall called that light "freedom light." Something very precise lies hidden beneath the happy imprecision of the formula: the bringing to light, the liberation of the interiority captive in the darkest depths of the self. Paris offered Chagall what his stuttering dream needed to take shape: a pictorial language, a syntax of the visible. Thanks to this encounter, Chagall escaped—as did Soutine—from what is the hell of art in Central Europe and Russia, the hell of the voice deprived of speech, described by Aeschulus in *Agamemnon*: "In shadow, he groans in pain, without hope of ever drawing anything from an interior on fire… "

To take shape is to take root in history. The Indépendants and the Louvre: the path of every artist, even the most secretive, passes through the art of his times. The times, for the young Chagall, were the second generation of Cubists. The essential fact is that he had the wisdom to accept being the same age, in painting, as Juan Gris.

He needed courage for that. The Cubist language is materialistic, optical, general: Chagall's world is visionary, particular, local. The opposition seems, in this case, to border on incompatibility; expression and communication seem separated by all the distance there is between Vitebsk and Paris. No matter: as antagonistic as they were, only Paris could bring Vitebsk to light. Chagall did not like Cubism: he needed it.

I detested realism and naturalism, even in the Cubists. I wanted to introduce a psychic formalism.

Meaning: the psychic could only become perceptible through a formalism. "I admit that two and two make four is an excellent thing," wrote Dostoevsky, "but if one must praise everything, I will tell you that two and two make five is also a charming thing." $2 + 2 = 4$ is Cubism's formula; $2 + 2 = 5$ is Chagall's. But that supernumerary 1, which is the sign of the fantastic, only emerges against a background of order, as a derogation to the logical permanence incarnated by the equation and its functioning. "Your monsters are viable," Louis Pasteur said to Odilon Redon. French painting offers visual viability to extrapictorial dreams.

The Cubist bottles were straight: I leaned them over. I cut off heads…

The unreal manifests itself through a warping of the real, of that moment of realism that was Cubism. It was the defender of Cubism, Apollinaire, who first recognized the "surreal" in Chagall's Cubist-oriented work. But naturally, Chagall would take exception to the Surrealism developing when he returned to Paris after the war, in 1923.

Surrealism is automatism. Art requires control, but by the artist's gift.

Obviously, Chagall illustrates in a fairly radical fashion the conflict between the self and society, between the personal voice and the common speech, which every artist must resolve. On the one hand, the Russian climate, the Jewish milieu, the influence of Hasidism (that sort of Hebrew Franciscanism), the dreamer's temperament; on the other, the technical-ity of Cubism. And thanks to Cubism, Chagall's work did not stay lost in the limbo of formless reverie or the natural reserve of folklore.

But he had yet to precipitate things: that was the role of "chemistry." This is not the place to tell how Chagall reinterpreted Cubism, making use of the right it had won to dislocate and recompose forms in order to topple heads and hoist the ox up onto the roof, making Delaunay's orphic circle spin like the wheel of chance at a street fair. Let us simply note that, for a painter, to understand clearly is to misunderstand. His false interpretation is in itself creative. Only the historian or the scholar can allow himself to be right. Chagall's interpretation of Cubism reminds one of what happened to the names of the Greek gods when they passed from the universe of the archaic theogonies into that of the pre-Socratic philosophies. At first symbols of manifestations of the sacred, these names lost their meanings as the gods died or were forgotten. They became mysterious instead of clear, in such a way that they were finally used as symbols of mystery, or were attributed to powers still unnamed and as essential as the gods whom they succeeded.

The inventive artist is a wolf who presents himself to us hidden, sometimes rather badly, in sheep's clothing. When we see through the ruse, it is too late. Creation is a-historic, but it must manifest itself in the bosom of history. And one thinks of the fate of the Jew: escaping from time but only discovering his exceptional status by submitting to the rules of time, affirming his difference by the very degree to which he assimilates himself into his milieu—as French painting, in masking Chagall's universe, reveals it. To show oneself to be different through the common language, to resolve the paradox of the double belonging—the solution being precisely his work—is the artist's lot. Every creator is a Jew within his culture.

We retrace our steps through the French galleries, this time all the way to the Staircase of Honor. David's self-portrait:

It is beautiful like Cézanne. It kills all of Ingres.

Delacroix, THE WOMEN OF ALGIERS IN THEIR APARTMENT:

Magnificent, like his self-portrait. It moves me. His Raphaelesque folds are much better than Courbet's. Courbet thought about death too much; he was an invalid.

Now we have come to the great neoclassical hall.

Aie! Aie! Aie!

But he breathes freely again looking at THE RAPE OF THE SABINES and THE CORONATION OF NAPOLEON:

No matter what he does, David is never academic. One is born academic. Neither Delacroix, nor Courbet, nor Géricault is—but Ingres.

Chagall's gaze wanders among the David canvases,

MADAME RÉCAMIER, marvelous. There is some Manet in it. But in LEONIDAS, there is Poussin. What softness, wrapped over everything! Never any dryness. He points toward THE OATH OF THE HORACES.

No chemistry without acid:

Perhaps I might not feel so tenderly toward David if people weren't talking about Ingres so much these days.

The Cimabue in the staircase. The tone changes, as if we were passing from history to truth:

Cimabue! My love, my god! When I arrived in Paris, it was a great shock. Silence. It transcends everything. That devoutness... No, I am not talking about the subject matter, but about the touch. Cimabue is more penetrating than Giotto... You have to go to Watteau to find the equivalent. Rembrandt, Monet, Caravaggio, Masaccio, Cimabue, Watteau, these are my gods!

We descend the staircase. Passing before WINGED VICTORY, Chagall whispers to me:

It moves me more than Brancusi.

We pass a fresco, brought back from Ostia, HERO ARMED WITH A SWORD:

This was done by a simple artisan. Art is like a good child: it should not go to school. One must not try to draw well, paint well. School is harmful. When I came to France, there was no professionalism in me. I had no mission. For me, that has not changed.

A window, through which we glimpse the delicate gray of Paris. Chagall goes over to it:

There is why we left Vitebsk. It is all of Le Nain, it is Watteau. The French are not always great, far from it, but there is this gray, this landscape in them. Fauvism can be as violent as it likes, it remains—in a Dufy, for example—French. Van Dongen has much more talent, but he vomits it.

Chagall is determined not to leave the French domain. Despite his age, despite the kilometers we have already covered, he drags me to the other end of the Louvre, way up high, where the new rooms for the eighteenth and nineteenth centuries are located, and again it is a David MADAME TRUDAINE, that greets us:

The touch, marvelous! He is perhaps the first to have used such a light touch. The execution, it's everything; it is like the blood—the chemistry.

So saying, he goes over to the SEATED NUDE, MADEMOISELLE ROSE by Delacroix:

What nobility! Things like this, after all, are greater than Courbet.

There are Corots all around us. Chagall comes to a halt before LA TRINITÀ DEI MONTI:

Ah! What an artist! There, that is France. It leaves one speechless. There is a god. He transcends everything. It looks like nothing... . That blondness, that gray, that is France... What were the Impressionists trying to do, after him? He already did everything. A real painter. He has the chemistry. He is a prince. He can do anything. He is a Mozart.

Which does not prevent him from appreciating THE PLASTER KILN, by Géricault:

Terrific! The first Vlaminck.

In fact, Chagall's hesitations are never negative. When he prefers a certain painter to another, it is less to take from the latter than to give to the former. For instance, he vacillates between Delacroix and Courbet. Now he is before ARAB HORSES FIGHTING by the former:

It is painted like a Daumier. It is more distinguished than Courbet, one must admit.

Before THE ORPHAN GIRL, the comparison becomes clear:

What intelligence, what nobility! Courbet was a great man, but his belly was too big.

And again, looking at THE TURKISH SLIPPERS:

What distinction, what respect!

A little later, however, when Courbet's HUNTED ROEBUCK LISTEN-ING catches his eye, he says:

Marvelous. What delightful tonality! Perhaps it is better than Delacroix.

With Chagall, hesitation is laudatory, ascensional. But he does not have to grope for contempt. A Puvis de Chavannes makes him grimace:

This is Ingres' heritage.

Before canvases by Huet, Diaz and Decamps:

Let's hurry, let's hurry!

Raffet offers us his MARSHAL NEY, a perfect example of simple-minded imagery:

This is Russian, I say.

Polish, if you please.

And he adds:

All pompiers are alike . . . . But perhaps the Russian ones are the most dreadful.

And here is our very own Russian, Meissonier, and his little pictures painted with a magnifying glass:

Nightmares!

But after all, why?

A matter of chemistry. No talent. Like a singer with no voice. It is dreadful.

At times, I have trouble understanding him. He shakes his head, sighs, mutters: *Nightmare!* before a Gustave Moreau, or an ironical *the famous Decamps, the famous Rousseau.*

With pauses for delight. Constable, HAMPSTEAD HEATH:

That is Monet, there. I'm not mentioning Pissarro, because he is nothing.

Or Daumier, THEATER SCENE:

Admirable! What is the secret of his greatness?

Surprises, such as his reaction to STILL LIFE WITH WHITE PITCHER by Monticelli:

One feels like stealing it. What an artist!

Or his indulgence toward Millet and his RECLINING NUDE:

He is not pompier. He has good qualities, he has Stimmung. But it is finished, like Maeterlinck, like Levitan. It no longer touches one. Corot, yes.

His HAYDÉE:

The breasts are sagging, but the painting rises. What a genius one has to be! A little scumble. It looks like nothing at all... That is what is lacking in Russia, in Germany: they always dot their i's...

My God.

Chagall has just caught sight of Watteau's THE EMBARKATION FOR CYTHERA:

The grandeur, the concept, the madness of that thing!

Of a JUDGMENT OF PARIS, he says: *Cézanne did things like that.* And of the neighboring Pater: *I cannot stand that.* Boucher, Lancret, Fragonard, he does not even look at. It is GILLES that attracts him:

That surpasses everybody. That comes close to Rembrandt. I would give all of Corot for that pair of pants. It sings and it weeps, like Cimabue. Corot has the song but not the tears. What one feels in GILLES is not the feeling of death, but of the end of life.

At a stroke, Watteau defines the limits of French painting by transcending it. Next comes a series of Chardin still-lifes, of which THE RAY:

The great French school comes from there. Scientific art... To end with Derain. I say: congratulations, hats off. But moved? No.

Thus, there exists another chemistry or, if you like, another aspect of the chemistry. The first allows us to enter into the historic, the visible; the second leads us out of it or, at least, orients the work toward a beyond-the-visible, a place common to all transcendent art:

The great chemistry is the same, always and everywhere, Chagall says before a Fayum portrait. *This Fayum portrait and a Corot are the same thing.*

The "great chemistry" is that by which we rejoin the community of nature, the "little chemistry" being that by which we rejoin the human community:

The only pleasure I have: when the chemistry I produce in my canvases approaches the chemistry of nature. Like Monet, or the old Titian... But one must live through one's times to reach that point.

For Chagall also, chemistry today is, above all, a matter of color. It is color that digs a tunnel to the untemporal in the canvas. Color depth: *The color must be penetrating, as when one walks on a thick carpet,* he wrote some time ago.

I didn't even show my paintings to my friend Cendrars. I always used to think: we don't have many friends on earth; only our wife, because she has nothing against us. As a boy, I showed my paintings to my mother. She thought that I had talent but that painting was too difficult. She wanted me to become a photographer. As for my father, he was in another world.

A rather unusual circumstance explains this remark: on our way out of the Louvre, we are going through the Mollien Gallery, where Chagall is being exhibited at this very moment. A terrifying ordeal, dreamed of—not without fear—by Cézanne, Matisse, Picasso, and so many others. I can vouch for the fact that Chagall talks about himself without indulgence:

No draftsmanship. It could have been done with the fingers. The color, that is what gives it the Geist. No stylization, no maestria, no pursuit of gesture.

The weakness: the way an old man is young. Ordinary. The more ordinary Delacroix or Corot are, the more they are geniuses. What really counts? Who can say? It is like a child asleep in a bed. The color. You buy it in a store. The themes? I borrowed from the Bible because it is a first-rate book. There is no science in me. You must not draw well. Leave your talent alone. Ingres draws well, and it is a nightmare. I could have done my lines differently, on the right instead of the left, up high instead of down low, it would have been the same thing. To the excited, I feel like saying: calm yourselves, be like Corot, be ordinary! Stanislavski used to say to his actors: calm yourselves, drop your shoulders, then we will be able to see your true colors. It is like pissing: if it does not come, it is because you are sick. I do not like the grand gesture. In THE THIRD-CLASS COMPARTMENT Daumier has no gestures: fortunately, he did not know it.

On the First Day of the Six-Day War
1967[2]

This letter was sent by Chagall to *Di Goldene Keyt* (the Yiddish cultural journal published in Tel Aviv and edited by Chagall's friend the poet A. Sutzkever) at the outbreak of the Six-Day War, June 6, 1967. A long waiting period preceded the war, raising deep worries among Israel sympathizers around the world.

Would that I were younger, to leave my paintings and brushes, and go, fly together with you—with sweet joy to give up my last years.

I have always painted pictures where human love floods my colors.

Day and night I dreamed that something would change in the souls and relations of people.

I have always thought that, without human or biblical feelings in your heart, life had no value. Now the Semitic nations have arisen, jealous of our hard-earned piece of bread, our burning national ideal, our national soil. They want to show that, like other nations, they are also anti-Semites. They want to choke us as the Pharoahs of old. But we crossed the sea of the ghettoes, and our victory was eternalized in the [Passover] Haggadah.

We now stand before the great world trial of the human soul: will all dear visions and ideals of human world culture of two thousand years be blown away with the wind?

History again puts the torch and sword in our hand, for the world to tremble when it hears our prophetic voice of justice.

Thousands and thousands of simple people here and everywhere are with you. Only "leaders" with no heart are with our enemies.[3]

Perhaps I am of an age to bless you, and instead of crying—to comfort you. I want to hope that the land of the great French Revolution, the land of Zola, Balzac, Watteau, Cézanne, Baudelaire, Claudel, Péguy, will soon raise its voice to stop the world shame. I hope that America with its democracy, the land of Shakespeare, and also the land of Dostoevsky, Mussorgsky—the land of my birth—will begin to scream that the world must stop its "manners" and give the people of Israel one chance—to live free and create free in its own land.

Anyway, no one will be able to create freely anymore if the nations let their conscience go to sleep. The last drop of talent will evaporate and their words will remain hollow.

To let Israel and the Jews be choked—means to kill the soul of the whole biblical world.

No new "religion" can be created without this drop of heart's blood. And we will see if we are worthy of continuing to live or of being destroyed by the atomic bomb.

My word of consolation is in my eyes, which you cannot see now.

And my blessings are embossed in my windows of the Twelve Tribes, now hidden in Jerusalem...

Our Streets of Vitebsk and Vilna
1967, 1969

Elkhonen Vogler (1907–1969) emerged as an original Yiddish poet in Vilna in the 1930s and was, with Sutzkever, a member of the literary group Yung Vilna. After the travails of World War II, he settled in Paris, a lonely poet. There Chagall met him. His poetry evoked the landscapes of Chagall's Jewish *Litah*. His sad existence represented to Chagall the end of the Yiddish-speaking world.

ABOUT THE YIDDISH POET ELKHONEN VOGLER (1967)[4]

For hundreds of years in cities and shtetls, on streets and squares, in houses and schools, your language has been heard. Sky and clouds, fields and forests have listened to your language.

Our fathers and mothers cried their lives out in Yiddish. In *Heder*, with the rebbe, the flies dashed to the window, begged, shuddered—when we children repeated Yiddish lines.

And you stood at a distance and saw it all, painted and recorded it close up.

The world finally perceived that all the cities and shtetls it destroyed have remained only in our dreams, paintings and songs. Our foes wanted to put a candle at our head as at the head of a dead person; they assumed we would stop singing and painting, we would not even have any more tears to weep.

Our house of wood and bricks is destroyed, but not the Jewish people. And there is no force in the world that would prevent us from believing in miracles. And you, Yiddish poet and artist, know that new cities and shtetls, new parents, dear and our own, descend to us as from Jacob's Ladder. As great as your genius—so great is the miracle. As pure as your paint and your word—so great is your world. And if you weep—they are tears of joy and creation.

Our streets of Vitebsk and Vilna arise somewhere else—in Tel Aviv and Jerusalem. They arise in our hearts and wherever the Jewish truth, the human truth, lives free.

May our spirit be strong and clear, holy as the music of our books, as the look of a child, may we be able to go our own way which has been, from the beginning, both a Jewish and a human way.

ON THE DEATH OF ELKHONEN VOGLER (1969)[5]

It may be late or not too late to express my grief at the death of poor Elkhonen Vogler. Poor? After all, he was a genuine Yiddish poet, but so lonely among Jews.

A stranger to others and perhaps even to himself.

How many times did I want to make him happy—and I didn't know how. I tried to make a few drawings for his book and I don't even know if the book appeared. Everything around him was delayed. He didn't know how to recover. Deep in me lies a thought that he made a mistake: he didn't go to Israel at least for a short time—to draw another strength from there.

His poetry was without beginning and without end, as genuine poetry must be (and all that was in Vilna—it is harder in Paris).

To whom shall I convey my grief? He had no family of his own. I send my grief to all of you.

The Tapestries in the Knesset in Jerusalem
Speech at the Unveiling, August 1969[6]

Over forty years ago, I was invited by the French publisher Vollard to paint the Bible. I was then confused: I didn't know how to begin the work. I was so far from the biblical spirit, in a foreign land . . . .

Fortunately for me, the Mayor of Tel Aviv, Meir Dizengoff, appeared before me like a flying angel, and invited me to come to Eretz-Israel.[7] Since then, I have grown close to the Land of Israel, and have created the Bible [illustrations]. Since then, I am born again; I became a different person. It is difficult for me to explain it in words, and do I need to?... Since then, I have always had the desire to express signs of devotion, however and whenever I can.

I have made many voyages to the Land of Israel. And every time, it has meant an even greater closeness; and here and there I left a sign of it. Finally, I am[8] in the new building of the parliament of Israel in Jerusalem—the Knesset—on its floor and on its walls. I am in the Knesset with its dear Speaker Kaddish Luz, who has so inspired me.

But it is not for me to talk about myself and my work. My goal, as I said, was to get closer to the land, to the biblical homeland of the Jewish people, to the land where there is an understanding of life and a right to life—a creation in the spirit that hovers over every page of the Bible and hovers here in the air, in the fields, in the sky, and in the souls of the inhabitants.

When the world, including our so-called "foes" (who are rather their own foes), understands this; when the world feels this—a new peace will come, not just here but in the whole world, as envisaged by our Prophets.

But, in the meantime, the reality is tragic: the vision of peace is still a mirage.

Art of genius and its luminaries are so rare... People prefer to embrace evil and injustice rather than love.

I pity our enemies who waste their time and their lives on their crooked ways and try to burst through closed doors which are actually open. The key to the doors is love, which is sown here at every step by the forefathers of the people, who returned here two thousand years later, from their ghettos and pogroms. They returned to live with a renewed love and brotherhood with the surrounding Semitic peoples. There are many kinds of art without genius, as there are lives lived in vain. But here, even a child's eyes are covered with an ideal. And the ideal of my soul is to be close to the spirit of the Biblical Land.

From my whole heart, I would call to friend and non-friend, whose soul glows, to open their eyes and hold out a hand, to give content to our short life, elevate our life and creation to the height of nature.

Some may not understand my fragmented words, but perhaps you will sense the pulse of life throbbing in the place where the wind of truth traversed... And our would-be enemies would angrily drop their weapons of annihilation, for they destroy first of all their own souls.

My voice echoes the voices of my parents and forefathers. The world must listen to the voice of that people who gave content to life—and thereby the world will endow itself with content of life.

There is no art or creation or life without love. Love lives in this land, and everything that is love is great and sublime. At my age, I tend to look with some sadness at everything—friend and foe.

Let my work here, whatever it may be, serve as a small part of my soul's devotion to the Land—this land of justice and biblical peace.

The Biblical Message
1973[9]

Ever since early childhood, I have been captivated by the Bible. It has always seemed to me and still seems today the greatest source of poetry of all time. Ever since then, I have searched for its reflection in life and in Art. The Bible is like an echo of nature and this is the secret I have tried to convey.

With the ebb and flow of my powers, throughout my life, although I sometimes felt I was someone else altogether, that was born, one might say, between heaven and earth, that the world is for me a great desert in which my soul wanders like a torch, I did these paintings in unison with this distant dream. I decided to leave it in this House[10] so that men may try to find a certain peace in it, a certain spirituality, a religiosity, a meaning to life.

To my way of thinking, these paintings do not illustrate the dream of a single people, but that of mankind. They are the result of my meeting the French publisher, Ambroise Vollard, and of my trip to the Orient. I thought I would leave them in France, a kind of second birthplace for me.

It is not up to me to comment on them. Works of art should be able to speak for themselves.

People often talk about what way, and in what forms, and in what Movement color should be placed. But this color thing is innate. It does not depend on the manner or the form on which you place it. Nor does it have anything to do with the mastery of the brush. It is outside of all Movements. The few Movements which have endured throughout history have all possessed that innate color... the movements are forgotten.

Are not painting and color inspired by Love? Isn't painting only the reflection of our inner self, and in that sense it goes way beyond mere mastery of the brush. It has nothing to do with it. The color and its lines contain your character and your message.

If all of life moves inevitably toward its end, we must, during ours, color it with all our colors of love and hope. Within this love are found the social logic of life and the basis of every religion. For me perfection in Art and in life comes from this biblical source. Without this spirit, the mechanics of logic and constructivity in Art, as in life, cannot bear fruit.

Perhaps the young and the not-so-young will come to this House in search of an ideal of brotherhood and love such as my colors and my lines have dreamed it.

Perhaps they will also speak the words of this love which I feel for everyone. Perhaps there will be no more enemies, and like a mother bringing a child into the world in love and pain, the young and the not-so-young will build a world of love with new coloring.

And everyone, regardless of their religion, will be able to come here and speak of this dream, far from evil and confusion.

I would also like to be displayed in this place works of art and documents of high spirituality by all peoples, so that people may hear their music and their poetry as dictated by the heart.

Is this dream possible?

But in Art as in life, everything is possible provided it is based on Love.

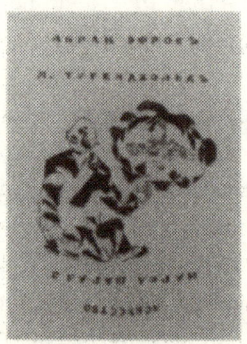

A. Efros and Ya. Tugendhold

THE ART OF MARC CHAGALL

With thirty reproductions of the artist's paintings and graphics
on separate pages and in the text.

Moscow

Publishing House "Helicon"

1918

The book is composed with the help of the
Circle for Jewish National Aesthetics "Shomir"

The publisher's logo by El Lissitzky

The First Book on Marc Chagall
1918

A. Efros and Ya. Tugenhold: *The Art of Marc Chagall*

The first book on Chagall was written late in 1916 or early 1917.[1] It appeared
in the difficult conditions of the early revolutionary days in the publishing house Helicon in Moscow in 1918. During the war, Chagall performed
his miliatary duty in an office in Petrograd (former St. - Petersburg) and
was actively painting and exhibiting both there and in Moscow. The authors
were in touch with Chagall and he illustrated their book, notably with the
famous crooked smile of his self-portrait on the frontispiece. The book
was published in 850 numbered copies with the aid of the Circle for Jewish
National Aesthetics, one of the organizations that emerged during the war
to promote the Jewish cultural renaissance.[2]

The art critic Yakov Aleksandrovich Tugendhold (1883–1928) lived in
Paris between 1905 and 1913. When Chagall arrived in Paris by train in
1910, he came with a sheaf of paintings and a suitcase to Tugendhold's
room, and they became close friends.[3] Tugendhold provided contacts for
Chagall in Paris and Russia, and was one of the first to write about him.

In 1915, at Tugendhold's suggestion, the celebrated Russian art collector Morozov bought Chagall's paintings for 300 Rubles, a huge sum at the time, which made it possible for Chagall to get married. After the Revolution, Tugendhold was appointed Plenipotentiary for the Arts in Simferopol (Crimea), a similar position to the one Chagall held in Vitebsk.

Abram M. Efros (1888–1954), an intelligent art critic and translator ("The Song of Songs," 1909), began writing about Chagall in 1915. In 1920, Efros brought Chagall to the newly created Yiddish Chamber Theater in Moscow, of which he was one of the founders. During the Soviet period, he wrote significant criticism of the theater and art in the theater, and eventually became a master translator of Dante and Petrarc, and a professor of art history in Moscow.

The book was translated into German by Frieda Rubiner,[4] the widow of the Expressionist writer Ludwig Rubiner; Chagall befriended them both in prewar Paris. The book reflects the early reception of Chagall, and it had a defining impact on the discourse about Chagall by both critics and himself. This English translation first appeared in *Marc Chagall and the Jewish Theater* (New York: Guggenheim Museum, 1992). Here, various corrections and annotations were made, and the original order of the book restored.

Abram Efros
The Emperor's Clothes

Here is a book about an artist—young but already famous—perhaps the most brilliant of our *hommes d'aujourd'hui*, but one who has experienced a hard lot: to be recognized without being understood. Marc Chagall fell under the wheels of one of those quiet artistic revolutions that seem to occur unnoticed and coincidentally, but whose victims include the most unusual talents.

What happened? What happened was the deepest rupture, still unnoticed and unaccounted for, of the most solid relationships between traditional antagonists—the artist and the masses. Oh, the roles have changed in an amazing way! The imperially conservative masses—Their Highness the Masses, the masses, slandered and adored, whom all revolutionaries of art have cursed and yet tried to captivate; the masses surrounding the artist like guards around Saint Sebastian, the masses marching over the corpses of innovators, the implacable, stubborn, pursuing, stinging, branding masses—what has happened to them in our time?

We see before us those strange idyllic years when the masses began obsequiously to accept everything the creative caprice of the artist offered them. They became his searching slave. They agreed to everything. They blessed everything with their thousand-mouth blessing: nothing appalled them—and nothing surprised them! The grief of many young artists, who wished, in vain, to have their own period of rejection, is understandable and legitimate: the masses really violated the good canons of rejection, established by the experience of so many heralds of new values in art.

Poor Chagall! He too experienced the meaning of this popular complacency, the worrying smile of devotion, and the frowning brows of attention. He too knew that if they hail a recognized writer so as not to read him, they hail a recognized artist so as not to look. Strolling through an exhibition, one figure throws to another, hurrying to sneak by Chagall: "Ach, Chagall... He is very talented"... "Yes-yes... Very-very"—and, relieved, they vanish into the next gallery, where they regain human language and, with a profusion of words, they burst into excitement before the *comme il faut* canvases of some Excellency.

The Emperor's clothes... Andersen's tale... Till the first fool cries out: "The Emperor is naked"... Well, this is so understandable! Art blinds like Lady Godiva with her nakedness. That's why experienced viewers and true appreciators, art historians and art critics—all wear glasses and increase their size every year. But the masses can glue their eye to the forbidden crack without fear: they won't go blind because they don't see anything anyway.

Art criticism is often an act of grace in relation to the profane spectator, and an act of justice in relation to the artist; it teaches the former to see and gives the latter an opportunity to be understood. Must it linger also at the deaf and dumb lawsuit between Chagall and his viewers? It seems that the time has come to stand up between them, especially since the artist is right and, this time, the viewers are not so guilty—for Marc Chagall put before them truly the most difficult problem: *about the boundaries of what is permitted in art.*

Ya. Tugendhold
The Artist Mark Chagall

"Sasha is three years old—three thousand, and perhaps three times three thousand, Sasha doesn't measure his age in years."

Remizov,[5] *Maka*

I.

In French exhibitions of recent years, the works of the young artist from Vitebsk, Marc Chagall, attracted my attention. Fiery-colored like the Russian Lubok,[6] expressive to the point of grotesque, fantastic to the point of irrationality, they stood out not only among the works of Russian painters, but also against the background of the young French painting. I remember the impact they made in the Autumn Salon among the "Cubist" canvases of Le Fauconnier and Delaunay, those Fauvist innovators. While the mind-boggling brick structures of those Frenchmen exuded cold intellectualism and the logic of analytical thought, what was astonishing in Chagall's paintings was some childish inspiration, something subconscious, instinctive, something unbridled—colorful. Next to the adult, too-adult works, as if by mistake, the works of some child, truly fresh, "barbaric" and fantastic, had landed there. Those multicolored, crooked huts with graves in the middle of the street and a fiddler chirping on the roof, that fiery-bloody "Golgotha" with Judas removing the ladder—could have repelled with their coarse expression, their savagery of theme, the loudness of their colors. But it was impossible not to see them or not to absorb their sharp aroma, because behind them, you felt the all-conquering force of a great talent, and a foreign talent at that. *"Tiens, il y a quelque chose—c'est trés curieux!"*—said the Frenchmen, and indeed, in Chagall, you guessed something inexplicable in European terms, and therefore "curious," as many things in the "barbaric" polychrome music of the Russian ballet seemed curious.

At another exhibition, Chagall showed works refined in their polychromy and ornamentation. Headless flying people, sentimentally inspired animals, houses outside of time and space, as in a sweet and wild childish dream, were painted in black and white, gold and silver, scarlet, cerise, and other unusual and subtle shades. Chagall's fantastics and palette seemed overly tense, unhealthy and delirious, but you couldn't doubt their sincerity—could such phantoms and such outbursts of painterly heat be invented *on purpose*?

Chagall roused interest; just condescendingly approved and almost boycotted by the powerful in Russia—he was accepted in the bosom of the Paris bohemia, invited to exhibit in Amsterdam, Brussels, Berlin. But the war stopped his rapid rise—Chagall found himself where he came from: in the god-forsaken Russian province, in his native Vitebsk. The result of his return to his native and familiar places was a series of studies of mundane life, surprisingly realistic, strong and calm, but quite different from each other.

Chagall is still steeped in searching, in frenetic pluralism, at the junction of many roads—like a child who has before him an infinity of influences, wishes and opportunities. But even what he has accomplished so far allows us to talk about him as an artistic phenomenon, as something authentic and original, which has already come to light and begun glittering fantastically.

II.

Can one "explain" an artist? Doesn't the creative spirit blow wherever and however it wishes? I think that one not only can, but must knock at the promising door and inquisitively seek keys to it. To say that an artist is simply what he is, as he is "made," means to say nothing. Perhaps, even the genius of Dostoevsky's psychologism is related causally to that single moment which he experienced on the gallows.

The attempt of a "literary" explanation does not diminish the artist. On the contrary, his artistic merits are diminished when he himself is so "anecdotal" that such an explanation is superfluous. One can explain Chagall in a literary manner, but he himself is not a story-teller, not an illustrator, but first of all *a painter*.

Chagall was born a Jew, grew up in a Lithuanian province,[7] matured in Paris. Those are three biographical moments we can account for in such a seemingly irregular phenomenon as Chagall's drôleries. Let us dwell on each of them.

Much that would seem "strange" in another perspective is explained by Chagall's national Semitic origin. I don't mean only the contingent meaning of this origin, not just that Chagall grew up in a Jewish milieu. Marc Antokolsky, to the end of his life, never learned to express himself correctly in Russian, nevertheless Stasov[8] was utterly justified, specifically á propos Antokolsky, in regretting the lack of a national element in the work of "Europeanized" Jews. Stasov wrote: "How much they could have presented to the rest of the world: original melodies, unique rhythms, characteristic expressions, and pristine tones of the soul!" Isaac Levitan had a lot of soft Jewish melancholy, but essentially represented a different strain of the Semitic soul—its ability to transform, to resonate with its surroundings: in Levitan's landscapes, the objective melancholy of Russian nature, as sung in the poetry of Tyuchev and Balmont, found its highest affirmation. Similarly, we can call Israels and Pissarro Jewish artists only insofar as the former sounded a note of sorrowfull intimacy; and in the *plein air* of the latter, there nestled something soulful, unlike the positive impassivity of his fellow Impressionists. But this "soulfulness" is in any case not a primary, but a secondary phenomenon of the Jewish soul. This sadness is acquired historically, yet not it, but the joy of the Song of Songs lies at the source of Jewish culture.

However, could one talk in general about a national substance of the Jews in the sphere of art? Isn't it well known that there is no Jewish art because the biblical religion forbade the creation of "graven images," and the historical conditions of an ever-worrying life could not be conducive to the flourishing and consolidation of beauty? But first of all, as Stasov once observed, the accepted view of Jewish art as an empty place does not correspond with reality. From Stasov's time on, the collection and study of Jewish antiques has been well advanced and it has become clear that, if the creative talents of biblical artists did not materialize or did not survive to our day in the domain of *grand art*, they did find their application in small art—in synagogue art and domestic utensils, in embroideries of the curtains and coverings of Torah Scrolls, in golden, silver, wooden, filigree and enamel objects, in miniature manuscripts. Religion forbade the representation of man—so the artists depicted domestic animals (beginning with the frieze in the palace of Hyrkanos). Religion forbade the convex depiction of animals to avoid the temptation of idolatry—so the artists painted them in colors or concave. It was precisely in the flora and fauna ornaments that the decorative talents of Jewish art were expressed— decorative because another, three-dimensional, relation to the world was forbidden. Hence, its supernatural character, fully corresponding to the metaphysics that grew from the biblical consciousness.

On the other hand, Jewish art had to develop abilities to transform alien beauty: nomadic in its history, it absorbed elements of Phoenician, Assyrian, Hellenistic, and Arabic culture. Hence its "national" weakness and racial, ancient refinement.

In this sense, Bakst's art is undoubtedly "national." Decorative in its nature, eclectic, and yet penetrating all cultures[9] not archeologically but with its sensibility, eastern-spicy in its coloring and classically refined in its linear content—it is the product of some ancient, millennia-old prepa- ration, perhaps a reflection of that Hellenistic Judaism which covered the Jerusalem of Herod's time in glorious garb of the beauties of Japheth. In his beautiful essay *"Terror antiquus,"* Vyacheslav Ivanov observed this *an- cient memory* in Bakst's mien, though he glossed over his racial antiquity.

The same, it seems, should be said about Chagall. No matter how young he is—the heritage of the ages weighs on him. Just that: "weighs"; the ex- cessive weight of this burden explains his hypersensitive nervousness. This does not in the least contradict Chagall's childishness which I men- tioned at the beginning of this essay: when a child paints eyes not in pro- file but *en face*, he repeats an ancient experience of archaic wisdom. And isn't a *Wunderkind* just this spontaneous and mysterious manifestation of an alien experience, accumulated by inheritance, that dwells in him and plays with his childish fingers? Every one of us is farsighted and fantasizes in sleep; but in the sober morning, in vain do we hold on to the escaping dream! Chagall's art is of the night: he knows how to remember dreams; and in dreams, the present is entangled with the past.

The roots of Chagall's painting go into distant depths and its buds are swathed (and poisoned) by the present. In his pointed huts and even in the swirling clouds—there are echoes of Egyptian pyramids; in his palette, which I earlier mentioned as influenced by the Russian Lubok, there is something more ancient and stronger than the Lubok—some exotic color- fulness, as if the gamut of antimony, scarlet, fresh flowers and even the

very texture of his painting seems to be color-dense, cosmetically sensitive. In his paintings, there is no Man, that forbidden image and the like-
ness of God (he does not paint individual portraits), but there are people
and animals. People—poor, oppressed by Orthodox commandments, apoc-
hryphal fears, and stringent religious observance. Animals—meek, sentimental, like gazelles or, on the contrary, with the look of a predator. Like
the pig muzzles in Gogol, curious "muzzles" of bulls and calves peep into
his interiors, and then appear as demonic symbols of the sinful temptation that led Aaron to cast an idol of the golden calf at Mt. Sinai. There is
something erotic from Sodom, reminiscent of Bosch and Goya, in those
Chagallian animal faces.

Chagall's fantastics is saturated with the fears and superstitions of
Lithuanian Jewry that experienced the horrors of Chmyelnitsky's pogroms
and the Polish-Russian wars and lives with the prayerful mysticism of
Hasidism. Much in its fantastics is dark and enigmatic for me, as in the
Kabbala. But I feel in it, in those homeless and flying people, a burning
thirst for the mysterious, a tortured renunciation of the life of the contemporary ghetto, "rancid, swampy, and dirty" (Bialik). Of course, the
roots of Jewish mysticism go back to the depth of eastern religion, but it
flourished along with the persecutions of Judaism—in the discrepancy between the bitter reality and the flights of dreaming. In Wyspiański's[10]
tragedy *Wesele* ("The Wedding"), it is not the funny invitation of a healthy
girl, but the magic oath of the darkly exalted [Jewess] Rachel, daughter of
the innkeeper, that summons the ghosts to the wedding. She came to the
wedding precisely because she sensed the mysticism of the events in this
nuptial "singing hut." "*Ach ta chata rozspiewana!*" [Polish: "Oh, this singing
hut!"], she says to the poet and is the first to throw out the window the invitation of the autumn night, calling "everybody who suffers, who is tortured by fear, whose spirit strives toward freedom" to appear at the wedding. Because Rachel's soul, fettered by the mundane life of the inn, in her
passionate ecstasy, longs for a shining miracle.

This black night, the night of oaths and miracles, peers through the
window of Chagall's study *The Clock*. The heavy pendulum counts the cen-
turies-minutes of monotonous life, and tiny cumbersome figures seek
something in the uncanny nocturnal void...

In another study, two Jews, an old man and a boy, sit at a table dreaming
in the rainbow, green-orange circle of a lamp. The cheap lamp, smoking

like ancient incense, is flaming with the gold of a fire (in which the biblical Jews saw the emanation of God), and the gaze of the Jewish boy, drawn to it, is enflamed ecstatically: perhaps he sees the redeemer Messiah, the promised land... Chagall's work has neither literariness nor "civil grief,"[11] but does have some ardent and sorrowful *thirst for myth*.

III.

But Chagall's fantastics would not be national if it cut off its ties with its soil, the mundane life. There is in it the same note of strong realism approaching the grotesque, and abandoned irony approaching self-mockery, that had to lurk in the Jewish soul as a natural self-defense of life, as the instinct of historical self-preservation. Medieval miniatures of Jewish artists are full of humorous grotesques; humor fills the parables, fables, proverbs, even now inseparable from Jewish speech. In Bialik's poem describing the passionate waiting for Messiah, he didn't forget the details of the coarsely realistic, clumsily funny life:

> And the maid behind the oven,
>
> Blowing up the fire in the samovar,
>
> Pulled out her sooty face:
>
> Isn't the Messiah coming?
>
> Didn't I hear the thunder
>
> Of his Shofar?
>
> [*"When the Days Will Get Long: From the Visions of the Later Prophets"*]

That is not the way the Poles in Wyspiański's play wait for the galloping of the Archangel. Waiting for centuries in vain did not teach the Jews to combine the humor with the pathos of tragedy. The eternal wanderer, Ahasverus, whom Chagall liked to depict wandering over the blue cupolas and roofs of a Russian provincial town, saw so much in his historical age and got so used to everything that nothing will crush his eternal passage:

> Toujours le soleil se lève,
>
> Toujours, toujours
>
> Tourne la terre où moi je cours
>
> Toujours, toujours.
>
> > [*Béranger, Le juif errant*]

This is the world irony, I would say, and the premature old man's wisdom that erupt in Chagall. And everywhere, at the threshold of houses, under snowflakes, and even on the roofs, his old fiddler, the eternal accompaniment of weddings and funerals, plays a melody, old as the world and monotonous, performed with a recitative... I remember my amazement at a study of Chagall's showing a pregnant woman and a pregnant horse. "Is it my fault it always happens like that?" answered the artist. I also recall another work named "What Happens at Home" ["The Birth"]— a crowded Jewish interior where people eat, pray, and give birth, and above it all, as in a dream, phantoms of people are flying as if falling from the opened sky. Rozanov[12] who attached himself so one-sidedly to the "wedding" essence of the biblical soul, would have seen in this painting by Chagall a synthesis of "all of Israel," a bedroom of world history with its "womb" and "offspring bearing." But this is something else; this is the synthesis of the eternally living mundane life and the fantastics hovering above it. Chagall's interior where people eat, pray, and give birth and where, instead of a ceiling, there is a thick blue sky—it is the same "singing hut," the singing hut of the homeless-fantastic mundane life, by some miracle hovering between sky and earth...

Here we approach the very essence of Chagall's talent; he sees the real world sharply and senses another world beyond it. In the cynical grotesques of Chagall, there is the fairytale quality of capriccio; in the small provincial mundane life, he grasps some great being... In this sense, Rozanov's retrospective formula "Zion, Babylon, and Vilna"[13] is really applicable to Chagall if we substitute Vitebsk for Vilna. Chagall grew up in a crowded provincial ghetto and the images of mundane life pursue him obsessively, even when he describes the subtle and lyrical aloofness of the loving Pierrot and Colombina. But apparently there is some clearing in the forest of "provincialism": from *his* street, *his* home—into the boundless mystical. The dirty girl Aldonza is no less inspiring than the beautiful Dulcinea because she leaves room for a dream. Hoffmann,[14] who grew up among philistines, apple-sellers and the Tomcat Murr, was a bright storyteller; and Gogol found fantastic curios in the stupidity of Russian mundane life.

Chagall senses the supernatural, the mysterious, not only in Jewish life, but in mundane life in general. He is a student of Bakst and Dobuzhinsky, but in the *authenticity* of his provincial observations, no doubt, the student surpassed his teachers. For in Chagall's "provincialism" you don't find

Dobuzhinsky's graphic precision, his metropolitan mockery of the provinces; but there is some spiritual participation in the described milieu,
an artless naiveté of observing. Dobuzhinsky senses the mysticism of
the big city, whereas in the province he is captivated by the funny and
old-fashioned. Chagall senses the mysticism of the provincial even in the
funny and contemporary. His province is a fairy tale, sentimental and cynical at the same time, boring and mediocre—and yet fantastically bright.
He has holidays when dancing grass grows green in the sky and huts sway
upside down, and funerals where the sky is covered with a black crepe.

His little churches, mills, market fair showbooths, many-colored hats
are like children's toys; his clumsy little humans at weddings and funerals
are like marionettes; and even inanimate objects, lamps and tables, seem
in his paintings to be mysteriously alive. Chagall could have realized on
stage what the contemporary theater needs more than anything—*psychological decoration*, in which mundane life style would seem real and inspired
from within, like things in Remizov's world—through the prism of the girl
Sasha, "who is three years old, three thousand, and perhaps three times
three thousand" *(Maka)*. For Hoffinann was right: only *"a childish poetic sensibility"* can introduce us into the true world. But, in Chagall's early work,
there was an unhealthy childishness—an exaggerated hyper-sensitivity of
"three thousand" years, and a tense worry of the contemporary Jewish
Pale. As if some bloody, pogrom-inspired fears poisoned his childhood,
and his fantastics often seemed like a feverish delirium of a sick child...

IV.

Paris exerted a positive influence on Chagall. He remained himself, but
acquired what he lacked—form. From childhood on, he had a sensibility
for color and linear patterns, but in his images, there was no "plasticity"
that brings images closer to semblances, which religion had forbidden
since ancient times. In his works, there was no flesh, and his decorative
mysticism was not sufficiently convincing. He was in danger of remaining
a *"Wunderkind"* in short pants. His sojourn in Paris brought him close to
Aryan idolatry without depriving him of the national-eastern qualities (of
color and ornament), it made his work more condensed by acquiring a
sense for volume. The stone-gray landscape of Paris taught him to feel the
borders of objects to a much greater extent than the crooked walls of
the colorful provincial colorful houses.

Chagall passed through the school of Cubism, but just that: he passed through it without getting fossilized spiritually as did many others; for him, form didn't become a sovereign fetish. A good example of this influence is the outstanding study *The Sweeper*—a hard metal-formed figure among heavily swirling provincial dust. Only now, having seen Cézanne and El Greco, was Chagall able to paint such architecturally ornamented, compositionally solid, and truly monumental biblical images as his dour religious Jew in a black-and-white tallis, resembling a biblical Prophet, or some other artisan on the background of a pyramid of heaped-up huts.

But this, of course, doesn't mean that Chagall began painting à la Cézanne or Picasso—his mode of observation emerged from the Paris crucible with all its erstwhile originality. The black-and-white harmony of *The Praying Jew* perhaps reflected the beauty of black-and-white velvet of the synagogue seen in childhood. The influence of Paris was manifest precisely when Chagall returned to his home province. He painted the same motifs which had earlier captivated him, only now they reflected not just a "childish poetic sensibility," but also the mastery of a mature artist. In the blue domed temple and little houses covered with snow of his Eternal Jew—there is a beautiful, sharp hewing of surfaces. The dark, dirty smocks of his Jews became formed and articulated in hard, sculpted folds with bluish rusty shades. Without losing any of its mysticism, the whole Chagallian world became materially tangible: Chagall learned to see dreams while awake, in the middle of the sober day.

But his return to his homeland also brought some humility to his observation, softened his satirical edginess and screaming colorfulness. Such are his Vitebsk sketches of 1914. In those provincial streets, under a somber gray sky, with the heaped-up wooden houses, delicately puffed-up trees, native shop signs, and poor thin horses, you no longer hear the anguished scream. You sense in them some subdued, humble love. His *Barbershop* is veiled in calm—one of the best interiors I have seen in exhibitions of recent years, and I. A. Morozov[15] did well to buy it—a provincial barbershop filled with a meek sun, dusty air, and the pitiful smile of cheap wallpaper...

The ennobling of Chagall's colors was especially reflected in the sketches of Vitebsk women. Here is a woman in a yellowish coat, pale pink skirt, against the background of a gray wall and black rags; from this coarse and poor piece of life, Chagall created a refined "legend" of cool harmony. And here is a woman ironing with a black ornamented iron, among the decorations of the wallpaper and the green-scarlet curtain—a work of subtle Degas-like beauty. The stamp of a master lies on many other studies—soldiers with bread, painted with an amazing confidence, guitarists substituting for the former fiddlers, and even on the series of provincial Pierrots and Columbinas. Somebody said that you can recognize a colorist in his gray hue, indeed Chagall's gray-black gamuts testify to his coloristic taste.

Chagall remained the same decorator and ornamentalist his race made him. But his work began to liberate itself from the flood; his people stopped flying in the rooms. In reality itself, in the truth of three dimensions, he began to guess the mystical life of colors and lines. The young and homeless Akhashverush stood with both feet on the ground—wet, warm, fruitful. And though, as before, he is different in every painting, still this nestling to mother earth is a hopeful sign of his creative blossoming.

He has to preserve his Hoffmannesque "childish poetic sensibility," so rare in our adult, too adult, time, and his sharpness and fantastics. But he will finally have to overcome his nervousness, his anguish. When the legacy of "three thousand" years stops burdening him, but becomes his epical tradition—his wonderful art will become religiously appeased and luminous, and, therefore, also objectively valuable.

Abram Efros
Chagall

I. THE NATURE OF HIS ART

I.

He enters the room the way practical people walk in, with confidence and precision, overcoming space, striding forcefully, testifying to a consciousness that the earth is earth and only earth. But look: at a certain step, his body totters and snaps drolly; like Pierrot collapsing in half in a puppet theater, fatally stung by betrayal and bending slightly sideways, cracked, with an expression apologizing for some guilt unknown to us. Chagall approaches, shakes hands—and sits down obliquely, as if falling into the chair. Chagall has the beaming face of a young fawn; but in conversation, the kindly softness sometimes evaporates like a mask, and then we think that the corners of his lips are too sharp, like arrows, and he bares his teeth tenaciously, like an animal, and the gray-blue kindness of his eyes too often shines with the fury of strange explosions, perspicacious and blind at the same time, making his interlocutor think he is probably reflected in some fantastic manner in the mirrors of Chagall's eyes, and perhaps will later recognize himself in one of those green, blue, red, flying, disheveled, folded-over, twisted people—in Chagall's future paintings.

And when hours pass in conversation, talking about the dear mundane world, work, his wife, his child, Chagall suddenly boils over with some prophetic phrase like: "We talk only as if before God, our way is faultless because it is God's way..."—we are no longer amazed; we even understand Chagall, we can see what strong but rational-intangible threads link Chagall's phantasmagoric expressions with his stories about dear daily life, illuminating it and permeating it with light, and opening, behind the first plane of his words, a second, third, fourth, and more planes—the planes of his soul. They are as inevitable in Chagall and as essential to his flesh and blood as those unexpected gray strands cutting through the bright curling hair of the not-yet-thirty-year-old artist.

II.

His art is as difficult as Chagall himself: to love him, you have to get close to him, and to get close, you have to go through the slow and insistent temptation of penetrating his hard shell. Because the first impression gets helplessly entangled in the contradictions and idiosyncrasies of Chagall's art.

That Chagall is very talented can be seen right away; but why does he do all those strange things? Why is this marvelously painted old Jew green? And another has [a] red [beard] and green hands? And a third has an identical miniature Jew standing on his head, just turning to the other side? In the belly of a horse we see an unborn colt, and two human figures protrude from under his hooves? The head of an old woman leaped off and is flying upward, and the headless body swiftly sinks down to a cow standing on the roof of a house? And the girl with a bouquet—a boy glued to her lips, folded up in the air, around her head, like a cat hurled upward? An ox has a man's jacket and human hands, and sits pensively leaning on his elbow, between two bare feet dangling from his shoulders, which probably belong to that feminine head covered with a kerchief, the nape of her neck hanging down, who spits into his mouth? And the man looking through a window at Paris has a Janus-head—one face forward, one face backward; and the cat with a girl's face looks from the windowsill at two people lying with their heads end to end at the foot of the Eiffel Tower and as tall as the tilted multistoried buildings all around?

What is it—disease or mischief, that particular aesthetic mischief of the young, with which so many great artists began their creative path.

Perhaps all we now need to do in relation to Chagall is just to forgive his present boldness for his great future? Or is there some third point of view from which another "angle on Chagall" opens up, in which his present creation is no longer a madness or throwing dust in your eyes, but is artistically justified and psychologically convincing in its mundane absurdities, and where the questions of inexperienced people—"why does he do it?"—will be met by us, the viewers "who came to Chagall," with the same astonishment with which Chagall himself meets the visitors to his exhibition who pour onto his pictures their: "Why?" and "What for?"

—Yes, exactly.

III.

It is hard to get close to Chagall because you have to overcome his contradictions, to be able to synthesize them. Behind the elements of his art thrusting out in all directions, you have to find one axis and a general guiding force dominating the multitude of colorful parts. Chagall—a master of mundane life, but also Chagall—a visionary; Chagall—a storyteller, but also Chagal—a philosopher; a Russian Jew, a Hasid—but also a pupil of French Modernism; but also, in general, a cosmopolitan fantasist, soaring like a witch on a broomstick above the globe and in his swooping flight carrying behind him a multitude of various particles from a multitude of various lives which descend in a swarm on his canvases when times of meditation and creativity emerge, and the flowing and roiling elemental force of Chagall's visions is graphically transformed into images and colors.

Had Chagall been only a visionary, it would not be difficult to accept him, as it was not difficult to accept the visions of Churlanis. It would be even easier had Chagall been a pure depicter of mundane life even if he was the most leftist and radical among the artists creating forms of new realist painting today: we are already experienced enough with various "deformations" not to be scared of them, and perhaps even to find some charm in them. Finally, it would not be difficult to be tempted by the possibility of deciphering a convoluted and complex allegory if Chagall's headless and green people were only allegories that can be changed into a simple and easily understood parable, like the monsters, scarecrows and cripples in Goya's etchings.

But Chagall has neither this nor that nor the other. His visions live entirely in the confines of the simplest mundane life, while his mundane life is entirely visionary. The people and objects of daily life are permeated with the nature of specters, but these Chagallian specters are by no means shadows with no mass or circumference or hue, and whom chopping or stabbing is as senseless as chopping or stabbing the air. Chagall's spectral daily life has all the palpability and weight of normal objects and bodies. And if, nevertheless, he is governed by some law which tears him apart and brushes people, animals and objects around the air, confounds all logic and sense of earthly proportions and interrelations, the poor law of allegory or the low law of a crossword puzzle is least guilty in it; we face here not a logical game, but an authentic, unconditional seeing of an immense internal saturation.

IV.

You can understand Chagall only through *empathy*, not through *comprehension*. The law of deformation which gives such a strange countenance to

Chagall's works—that law which moves the absurdities and strangenesses of children's stories, inventions, and fears—is the same law that creates the phantasmagoric world of Jewish national mysticism which endeavored in the great movement of Hasidism miraculously to transform the mundane life of poverty and suffering of shtetl existence.

The favorite and primary link between events in stories children tell is the word "suddenly," which is not at all mechanical or external—otherwise the pure truthfulness of childish fantasy would have brushed it aside; on the contrary, the word "suddenly" expresses the very essence and intimate nature of that elemental force of unlimited possibilities which, in the child's eye, abound in the world; the word "suddenly" merely warns the listener that this omnipotent, elemental force will splash one of its caprices on him. If we translate this "suddenly" into adult language, we get "miracle." But not "miracle" in the sense of an unusual and rare exception violating the laws of nature, but "miracle" as a habitual element of daily life, a "miracle" that denies the very possibility of "life without miracle," and asserts that "anything may happen and does"; and this is precisely the world perception which has created the practical miracle-making of Hasidism in the modern history of the Jews.

Such an internal belief that "anything happens" speaks in Chagall's work. Therefore, you can penetrate his art without breaking your neck on the shell, only if you evoke in yourself the vestiges of childhood dreams, reviving in your soul those forgotten sensations, when the fear of a dark room lived in us, for we knew that the hairy hands of some monster may penetrate the desolate and black walls and drag us off, and the old chair may suddenly bare its teeth and pounce on us.

What's the difference between the demands offered the reader by Hoffmann's fantastic world and the fantastic world of Baron Münchhausen? Isn't it that Hoffmann requires belief in his unrealities, and Münchhausen demands disbelief? Isn't this the foundation on which they build their respective effects? Like Hoffmann, Chagall needs a spectator who believes in him, his spectator must be able to succumb to the unrealities of his paintings and visions, to entrust himself to their special logic just as he can abandon himself to the flow of Hoffmann's inventions. That is why when a naive spectator approaches Chagall with his naturalistic criteria and angrily points out "Chagall's absurdities," the artist can only wonder bitterly: he truly understands nothing in his spectators' indignation, for they do not measure his art with the same yardstick as he. An axiom in the cognition of art states that the art of every master is a country with its own special laws; to understand an artist in this sense implies succumbing to those laws and approaching the external manifestations of his work—paintings and statues—from the inside, from the creative will of the artist. That is why, if Chagall's art is invincibly chaotic and hopelessly senseless when approached from outside and measured with the illegitimate yardstick of realistic-mundane painting—it is clear and opens up to you almost schematically, if you follow its own internal logic.

V.

In the development of Chagall's art so far, three periods clearly emerge before our eyes. External boundaries determine the first as a preparatory, provincial-and-Petersburg period, when Shagal came from his Vitebsk Province to St.-Petersburg to study painting, attended Bakst's school, and worked on his first independent paintings. The second period—abroad; Shagal left for Paris, where he became "Chagall," impressing the turbulent Bohemia of La Ruche with his unusual canvases which promoted him to the ranks of the most interesting "masters of tomorrow," and were triumphantly taken to exhibitions of the new art in Berlin and Amsterdam. This is the period where such chimera canvases were created as "Paris Through the Window," "The Carter," "The Calf Seller," "The Brides," and so on, with their headless bodies, two-faced heads, and flying cows. Finally, the third, contemporary period—the period of his return to Russia at the outbreak of the Great War, when Chagall created his "Vitebsk Cycle": "The Barbershop," "The Shtetl Lyozno," "In the Provinces," "On the Outskirts of Vitebsk," "The Praying Jew," "The Birthday," "The Guitarist," and others.

The internal line of his creative work passed through those chronological boundaries amazingly whole. Chagall had no interruptions, no treading water, no deviations. The originality of Chagall's art was evident from the beginning, and went its own way, where the boundaries of the above-mentioned external periods of development indicated only turning points in the interrelations of the two major elements of his work. These elements, inseparably linked to each other from Chagall's first steps, are the genre of mundane life and visionary mysticism. Chagall's earliest paintings created the basic "Chagallian" impression: the unreal countenance of real life. The Chagall of those works is a dreamy child who grew up in a

Hasidic family in a Jewish shtetl. But childhood and Hasidism mean a dream multiplied by a dream; this is the source of the boundless ore of Chagall's fantasy. And the mundane life around him is the life of a small town in Vitebsk Province, that is, the very quintessence of everyday life, the very thick of the most pitiful poverty and opaque existence.

Chagall's dream and the shtetl existence had either to break each other or find a higher and integral connection. Art gave Chagall the redeeming synthesis. Chagall's painting showed the light in the humble poverty of the people, streets, cattle, and huts of his little Lyozno, which he depicted with all the acuity of love for his hometown. Chagall's childish vision and Hasidic mysticism discovered a world of miracle in the daily round.

There are two paintings, "The Wedding" of 1908, and "The Funeral" of 1909, where we can observe precisely and profoundly how his hometown existence is transformed in the young Chagall, and how he constructs his canvases. First of all, it is a simple story about a simple event from simple life. A story with no details and no makeup, laconic and clear. "The Wedding": two musicians walk in the street, behind them come the bridegroom and bride, followed by an old man and woman and two children, and three more relatives bring up the rear; a water-carrier and a merchant, a woman and a couple of kids have stopped in the middle of the street and are watching the procession, and in back, a Jew with long coattails excitedly shakes his hands in the air.

The protocol of daily life! But what a remarkable face it all has: as in children's drawings, people are higher than the buildings because people are more important than buildings, and the perspective of the street is sharply reared up for, otherwise, not everybody would be seen, and not everything would be clear to us spectators—and is it possible not to show us anything in this Lyozno heaven, including the street lamp, raised like a torch above the procession? As in Hasidic legends, the figures of the Jews in Chagall's country are unusual and transformed: yes, those are shtetl Jews, but they are apparently made of some special material, and we won't be astonished if the whole procession suddenly rises up into the air where the fiddler will go on chirping and the bridegroom will take the bride—we shall not be astonished because what we see is "life inside a miracle," and perhaps the Jew with long coattails, shaking his hand is prophesying about this miracle, about the birth of the Messiah out of this new couple, for believers expect Messiah from every wedding.

In "The Funeral" ["The Dead"] Lyozno existence reveals its mystical nature even more clearly: again everything is simple and everything is chimerical, but too simple and too chimerical. In the middle of the reared-up street, between the huts, lies the corpse in a shroud, surrounded by burning candles; a giant gravedigger raises his shovel, and a woman spreading her hands high whisks aside, and above them all, astride the roof of a house, a strange Jew, bent over his violin, draws a melody—in harmony with the wind howling under the glowering sky, tearing up the clouds, and shaking the leaves with a shoe and sock hanging over the huts instead of signs.

It is amazing that, even in those early years, Chagall uses color and hue as means of characterizing and influencing the psyche of the viewer, and not just for conveying the realistic-existential coloring of the objects. Chagall goes hand in hand here with the most progressive and sensitive masters of our art. The painting of our days consciously began to use the influence of color not only on the eye, but also on the spiritual world: the painterly texture of the picture is assigned the task of evoking a direct re-action in the internal world of the spectator by circumventing the plastic image, playing on the spectator as on a keyboard with color, line, layering of paint, and curve of the line; sometimes the artist even tries to *character-ize* an object by the very selection of colors. Chagall promoted this "psy-chic value of color" from the start—subtly and freely. And perhaps it was because of their "color mystique" more than anything else that the realis-tic life in his pictures is permeated with the order of a different, miracu-lous existence.

VI.

When Chagall turned up in Paris and had a chance to get close to the very center of world art, the balance between the everyday life and the visionary elements of his art was deeply disturbed. Above the little world of Lyozno with its small dimensions and domestic density hovered the monstrosities and spaces of a Cyclopean city. On the other hand, what Chagall encoun-tered in the art world of Paris shattered all the everyday clamps of his im-ages and themes. Chagall's mysticism, in its very essence, in its striving mystically to transform the countenance of daily life, carried a centrifugal force striving to rend the frozen forms of observable existence. However, that early Chagall was still too attached to "the earth," to "his Lyozno," not to hold the destructive impulses of his fantasy in check. But now, Paris removed all his shackles, and his Lyozno daily life was literally torn to pieces by the unlimited explosion.

Chagall landed in Paris at that moment when Cubism was at the zenith of its triumph and influence. That is, from the outside, in the form of a mandatory aesthetic program, Chagall confronted those aspects of Cubism to which his own art strove from inside him. Cubism splintered the whole visual world into pieces and parts in the name of an abstract aesthetic principle; but the mysticism of Chagall's creation, albeit by different laws, also attempted to tear up the cover of daily life. If, by its nature, the cold, heady force of Cubism was strange to Chagall's fiery immediacy; in its results, the triumphant Cubism gave it exactly what it needed. Most important, in the eyes of the masters of the new art, Cubism destroyed the value of any re-creation of objects in their normal, "everyday" aspect; the mandatory, essential "deformation" of objects was pronounced as the basic principle of art. Thus, the doors were wide open for Chagall's fantasy. The raging force erupted. Some terrible cataclysm crumbled Chagall's native world of shtetl Judaism.

That cycle of chimerical canvases, described above, which created Chagall's resounding fame among the innovators and their adherents, and evoked a similar rage in the philistines and Naturalists—that cycle is a truly shattering confession, a stunning story of a fiery storm which gusted over Chagall's art in Paris. "Foil... Clowning..."—but I don't know anything more palpable and visual in its power of persuasion and sincerity than those extraordinary paintings. It truly took a lot of internal courage and artistic talent to imprint the rage of the storming force so directly and plastically. Perhaps those who value this cycle above anything else in Chagall are not so wrong, for such a conjunction of tense depth and artistic significance did not recur in him later on. Incidentally, this assessment would be true only if what Chagall disclosed to us here did not have such an exclusively narrow, personal character, if that broad, generally significant value of the internal experience which marks his creativity in the two other periods was expressed here.

Be that as it may, in any case, the purely artistic organization of those Paris compositions is no doubt remarkable. Channeling the minute chaos of formless visions into a plastic frame, it was possible only by a strong artistic welding of all parts of the picture. Cubism helped Chagall here too,

for if Cubism is especially strong in anything, it is in the iron functional-
ity of its artistic constructs, in that utterly granite solidity which charac-
terizes the constructions Cubism erects from parts of objects that had dis-
integrated into their components. Chagall knew how to achieve the same
thing—he channeled the flood of his anarchic force into the sturdiest
artistic shores. The raging colors and precise rhythms of the Paris canvases bound it as with a steel hoop, and their magnificent organization
calmed the viewer's eye, excited by the internal chaos of the picture.

VII.

Chagall was faced with a choice: either return his art to the forms of the
real world or stop being an artist. You cannot float in the melted stream of
fuzzy mystical visions for years, for this fire not only illuminates but also
consumes. A third solution is possible: mannerism, when, with a gelid
hand and ashen heart, the artist produces imitations of himself and offers
false visions as true. But of course, Chagall, with his unusual ultimate sincerity, could not become his own follower.

His return to Russia at the start of the war was a cure for Chagall. Like a
prodigal son returning to his father's home, he returned to his Jewish
shtetl world. He attached himself to it with the same zeal and fervor of
spirit with which, in Paris, he crumbled and eroded its poor forms. The
Vitebsk cycle of Chagall's paintings emerged in a feverish and whining
sweep and Chagall's devotion to work, always great, here knew no bounds.
Chagall creates dozens of canvases, and each is like an embrace, arms
stretched out to everything Chagall saw again in his homeland. He culti-
vates and lavishes all the subtlety and delicacy of his amazing palette and
the nobility of a refined painting to record respectably the face of his re-
acquired homeland.

The tattered parts of Lyozno daily life are re-united; and "the soul of
things" that stormed in the general stream return to their objects; and in
Chagall's painting, the previous Jewish world re-appears. Chagall paints
every alley, every person, every house of his home places. In the Vitebsk cycle, his whole family parades before us, young and old, childhood friends,
neighbors, street urchins, beggars, houses, huts, trees, grass, cattle—Chagall
even paints the forbidden pig affectionately, for truly everything is blessed
and holy in this re-acquired daily life. And at the same time, what a difference from the daily life of his first, pre-Paris period! If there, Chagall's

mystical force strove to break out of objects, here it strives from the outside to get into things.

In "A Wedding" of 1908, people still walk on the earth and we only feel that at any minute, they may leave it and soar in the air, where the true nature of their being draws them; whereas in the paintings of the Vitebsk cycle, these people, on the contrary, are still soaring in the air, as in the paintings of the Paris period, but they are already descending to the earth and soon will have to land finally and stand on their feet. Thus a young couple hovers over the shtetl in the painting "To My Wife"; thus an old Jew with a sack soars over the town in "The Outskirts of Vitebsk"; thus above the girl with a bouquet in "Birthday" a young man has frozen in the air kissing her lips. Even whatever has landed on the earth still has some instability in these paintings, a lack of firmness typical of first touching the earth after a long flight, as if the earth's gravity had not yet fully embraced this new Chagallian daily life. In this sense, we must note how fragile and light people and things stand on the Vitebsk canvases, and how even houses and rooms are still unstably attached to the earth. That is the source of the strange coloring of objects, the green, violet, red bodies and faces of people: this is the heritage of the Paris whirlwind, its mystical colorfulness, the glow of its colorful fires.

VIII.

Today, Chagall stands in the very heat of his Vitebsk period—what the results will be we can only vaguely guess. There are reasons to think that Chagall's present road leads him to that "Grand Art" of transformed daily life indicated in several of his recent big works—in the magnificent "Praying Jew," in the "Green Old Man," and such; here the shtetl Jews have grown into enormous national figures, deeply rooted in their mundane typicality and, at the same time, endowed with all the internal significance of a symbol.

However, new traits have recently begun to break through in Chagall's works, traits of an even denser, hotter, hastier, voluntarily obsequious submission to "the tyranny of small things," the rule of dear daily life. I saw a new series by Chagall: a *Dacha* cycle. A man living in a dacha with a front yard with green trees, on the balcony hang red dotted curtains, on the table a golden samovar, and in a wicker basket, scarlet and blue berries—here he is, *Man in Paradise*, as if, after a hard earthly road, abiding "in a place of light, a place of grains, a place of peace"...

Is it a final reconciliation with everydayness that the subdued artist has to go through? But what will then link his "Grand Art " with the "apology for a dacha?"

How can we know... ? Except for guesses, what does Chagall leave us? We must admit courageously that there is nothing more hopeless than predicting his future, for among our artists, there is no spirit more free and unexpected in his creative idea than this God-intoxicated Chagall...

II. THE PALETTE. GRAPHICS

I.

Russian art can be called art in makeup. You must not get too close to it; otherwise, instead of a hero, you will face N.N. in makeup. Russian artists are charming storytellers, clever stage directors and sensitive psychologists. But how many of them can also be called masters? In Russian painting, you enjoy the insightful vivacity of portrait characteristics as much as the accuracy of scenes from everyday life and almost frightening clairvoyance of historical resurrections; Russian paintings can be read inexhaustibly. But do not get close to their canvases! Beyond the figures and objects, when your eye detects the rough surface of a hastily painted canvas and your gaze follows the clods and ruts of the daubs—what spleen overcomes you among this swampy overflow of paint! With fatal clarity, you will distinguish that the traits that captivated you are not art, but only the makeup of art, in which all effects are calculated on "looking from afar," "looking from the distance," "looking from an auditorium," through the deluding prism of the footlights. The unstable layers of paint hold shakily onto the canvas, the color is exaggerated, the tone is approximate, the contour is dangling.

Art in makeup... I remember Verhaeren[16] in the Tretyakov Gallery seeking masters of the brush and finding only makeup artists. We had nothing to respond to him when he filtered our painters through the golden sieve of the French palette—a palette of masters and mastery—and hall after hall and artist after artist flew somewhere into non-being. We ourselves often called our art *Provincial* but we believed that a provincial aware of his provinciality was not hopeless. Yet we nevertheless did not value our art *so* poorly.

Verhaeren's judgment was the judgment of the metropolis of art on a provincial school; and when, stooped and pulling the hanging threads of his endless moustache and dropping precise evaluations, the poet ran from an ancient icon to Shchukin's "Lady in a Cap," and drew in the air with his long fingers before Levitsky's "Anna Davia"; when, throwing his glasses on his nose before Sylvester Shchedrin, Fedotov, or Ivanov, he pronounced ambiguous aphorisms about Cézanne, Corot and the Dutch; and later, *without stopping*, slowing down pensively only before the bursts of snow of Surikov's "Morozova," swept by even Repin, Levitan and Serov, to nod affirmatively before Vrubel's "Portrait of My Wife," and finish with a deeply satisfied "Voila!"... before Somov's "Lady in Blue"—the circle of *art* was drawn by him with authority and conviction.

Should we reconcile ourselves to that? But what can we do? That's how it is, you cannot circumvent or get around it; our art is the art of painters but not of masters; it has no taste for métier; and every name that augments the short dynasty of Russian masters of the brush is a true event.

II.

How did the provincial Chagall turn out to have that rarest gift denied so many great and praised talents? An accidental caprice of fate? Or the buds of a French seed falling on the sickly-sharpened sensibility of Chagall's talent? Be that as it may, the numerous pleiade of the young generation of our artists counts only one master, and this master is Chagall.

A skillful and excellently-precise brush; now fondly licking, now scratching; now bathing in the even ripple of the daubs, now scattering marvellous "Chagallian" little dots, drops and patterns, joyful and resounding, scarlet, green, yellow, leaping and coiling, like deposits of posies and Chinamen on the joyous wallpaper of our half-forgotten nursery; the surface—exquisitely worked—now rough, sometimes protruding with the bald spots of the background, sometimes swelling with layered hills of paint; an even and smooth growing and waning of the tone, precise and finished, reminiscent of the growth of a range of sounds under the fingers of a flawless pianist; and a special soft film of velvet, or even the delicate down of a peach, lying over everything and evoking in the spectator a wish to touch and caress the painting, to feel its grain with his fingertips—this is Chagall's palette, transforming the colorful cover of his paintings into a kind of geographical relief map, where you can travel long and fruitfully, conscious that the irregularities, convexities and concavities of every centimeter are utterly justified.

A magician among the images and visions of his paintings, among his tubes of paint, ringing his brushes and knocking his easel, he also conjures up the image of a veritable alchemist in a pointed hat knocking his retorts and test tubes, where the philosopher's stone crystallizes in smoke and flame. What a stew of spices had to be activated to create the painting of "The Green Lovers," "Mariasenka with a Dog," "The Sweeper," "The Praying Jew." Only such an elasticity of artistic means of depiction, operating with "infinitely small" units of painterly elements, allowed Chagall not to get lost in the whirlwind fogs of his spectral existence, to fill the skin and bones of the simplest beings and objects with the movement of some flaming and tenuous matter; and force us spectators to believe that the axioms of the regular painterly experience—that presumably a body has "body color," a large object is larger than a small one, things are not but seem, etc., etc.—are just a boring delusion of tired routine which he, Marc Chagall, has the authority and power to waive.

III.

We are talking about Chagall's painterly art at its peaks and in a static perspective, relying on the best successes of his recent experiments. Obviously, the history of the unfolding of Chagall's mastery would have brought some qualifications into our description.

However, even in this most recent and accomplished stage, Chagall is not faultless in one respect. He cannot be coarse. He is not sufficiently courageous. Like an adolescent boy, he hasn't yet emerged from the immature plumpness of his limbs. He cannot force his brush to scream and shock. He does not command resounding and terrifying tones. He may be angry, raging, sometimes even furious, but not fearsome. Like the youth Jeremiah, summoned by God to serve as a prophet, he could have repeated: "Oh, Lord Yahweh, look: I cannot prophesy for I am still a youth"... Blessed be he, that his current period—of reconciliation with mundane life—requires only an elegiac tenderness and a calm joy, and there is room and order for all the delicate and skillful devices of his palette. But let us recall his Paris cycle—a cycle of storm, shock and chaos. So what? Our reproach relates primarily to this period. It is not the roar of apocalyptic storms—Chagall whistles on a lyrical pipe; he found sharp, confused and penetrating tones, for let us not forget that he is a *master*; with the ebb and flow of his rage and passion, he hurls at us with a wind-up the whole great force of his clairvoyance and talent. But it is not the same brush with which the artist engulfed in the horror of a cataclysm and torn by his spiritual pain, hits the trembling and sighing canvas with both hands. There is some discrepancy between the tossed-about, torn parts of objects hanging in the voids of the canvas, and the insufficiently simple and rigorous, over-subtle and aristocratic texture of his painterly script. When even the air cracks and shrinks and settles in Cubistic folds and edges, as in his Paris works, then Chagallian anxiety and confusion is not enough.

One thing we don't yet know: is this softness and lack of courage in Chagall's nature, and will lyricism forever be the primary force of his creativity? Or, forged and reinforced with time, Chagall will find another language for the fiery and fateful visions of his creation! If that happens, and if the boundaries of his ability and powers thus expand, then Chagall will appear before us as one of the most accomplished talents of our art.

IV.

A painter turning to graphics becomes a philosopher of his own work.

This will be recognized when we recall that graphics is the most abstract and generalizing kind of art. It is more calculation than impulse, more thought than feeling, more prose than poetry. Therefore, painting is always more mysterious than graphics; and an artist, shifting from the palette to the pen, *exposes* himself and carries his true face out of the dusk into the light. Perhaps we must even say that the graphics of a painter is only the formula of his painting—a condensation composed of the main features of his art.

Chagall turns to graphics suddenly, often, and in a storm. The painterly series and the graphic series intersect and interact. In their parts, motifs and topics, they are amazingly close. There are graphic themes which later became paintings; there are paintings that were eventually transposed into paper and ink. Chagall is a graphic artist as much as he is a painter. Therefore, his graphics is not a peripheral branch of his art. It leaves no room for the accidental. Those are not fruits of creative pauses or fuzzy ruminations, drawn on pieces of paper as most artists draw them, if they are not masters of graphics by profession. Chagall's graphic works are even denser, fuller, and more saturated than his painting. This is how they should be, for if, on canvas, Chagall creates his images, on paper he thinks about them, investigates their nature. In this sense, it is very significant

that Chagall is now especially and eagerly absorbed in graphics. Sometimes it seems that this profusion of graphic material indicates that Chagall faces the closure of the current period of his painting, for the artist is
too *cognizant* of his work to be able to stay long enough with the current
themes and devices. However, it would be most incautious to exaggerate
the meaning of this. Chagall never becomes analytical, classifying, brainy.
He is always ardent; and even if his graphics is just a philosophy of his art,
it is cognate to that *fiery* philosophy with which the Kabbala seared the
thought and heart of Judaism, running God's chariot, the *Merkava*, through
the spheres of the universe; it is cognate to the ecstatic world-view of Hasidism and in the Christian domain—to the systems of the Church mystics.

Therefore, Chagall meditating on his visions, Chagall the graphic artist,
is perceived even more sharply than Chagall the painter. Reading Chagall's
graphic "book," you read a master's compendium of his art—precise, laconic and lucid: about the world of spirit gliding through the world of matter, about the disintegration of daily life exploded by the raging of hidden
forces, about the delicate and intimate earth gathering and coalescing the
scattered parts of beings and things. But here everything is exposed, here
there are no unfinished words; this is Chagall as he is.

In his painting, the color and tone of the paints, the lightness and accuracy of his brushstrokes, the clever network of daubs—obstruct and skim
the *rage* of his spirit which fills the canvas; they seduce with their own soft
beauty. In graphics, however, the furious dynamism of his art appears before us entirely bare. Black clods, black grains of dust, black ornaments,
black nets, black pieces of figures and objects, *tense as if screwed to the ut-
most*—they truly jump onto the spectator, sweep him into their whirlpool
and carry him off. In the images of his painting, Chagall is often uncertain;
even more often, we perceive him with uncertainty; parts of the painting
seem to us overly vague, the visions caught in mid-flight, by one wing
Chagall's graphic solutions are crystallized to the highest degree, absolute
and final. We think about it first of all when, using Hugo's definition, we
say that Chagall created a new tremor in art.

v.

Painting and graphics are, in principle, mutually opposed and hostile; but
in the work of one artist, such relations between them cannot exist because the living personality of the master reconciles them. In this case,

they sometimes even color each other. Traits of graphic schematization and sharpness appear in the paintings; while, in the graphics, we may observe a certain painterly gamut of tones and glimpses of chiaroscuro. Such is the case with Chagall. For his painting "The Birthday" may serve as a telling example of this kind which emerged in the very heat of his latest graphic "Chagallesques" and obviously bears the imprint of graphic art. But Chagall's graphics, too, is the graphics of a painter, even by virtue of the fact that typically it has neither contours nor one continuous blot.

Chagall has a device that became famous and evoked imitations by his friends and foes, and which constitutes the axis of his graphic technique; thanks to it, the appearance of an image on paper has the following visibility: from the paper, separate black threads of lines begin to emerge, of various degrees of force and delicacy; moving toward the center, they grow denser, tighter, harder, shift into spilling blots, form with them the supporting parts of the image, endow them with a final finish; then they flow onward, again lose density and mass, splay out, become more transparent, thinner, gossamer, again shift into bundles of strings, and in separate threads, disappear altogether in the surface of the page.

Needless to say, how painterly in its essence is this device which Chagall uses with amazing, unparalleled mastery. It predetermines both the lack of a counter-line and the possibility of a timely use of the graphic chiaroscuro. Thanks to this device, the line of the contour in Chagall becomes really only "implied." Between one part of the image and another, there is no direct link. Only in his mind and involuntarily, through the white blanks of the page, from one net of threads to another, does the spectator carry the line boundary and define the image. For such an image—and this is the second most important result—the white blank of the paper in Chagall's graphics is not *a background* for the image, but *its part*, a living, active substance that forms and individualizes it. Hence, also, the characteristics typical of Chagall: the torn and splayed edges of his figures, the tone of dense and rarified dots—grains of dust around his objects, the rhythmical series of flowers, circles, diamonds, with which he floods the costumes of his graphic heroes; all these are variants of the basic order as well as echoes of a "Rembrandtian" chiaroscuro of strokes and nets which, here and there, runs through Chagall's page.

Currently, Chagall has moved into illustrations. He made a delightful graphic setting for children's stories. Such a Chagall we didn't know before. The paper seems to have swallowed the thick and restless lava of his regular black masses. The boundaries and blots are scattered accurately and even niggardly, reminiscent of the dry pattern of branches in the evening sky. Chagall's pen has become laconic and lucid, he has *subordinated* it to himself, for he himself succumbed to the text of the stories. His painting attained transparency in its obedience to daily life—it seems that the burden of illustration will supply a purifying simplicity to his graphics.

NOTES

PREFACE

1. Many of the Yiddish essays were published in the Yiddish quarterly *Di Goldene Keyt*, Vol. 60 (1967) in Tel Aviv, but they are virtually unknown to non-Yiddish readers.

2. We included almost all available texts, with a few exceptions that would be repetitive in this context.

3. Some of our translations first appeared in the Solomon R. Guggenheim Museum exhibition catalogue, *Marc Chagall and the Jewish Theater* (New York: Guggenheim Museum, 1992).

INTRODUCTION

1. There were exceptions, such as Andzia Yezierska, a Polish immigrant to New York who wrote novels in English, and the French philosopher Emanuel Levinas, who came to France from his native Lithuania as an adult, yet he wrote philosophy rather than fiction.

2. This biographical sketch is based on my book, *Marc Chagall and His Times: A Documentary Narrative*, Stanford, Calif.: Stanford University Press, 2004.

3. Cf. Yeshurun Keshet, "Marc Chagall: Toward an Evaluation," *Di Goldene Keyt*, No. 60 (1967), pp. 34–40.

4. College, in Russian: *Uchilishche*; sometimes translated as "academy"; yet Chagall hated academies in art.

5. See Benjamin Harshav, *Language in Time of Revolution*, Berkeley: University of California Press, 1993; paperback edition: Stanford, Calif.: Stanford University Press, 1999.

6. The terms must not be read as evaluative; they are simply describing the situation when observed from within, or from the Jewish past.

7. In 1932, Walden fled to the Soviet Union and died in a Stalinist prison.

8. Some portraits of religious Jews dated "1912" were surely made in Russia, hence not earlier than the fall of 1914.

9. See my interpretation of this painting in *Marc Chagall: Les années russes, 1907–1922*. Paris: Musée d'Art moderne de la Ville de Paris, 1995.

10. The designation "French" derives from Chagall's own information. When the painting was bought in 1937, he answered the questionnaire of the Art Institute of Chicago with: "Nationality: French," apparently referring to his recently acquired citizenship.

CHAPTER 1

1. Here we included only the major public statements. Chagall's personal struggles and achievements in Vitebsk are reflected in further articles and documents collected in *Marc Chagall and His Times*, Chapter 6.

2. Translated from Russian. Published in *Vitebsky Listok* (*The Vitebsk Leaflet*), 1918, No. 1030, November 7.

3. The Bolshevik Revolution took place in St.-Petersburg on October 25, 1917, according to the Old Style (the Julian calendar). After the Revolution, the general European, or Gregorian calendar (called New Style), advanced by thirteen days, was adopted and the Revolution was celebrated on November 7, though the name still remained October Revolution.

4. Translated from Russian. Published in *Revolutsionnoe Iskusstvo* (*Revolutionary Art*), Vitebsk, 1919, Collection 1, pp. 2–3, March (or April).

5. Translated from Yiddish. Written on the Moscow Yiddish theater's tour of Western Europe and published in *Di Yidishe Velt*: Monthly for Literature, Criticism, Art, and Culture, Vilna: Kletskin, No. 2 (May 1928). A shorter version of this text translated from a translation (English from French from Russian from Yiddish from Russian), can be found in Chagall's *My Life*.

6. The art of Granovsky's theater and Chagall's murals are discussed in my essay in *Marc Chagall and the Jewish Theater*.

7. An allusion to stereotypical lower-class manners and the lower-class kitschy Yiddish theater.

8. Chagall bought "Dutch sheets," which he sawed together and painted on them his murals.

9. The eighteenth-century synagogue painter in Mohilev Province, Chaim Segal. The lineage to Chagall is possible (his ancestral town Lyozno was in Mohilev Province) but is not supported by any surviving evidence. On the other

hand, *elter-zeyde* (great-grandfather) may simply mean "forefather, ancestor," with no hereditary commitment.

10. "Jewish truth" connotes: well-founded, reliable, supported by the community.

11. Russian pornographic curses, widespread in daily usage.

12. The goblet of tears and suffering is overflowing—an old Jewish motif, memorably embodied in a Yiddish poem by Shimon Frug.

13. As he often was, Chagall was confused about his dates; the invitation came toward the end of 1920.

14. HaBimah, founded in Moscow in 1917, was a theater performing in the recently revived Hebrew language, hence a rival of Yiddish. It was trained and directed by Evgeny Vakhtangov, a disciple of K. Stanislavsky. After a tour in Western Europe in 1926, HaBimah stayed in the West and eventually settled in Palestine and became Israel's National Theater.

15. Here, Chagall gives Jewish names to the Jewish traditional figures, which he had presented in Moscow as: Music, Theater, Dance, and Literature.

16. Some scholars claim that he painted the ceiling as well. Clearly, there is no evidence for it neither here nor in the description of his murals that Chagall included in his resumé of 1921.

17. Aleksey D. Diky (1889–1955), a theater director who worked in the first studio of Stanislavsky's theater MKhAT.

18. Nakhum Zemakh (1887–1939), founder of HaBima; settled in the United States in 1926.

19. Sh. An-sky (pseudonym of Shloyme-Zanvl Rapaport, 1863–1920), a native of Vitebsk Province, was a scholar, folklorist, and writer, and author of the celebrated play *The Dybbuk*. An-sky organized an expedition to collect folk art in the Pale of Settlement.

20. A hall for public events in Moscow.

21. Translated from Yiddish. Published in *Shtrom*, No. 1, Moscow, 1922. For lack of a good literal translation of the title, this text is sometimes referred to by its Yiddish name *Bletlekh*. The word means "little leaves" as well as little pages of paper, as for jotting down notes. This article was later included, with minor changes, in the first version of Chagall's memoirs, *My Own World* (see *Marc Chagall and His Times*, Chapter 2).

22. Ironic reversal, meaning: the old-world, old-fashioned Jews.

23. Moyshe Litvakov (1875–liquidated in 1938?), Yiddish writer and editor. He was a former Zionist and territorialist; after the Revolution, he joined the Communist Party and became a leader of the Yevsektsiya (Jewish Section of the Communist Party) and editor of the newspaper *Emes* (*Truth* = the Yiddish *Pravda*). Litvakov demanded the uprooting of Jewish religious observances and

nationalism. Chagall alludes to Litvakov's sharp attack in 1921 against the Moscow Yiddish writers, who tried to build a secular Jewish culture based on images of the old. Litvakov chastized them for not participating in his Communist newspaper.

24. La Ruche, a "beehive" in Paris, where many immigrant artists lived; Chagall had a room and studio there in 1911–1914.

25. A movement for the establishment of "Jewish Art" was active among Chagall's colleagues at La Ruche. Chagall may have been one of their models, but he himself preferred his contacts with French art and culture.

26. Herwarth Walden (Georg Lewin, 1878–1941), influential editor of the Expressionist journal *Der Sturm* in Berlin and owner of a gallery of the same name, where artists of the international avant-garde exhibited. In 1914 he organized Chagall's first, large one-man show in his gallery. With the rise of Hitler, Walden fled to the Soviet Union and was later liquidated by Stalin.

27. Albert Gleizes and Jean Metzinger, whom Chagall knew in Paris, were the authors of the first book on Cubism, *Du cubisme*, Paris: Figuière, 1912.

28. Sh. An-sky had organized an expedition to collect folk art in the Pale of Settlement.

29. See footnote 9.

30. Abram Efros (1888–1954), art critic, coauthor of the first book on Chagall, and artistic director of the Moscow Yiddish Chamber Theater, who invited Chagall to do his theater murals in 1920.

31. Isaac Levitan (1861–1900), a Jew, was a prominent representative of Russian Realist-lyrical painting. This is a mock-reference: The dead "academic" authority would decide what "academic ration" Chagall gets, i.e., how valued he was.

CHAPTER 2

1. Translated from Yiddish. Published in *Literarishe Bleter*, Warsaw, Nos. 49–50, 1925.

2. Peretz's influential Expressionist-Symbolist drama, also performed by the Moscow State Theater.

3. Translated from Hebrew. Lecture for an invited audience in the hall of the HaBimah theater, Tel Aviv, Sabbath evening, March 23, 1931, published in *Moznaim*, Nos. 46–47 (March 31, 1931) and No. 48 (April 16, 1931). Unfortunately, the original Yiddish manuscript was not preserved and the Hebrew text is somewhat florid and fuzzy in places.

4. These words, strange for Chagall, are probably inspired by the Zionist Revisionists, in whose Russian journal in Paris Chagall participated. He is probably alluding to Pissaro's non-Jewish wife.

5. Translated from Yiddish. Published in the Warsaw literary paper *Literarishe Bleter*, No. 30, 1934, and reprinted in I.A. Ronch, *The World of Marc Chagall* (in Yiddish), Los Angeles, Calif., 1967.

6. Baal-Makhsoves ("The Thinker"), pseudonym of Dr. Israel Izidor Elyashev (1873–1924), an influential Yiddish literary critic, whom Chagall befriended in Petrograd, Moscow, and Berlin. In 1922–1923, he edited the Klal-Ferlag Yiddish publishing house in Berlin.

7. Though Bialik was the foremost Hebrew poet, he loved to speak Yiddish (and wrote some Yiddish poetry as well).

8. Because modern Hebrew was a new language, "flowers had no names" (see Harshav, *Language in Time of Revolution*, p. 109). They had to be invented or adapted from flower names in the ancient texts.

9. The avant-garde poets in Eretz-Israel, notably A. Shlonsky, attacked Bialik severely, in the name of Modernism; yet they revered him at the same time.

10. "Magid"—the Preacher of Slutsk. Chagall's portrait of him was renamed "The Green Jew."

11. Chagall did not understand spoken Hebrew, especially if it was in the Israeli rather than the Ashkenazi pronunciation.

12. Ida Chagall was fifteen at the time. Bialik had a writing block since he arrived in Palestine.

13. Since the whole affair had a personal and biographical aspect, it is included in *Marc Chagall and His Times*.

14. Translated from Yiddish. Published in *World Conference of the Yiddish Scientific Institute: On the Tenth Anniversary of YIVO*, Vilna: YIVO, 1936. Chagall's letter to the YIVO of 1929 is included in *Marc Chagall and His Times*.

15. The YIVO, with highly limited means, had a humble home on Wiwulska St. 18.

16. Chagall's birthplace Vitebsk, now in Belarus. Chagall was barred from visiting the Soviet Union. Vilna Province, then in Poland, was the closest to the border of Soviet Byelorussia.

17. As an emigrant and renegade, as well as a modernist artist, Chagall was ostracized in the Soviet Union.

18. Apparently an allusion to former friends who felt forced to denounce Chagall in the USSR.

19. Enterpreneur of the modern arts and director of the Russian Ballet in Paris.

20. Wealthy, large-scale collectors of Western modern art in Russia.

21. He means ethnic and parochial, an object of ethnography, as in An-sky's collection.

22. He means the Jews of the internal Jewish establishments, the so-called "Jewish Jews." Assimilated Jews did buy his paintings, from Maxim Vinaver in St.-Petersburg to Solomon Guggenheim in New York.

23. Jewish lawyers disbarred by the Nazis for racist reasons.

24. A reference to Chagall's failed attempts in 1931 to influence the nature and standards of the budding art museum in Tel Aviv.

25. The Bezalel School of Art in Jerusalem, built at the beginning of the twentieth century, produced generations of Jewish artists. Chagall censures the "folkloristic" and overly "Jewish" artifacts promoted in Bezalel.

26. Translated from Yiddish. Published in the Paris Yiddish Communist newspaper *Naye Prese*, April 23, 1939; and in *Yidishe Kultur*, No. 7, New York, June–July 1939.

27. Implying that the war against Hitler is no longer a solely Jewish problem, but all of Europe is getting embroiled in it.

28. An allusion to his first teacher, the artist Yury Pen in Vitebsk, who painted in the precise realistic style of the Russian "Itinerant" artists at the end of the nineteenth century.

29. See Chagall's first two articles in this collection.

30. An allusion to Chagall's own contribution to the avant-garde style of the Moscow Yiddish Theater in the 1920s.

31. Famous collectors of modern art.

32. Albert Barnes, the founder of the Barnes Collection in Philadelphia.

33. He means centers of large Jewish populations and an autonomous Jewish culture.

34. The blue-and-white Jewish National Fund savings box, which used to stand prominently in Jewish homes to collect money for buying land in Eretz-Israel.

CHAPTER 3

1. Published as "Quelques impressions sur la peinture Française," *Renaissance: Revue trimestrielle de l'Ecole des Hautes Etudes de New York*, New York, II–III, 1944–1945, pp. 45–57. The English typescript was made ad hoc and never published.

2. This English version was arranged by Robert B. Heywood and published as "The Artist" in *The Works of the Mind*, Chicago: University of Chicago Press, 1947.

3. Chagall's original French text says: "Je suis un peintre inconsciemment conscient," yet the English typescript of 1943 has it: "consciously unconscious." Both formulations may express a similar idea, applicable to Chagall, but we felt that precision here is important.

4. Interestingly enough, he includes here the nine years of absence (1914–1923), eight of which he spent in Russia and a year and a half in Berlin.

5. Picasso. He did not launch his revolution in art with programmatic manifestos.

6. Apparently his childhood friend Viktor Mekler, with whom Chagall quarreled in Paris.

7. An allusion to Walden's being Jewish.

8. Walden had sold Chagall's paintings during World War I, when the painter disappeared in Russia. Indeed, it was assumed in Berlin that Chagall had perished in the war.

9. An allusion to F.T. Marinetti's slogan: "War—the only hygiene of the world."

10. The first version is translated: "flooding your internal world."

11. Chagall returned to Paris in September 1923, after a year and a half in Berlin, which he doesn't want to mention at a time of war against Germany.

12. One of the tenets of Surrealism was "automatic writing," transferred to painting as well.

13. The mystical and mythical aspect of Nazi ideology.

14. Vollard used to hoard works that he commissioned. Chagall's major works of engravings were not published until after World War II, after Vollard's death.

15. An allusion to the Inquisition and the expulsion of the Jews from Spain in 1492, which caused a Rabbinical boycott of Spain for 500 years.

16. In 1931, Chagall made a long visit to the Jewish presence in Palestine.

17. Communism.

18. Published in *Partisan Review*, New York, Vol. 11, No. 1, Winter 1944, pp. 88–93. Chagall uses many passages from his recent Mount Holyoke lecture (see above). J.J. Sweeney was the curator who organized Chagall's retrospective exhibition at the Museum of Modern Art in New York in April 1946.

19. Chagall dates his real beginning as an artist from the time he left his first art teacher Yury Pen in Vitebsk and began serious studies of painting in St.-Petersburg.

20. Actually, Chagall arrived in Paris in September 1923 (see note 11).

21. Translated from Yiddish. Published in *Eynikeyt* (*Unity*), biweekly of the American Committee of Jewish Writers, Artists, and Scientists, New York, February 15, 1944.

22. The center of Jewish life in Eastern Europe.

23. The Jewish Autonomous Region in Birobidjan, in the Soviet Far East, was an attempt to create a Jewish autonomous "state" in the Soviet Union, and was supported by pro-Soviet Jews in the United States, who wanted a Yiddish rather than a Hebrew Jewish nation.

24. The visit in New York of the leaders of the Soviet Jewish Antifascist Committee, Schloyme Mikhoels and Itsik Fefer.

25. Heads of two Hasidic dynasties.

26. Translated from Yiddish. Published in *Eynikeyt* (*Unity*), biweekly of the American Committee of Jewish Writers, Artists, and Scientists. New York, February 15, 1944, on the occasion of the liberation of Vitebsk from the German occupation.

27. A painting by Chagall, "The Rabbi," was burned in Mannheim as "Degenerate Art"; other "degenerate" paintings were confiscated by the Gestapo and sold in Switzerland.

28. An allusion to Chagall's first one-man show, held in Berlin in 1914.

29. Translated from Yiddish. The manuscript in Chagall's handwriting is in the YIVO archives in New York. The article was published in the Yiddish journal *Naylebn* (*NewLife*), New York, June 1944, with the added title, "The Art of the Straight Line and Clarity."

30. The problem that the "people" and the political left do not understand his (and any real, revolutionary) art preoccupied Chagall from the days of the Revolution. See his articles "Art on the Anniversary of October" and "The Revolution in Art" in this volume.

31. Scholem Asch (1880–1957), a major Yiddish novelist, widely translated into other languages. Asch lived in Poland, France, and the United States in the 1940s; he was ostracized by Jewish institutions (except for the left) for writing a trilogy on the life of Jesus Christ in 1943–1949.

32. Dr. Isaac Kloomok (1888–?), a Yiddish writer, arrived in the United States in 1902, was art critic of the New York Communist Yiddish paper *Frayhayt* and wrote about art in various Yiddish journals. He wrote a book about Chagall, published in both Yiddish and English.

33. Major Yiddish Soviet writers. Yikhezkel Dobrushin (1883–1953), a leader of the Yiddishist Cultural League, was the literary editor of the Moscow Yiddish Theater; he was arrested in 1948 and died in a Soviet concentration camp. Dovid Hofshteyn (1889–1952) collaborated with Chagall on a book of Expressionist poetry and drawings, *Troyer* (*Grief*, 1921); executed by Stalin in August 1952. Der Nister (Pinhas Kahanovich, 1884–1950), a major Yiddish fiction writer, lived with Chagall in the Malakhovka orphanage; arrested in 1949 and died in a prison hospital.

34. The slogan of Fefer's poetics.

35. Referring to Soviet, or Communist criticism of the "bourgeois," religious, and modernist features in Chagall's work.

36. In Yiddish: *iber-realistishe*, i.e., above realism, a higher realism, derived from Appolinaire's designation of Chagall's style as "surnaturel." The idea is similar to that of "Surrealism," but in the translation, we had to avoid that term so

as not to confuse it with the specific French movement, which emerged after Chagall's super-naturalistic paintings.

37. Nokhem Shtif (1879–1933), Yiddish linguist and literary historian. In 1914, he lived in Vilna and in 1915–1918 in St.-Petersburg, where he persuaded Chagall to illustrate a Peretz story for the Vilna publisher B. Kletzkin.

38. Chagall made thirty-four drawings for the Yiddish poetry of A. Lyesin (A. Walt), published in New York in three volumes in 1938. See their correspondence in Harshav, *Marc Chagall and His Times*.

39. Of the Red Army.

40. On their visit to New York in 1943.

41. Chagall dares to talk about the revival of Eretz-Israel at a Communist assembly, when Zionism was a colonialist conspiracy in their eyes and the very name "The Land of Israel" was taboo. Only three years later, in 1947, a drastic change occurred in Soviet policy toward Zionism, when the Soviet Foreign Minister Gromyko made a pro-Zionist speech at the U.N., and the Soviet Union aided Israel in its War of Independence.

42. The British White Paper of 1939 all but closed Palestine for further Jewish immigration and prohibited Jews from settling more land. Thus, they violated the promises of the Balfour Declaration to build a national "home" for the Jews in Palestine.

43. Quotations are from Chagall's article "Our Jewish Culture and Our Resistance," in the Paris Communist Yiddish newspaper *Naye Prese (New Press)*, May 24, 1938. Chagall conflates the Jewish plight under Nazi persecutions and the Communist resistance to fascism in the Civil War in Spain.

44. An allusion to the left fighting in the Civil War in Spain, perceived at the time as a battle against fascism.

45. This quotation is from his essay "Artists and Jewish Artists" (1939). See above, p. 60.

46. Specifically, he alludes to the influence of his avant-garde painting on the style of the Yiddish Theater in Moscow.

47. A charity collection box for coins, kept in Jewish homes.

48. Crossed-out sentence.

49. The parallel between the religious and revolutionary martyrs and visionaries is typical of A. Lyesin's poetry, which Chagall profusely illustrated.

50. The transformation of the "Old" in the "New"—the "new culture" of the "new Jew"—is a central theme of the time, absorbed by Chagall since his work in the Moscow Yiddish Theater. It may also be an allusion to Herzl's Zionist vision in *Altneuland (Old-New Land)*.

51. The poem is effective with its meter and rhyme; here we present only a literal translation.

52. Translated from a Yiddish typescript in the YIVO archives, New York. Apparently published as "Message aux peintres français," *Le spectateur des ans*, Paris, No. 1, December 1944, p. 3.

53. Bella Chagall died suddenly in upstate New York in September 1944, shortly after the liberation of Paris.

54. Translated from a Yiddish manuscript in Chagall's handwriting in the YIVO archives, in New York. For the Yiddish world in New York, for those who were shaken by the Holocaust, as well as for Soviet sympathizers, the war that was over was the war in Europe.

55. Soviet Russia.

56. Therefore, naturally from the left; and yet, he loved Jerusalem, hence was also an instinctive Zionist.

57. This sentence may refer to the disruptions caused by the Jewish Socialist Bund in Chagall's father's synagogue in pre-Revolutionary Vitebsk, breaking unity in the name of class warfare.

58. An allusion to A. Sutzkever's Yiddish poem "Moses," written in the Vilna ghetto; see A. Sutzkever, *Selected Poetry and Prose*, translated from Yiddish by Barbara and Benjamin Harshav, Berkeley: University of California Press, 1991, p. 159.

59. The beginnings of the U.N.

60. A direct allusion to Uri-Zvi Grinberg's Yiddish Expressionist poetry from the 1920s, presenting Jesus as "our brother," who was hanging for 2000 years, crucified on all the roads of Europe. Cf. Benjamin Harshav, "The Role of Language in Modern Art: On Texts and Subtexts in Chagall's Painting," *Modernism/Modernity*, Vol 1, No. 2 (April) 1994, pp. 51–87.

61. Chagall imagined a Communist assembly in New York as representing the "folk masses" and "the people."

62. Translated from Yiddish. Published in the Communist Yiddish newspaper *Naye Prese*, Paris, June 15, 1946, after Chagall's first return to Paris on June 4, 1946. Chagall had written several articles in this newspaper before the war, in 1938 and 1939. The circumstances of this speech are described in detail in *Marc Chagall and His Times*.

63. An allusion to the Jewish Communist partisans who fought in the French Resistance.

64. Translated from Yiddish. Published in *Parizer shriftn*, a periodical publication, the organ of the Jewish Culture Organizations in France (Union de la Culture Juive), No. 4, September 1946. The title is a quote from Isaiah 40:1. Hotel Lutetia was the headquarters of the Gestapo in Paris during the German occupation.

65. Translated from a Yiddish manuscript in Chagall's handwriting, found in the archives of his friend, the Yiddish art critic Leo Kenig, who resided at the time

in London. Preserved in the archives of the National and University Library in Jerusalem. Published in *Eynikeyt*, New York, July–August 1947, with the added title, "New Jewish Life—A New Foundation for Jewish Culture and Art." The title reflects the obligatory optimism of the Communist editors, quite opposite to Chagall's quote from Isaiah.

66. At the beginning of the Cold War, America helped rebuild Germany as a buffer against the threat of Communism, whereas the Communist propaganda opposed it, in the name of revenge.

67. Chagall refers to the Western appeasement of Germany after World War II for the sake of fighting Communism and "saving European culture."

68. An allusion to the Cold War and to the hostility of the Yiddish establishment in New York toward the left. Chagall felt especially offended by the "silence" that surrounded the publication of Bella Chagall's memoirs in 1945.

69. Chagall evokes the theory that the "nihilism" of modern art was at the root of Fascism.

70. Like the "automatic writing" of the Surrealists. See Chagall's dissociation from "automatic" writing in "Some Impressions Regarding French Painting," in this volume.

71. Chagall uses here the French word *matière* (materiality), the physical substance of a work of art, especially its paint. It is equivalent to the Russian *faktura* (texture of the painting).

72. Exodus 31:6, King James translation: "And in the hearts of all that are wise hearted I have put wisdom, that they may make all that I have commanded thee."

73. Small boys would walk home from *Heder* with a lantern in the dark.

CHAPTER 4

1. Translated from Yiddish. The text was preserved in Chagall's handwriting in the archive of the painter Moshe Mokady, then Director of the Art Division in the Israeli Ministry of Education.

2. Of the Israeli War of Independence, 1947–1949.

3. Translated from Yiddish. Chagall's manuscript was preserved in the archive of the artist Moshe Mokady.

4. Translated from Yiddish. The manuscript was found in Mokady's archives and apparently was never published. It relates to the public debates in Israel at the time.

5. He refers to the *Ma'abarot*, temporary camps of tents and shacks for new immigrants from the Holocaust and, later, from North Africa. Israel tripled its population in the course of several years.

6. Chagall applies to Israel the French model of centralized administration of art and culture.

7. Written in Yiddish in 1950. This English translation was published in the English version of *Siberia: A Poem* with illustrations by Marc Chagall, Jerusalem: Mosad Bialik, 1961 (in Yiddish). New English translation of the poem, preserving its meter and rhyme, in A.Sutzkever, *Selected Poetry and Prose*, edited and translated by Benjamin and Barbara Harshav, Berkeley: University of California Press, 1991.

8. The resistance fighters against the Nazis.

9. An allusion to the fierce "war of languages" that went on before the Holocaust between Hebrew and Yiddish. Eretz-Israel was the fortress of Hebrew, whereas Yiddish was largely oppressed.

10. Translated from Yiddish. Speech at a celebration honoring the Yiddish poet and partisan A. Sutzkever in Paris in 1955.

11. Chagall refers to his familiar Russian peasant hut, *khata*. In the original it is spelled *khupa*—clearly a mistake.

12. Chaim-Nakhman Bialik (1873–1934) was considered the national poet of the Hebrew literature revival in Russia. Since he arrived in Palestine in 1921, he wrote almost no poetry. See "With Bialik in Eretz-Israel" in this volume, p. 51.

13. English typescript of lecture. One copy indicates "February," the other "March" 1958.

14. Chagall came to America in June 1941 and returned to Europe in August 1948.

15. Actually in 1946.

16. "Chemistry"—a key term in Chagall's global judgment of paintings. He means a complete fusion of all aspects of a painting, rather than a mere "physical" mixture or coexistence of colors and figures; hence, the impact of its totality on the observer's eye.

17. An allusion to the action painting of Jackson Pollock.

18. This line, from Paul Verlaine's poem "Art poétique, " was often quoted by the Russian Symbolists and Formalists—to stress "musicality" above "meaning" in poetry.

19. More precisely, a wife and eight children. His father used to say: "I have to feed nine mouths."

20. A reference to the theories of Vassily Kandinsky.

21. English text in *Praemium Erasmianum MCMLX*, Amsterdam, 1961.

22. He apparently refers to his visit in Paris in June–August 1946.

23. Mayakovsky actually wrote: "If you wish, I can be exquisitely delicate,/ Not a male, but—a cloud in trousers!" (in the long poem "A Cloud in Trousers").

24. An allusion to Communism.

CHAPTER 5

1. Published in the exhibition catalogue, Marc Chagall, *Ceramics*, New York: Curt Valentine Gallery, 1952. Date: "Vence, September 1952."

2. Marc Chagall, *Chagall Lithographs*, George Braziller, 1960.

3. Translated from Yiddish. Published in *Di Goldene Keyt*, No. 60, 1967. There are minor omissions in the published Yiddish text, here corrected from the original English translation.

4. On his visit to Palestine in 1931.

5. Translated from Yiddish. Speech delivered at the Congress of the Center for Human Understanding of the University of Chicago, held in Washington, D.C. on May 2–4, 1963. Published with this title in *Di Goldene Keyt*, No. 50, 1964. The French text was published in *Lettres Française*, with an introduction by the editor Louis Aragon. An English translation from the French in *Bridges of Human Understanding*, edited by John U. Nef, New York: University Publishers, 1964, with the added title "Why Have We Become So Anxious?"

6. English typescript. The work was commissioned by the French Minister of Culture, André Malraux.

7. Published in the exhibition catalogue, Marc Chagall, *Le cirque: Paintings 1969–1980*, New York, Pierre Matisse Gallery, 1981.

8. An allusion to Hitler, in Charlie Chaplin's caricature.

CHAPTER 6

1. From Pierre Schneider, *Louvre Dialogues*, enlarged edition, Paris: Editions Adam Bird, 1993; translated from the French by Patricia Southgate, New York: Atheneum, 1971.

2. Translated from Yiddish. Published in *Di Goldene Keyt*, No. 60, 1967.

3. An allusion to the Soviet and Western Communist leadership.

4. Translated from Yiddish. Written on the publication of Vogler's book, *Spring on the Highway*. Published in *Di Goldene Keyt*, No. 60, 1967.

5. Translated from Yiddish. Published in *Di Goldene Keyt*, No. 66, 1969.

6. Translated from Chagall's Yiddish manuscript owned by M. Tsanin, editor of the Israeli Yiddish newspaper *Dos Naye Lebn*. Chagall's attached note reads: "Dear friend Tsanin, here is the draft of my speech. Please correct the mistakes. With warm regards, Marc Chagall." An abbreviated version was Published in *Di Goldene Keyt*, No. 66, 1969.

7. Eretz-Israel ("the Land of Israel"), or abbreviated and affectionate Eretz ("the Land"), is the traditional and Zionist name for biblical Palestine, even before Israel became an independent State. In 1931, Marc and Bella Chagall visited

Eretz-Israel at the invitation of Meir Dizengoff, the first Mayor of the "first Jew-ish city in two thousand years," Tel Aviv.

8. Meaning: my works are there.

9. English text translated from the French by Rhoda B. Miller. Published in *Marc Chagall 1887–1985*, Nice: Musée National Message Biblique Marc Chagall, 1973.

10. Musée National Message Biblique in Nice.

CHAPTER 7

1. There is no trace in the book of either the February or the October Revolu-tion of 1917; furthermore, Efros mentions that Chagall is not yet thirty (as he would be in July 1917). The description of spectators strolling through a large ex-hibition points either to the exhibition of the avant-garde group Jack of Dia-monds in Moscow in November 1916, where Chagall exhibited forty-five works, or to the "Exhibiton of Paintings and Sculptures by Jewish Artists," held in Moscow in 1917, where Chagall exhibited forty-three works. The YIVO copy of the book is numbered #9 and dedicated to a friend by Abram Efros on August 16, 1918, apparently shortly after its publication.

2. The name *Shomir* (in Ashkenazi Hebrew) connotes: to preserve, protect, i.e., preserve the values of the tradition.

3. See Chagall's reminiscences in "In Memoriam Ya. A. Tugendhold," written in Russian in Paris 1928, published in *Iskusstvo*, Nos. 3–4, 1928. English transla-tion in *Marc Chagall and His Times*.

4. A. Efros und J. Tugendhold, *Die Kunst Marc Chagalls*, Potsdam: G. Kiepen-heuer Verlag, 1921.

5. Aleksey Mikhaylovich Remizov (1877–1957), a prominent Russian Symbol-ist writer.

6. *Lubok*, a traditional Russian colored narrative folk print.

7. Jewish Lithuania, including today's Belarus.

8. V. Stasov, a major Russian critic who originated the interest in and collec-tion of Jewish folk art.

9. [Author's note:] I remember what Bakst told me: "I always set myself the goal of conveying the music of what is depicted *(ambience de l'oeuvre)*, having lib-erated myself from the bounds of archeology and chronology of mundane life." This colorful-musical empathy for the depicted epoch is first of all a sensuous perception, perception-as-assimilation.

10. Stanisław Wyspiański (1869–1907), a modern Polish dramatist. His major play, *The Wedding* (1901) uses an actual wedding of a poet with a beautiful peasant girl as a symbolic presentation of Poland's past, present, and future. The play

made an enormous emotional and political impact (Poland did not exist as an independent nation at the time).

11. An allusion to the Russian "Civil Poetry," focusing on defending the civil and social rights of the citizens.

12. Vasily Vasilyevich Rozanov (1856–1919), a Russian writer and philosopher who advanced unorthodox religious ideas, the religion of sex and procreation, and rabid anti-Semitism.

13. The essence of Judaism as represented in three historical centers: Jerusalem ("Zion") and the Bible; Babylon and the Talmud; Jerusalem of Lithuania (Vilna), as the contemporary center of learning. By substituting Vitebsk, Tugendhold shifts from rigid rabbinical learning to the secular creative revival.

14. E.T.A. Hoffmann (1776–1822), a major German writer, had great influence on Russian literature. His unfinished novel *The Tomcat Murr* (*Kater Murr*, 1819–1821) exposed the philistine society.

15. Ivan Abramovich Morozov (1871–1921), a major Russian collector of modern art.

16. Emile Verhaeren (1855–1915), a major Belgian French poet.

INDEX OF NAMES

The authorized representative in the EU for product safety and compliance is:
Mare Nostrum Group
B.V Doelen 72
4831 GR Breda
The Netherlands